Software Design Methodology

Hong Zhu

ELSEVIER
BUTTERWORTH
HEINEMANN

AMSTERDAM BOSTON HEIDELBERG LONDON NEW YORK OXFORD PARIS
SAN DIEGO SAN FRANCISCO SINGAPORE SYDNEY TOKYO

Butterworth-Heinemann
An imprint of Elsevier
Linacre House, Jordan Hill, Oxford OX2 8DP
30 Corporate Drive, Burlington MA 01803

First published 2005

The following figure supplied courtesy of Diagram Visual Information Ltd
Figure 4.2

The following figures supplied courtesy of ACM Publications
Figures 4.9, 4.10, 4.12, 4.13, 4.16

The following figure supplied courtesy of AAAI Press
Figure 5.10

British Library Cataloguing in Publication Data
A catalogue record for this book is available from the British Library

Library of Congress Cataloguing in Publication Data
A catalogue record for this book is available from the Library of Congress

ISBN   0 7506 6075 9

For information on all Butterworth-Heinemann publications
visit our website at www.books.elsevier.com

Printed and bound in Great Britain

Table of Contents

List of Figures

List of Tables

Preface

Design is vital to software development. For many reasons, software design is difficult. Teaching and learning software design is even more difficult. A great number of textbooks on software design have been written. Most of them are devoted to one specific software design method, such as object-oriented software development. However, few have addressed software design at a higher level of abstraction such as at the methodology level, which is what this textbook about.

In my personal experiences of teaching software design in advanced undergraduate courses as well as supervising student dissertation projects, I have found that students often have some misconceptions about software design. One of the common misunderstanding of software design is that there is only one correct solution to any given design problem. Many textbooks on software design have case studies and examples, but very few give several alternative solutions to one design problem. A related common misconception of software design methods is that properly applying a well-established design method will always results in *the* correct solution to a design problem. Therefore, many students jump to the implementation stage of their dissertation projects once a design is completed without carefully analysing and evaluating their designs, even fewer thought of making alternative designs and then compare them. Few textbooks on software design cover the topic of how to analyse a design and how to compare alternative software designs. Such misconceptions of software design methods can be corrected by learning software design methodology. Theories of software architecture, especially software architectural styles and analysis and evaluation of architectural designs, are at the right level of abstraction and especially helpful to correct students' misconceptions.

Another cause of difficulties in teaching and learning software design is that most students have no experience in dealing with large scale and highly complicated software systems. The theories of software architecture also provide a suitable means of communication to transfer the design knowledge of large scale software systems to the students. It can bring a large amount of software engineering, development methods, and programming knowledge learned in various courses together, and put them into one well-organised framework. It also significantly widens student's knowledge of software systems.

The book is based on my lecture notes prepared for teaching the Software Design module at Oxford Brookes University to software engineering and computer science students over the past six years. It is intended to be used as a textbook for such courses. Each chapter starts with a short introduction that gives the context of the topic and the expected learning outcomes of the chapter. Each chapter also contains a summary of the key points that the students should have learned from the chapter and a list of exercise questions to test students attainment of the knowledge and skills. Some of the questions are also suitable to be used as coursework. I have also included materials on advanced topics that are suitable for postgraduate courses. At the end of each chapter, a brief direction to the further readings and a list of references are also included so that it can be used by postgraduate students as a guideline for their independent studies after classes.

The diagram on how to use the book on the next page shows the interdependences between topics and may be helpful in selecting undergraduate or postgraduate courses. In the diagram, the prerequisite knowledge indicates what the students should have learned from other courses. Such knowledge aids understanding of the related topics. As shown in the diagram, the book consists of three main parts. Chapter 1 to Chapter 3 forms the first part that covers the basic principles of software design and their links to the general theory of design methodology, which has been developed as an independent scientific discipline. Part 2 consists of Chapter 4 to Chapter 8. It addresses the problem of how to develop software architectural designs. Part 3, which consists of Chapter 9 to Chapter 12, addresses the problem of how to analyse and evaluate software architectural designs.

Acknowledgement. Many people have contributed to this textbook. I would like to thank my colleague Mr David Lightfoot at Oxford Brookes University for the six years of enjoyable collaboration on teaching the Software Design module. My thanks also go to the students at Oxford Brookes University who participated in the module. Their feedback had a great influence on my selection and organisation of the contents of the textbook and setting the exercise questions. I am most grateful to Prof. Jiafu Xu at Nanjing University, China, from whom I learned the principles of software development methodology since I was a PhD student of him. He also read the manuscript of the textbook and gave many invaluable comments. I would also like to thanks Dr John May at the University of Bristol, Prof. Huaglory Tianfield at Glasgow Caledonian University and Prof. Kecheng Liu at the University of Reading for their invaluable comments on the draft versions of the book. Thanks to Prof. David Garlan for the permission of using the materials from his work. Finally, I would like to thank the editors of the book at Elsevier Science, Mr Alfred Waller, Ms Jodi Cusack and Ms Stephani Havard, for their patience and their friendly and professional advice during my prolonged preparation of the manuscript.

Hong Zhu

How to use the book

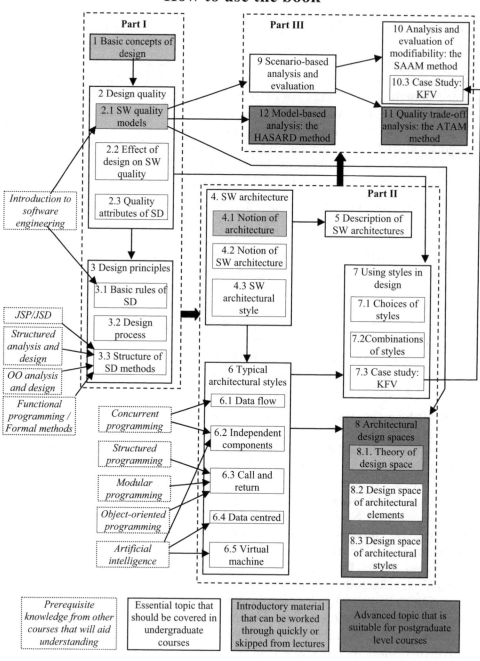

1 Basic Concepts of Design

Design methodology emerged in the 1960s as an independent scientific discipline. This chapter looks to the theory of design methodology as a source of inspiration to understand the basic concept of design in the most general context. The objectives of the chapter are:

- To understand the basic characteristics of design processes;

- To understand the elements of designs;

- To understand the factors that affect design processes and outcomes.

The chapter is organised as follows. Section 1.1 gives a brief introduction to the notion of design. Section 1.2 examines the main characteristics of design activities in the creative processes of design. Section 1.3 considers designs as plans to produce man-made artefacts, and identifies the essential elements of all designs. Finally, section 1.4 presents Mayall's axioms of design to outline the basic relationships between various issues involved in every design.

1.1 INTRODUCTION

The word 'design' as defined in the *Longman Dictionary of Contemporary English* (1987) has the following meanings. As a noun, it means:

1. *A drawing or pattern showing how something is to be made;*

2. *The art of making such drawings or patterns;*

3. *The arrangement of parts in any man-made product, such as a machine or work of art, as this influences the product's practical usefulness;*

4. *A decorative pattern, esp. one that is not repeated;*

5. *A plan in the mind.*

The word design is also used as a verb with the following meanings.

6. *To make a drawing or pattern of (something that will be made or built); develop and draw the plans for;*

7. *To plan or develop for a certain purpose or use.*

As Christopher Jones pointed out in the book *Design Methods: Seeds of Human Futures* [1], design methodologists have been moving away from 'drawings and patterns' in the notion of design, although it is perhaps still a common action of designers of all kinds. The literature on design methods began to appear in the 1950s and 60s. Since then, design methodology has become an independent discipline of scientific study. The Design Research Society[1] publishes a quarterly journal *Design Studies* in London by Elsevier Science, which provides an insight into design issues affecting a wide range of fields of applications for design techniques. Researchers in the general theory of design have tried to answer two interrelated fundamental questions about design. The first question is:

What are the essential characteristics of design?

---

[1] The web address of the Design Research Society is: http://www.drs.org.uk/

This question relates to understanding when an activity is designing and when it is not.

The second question is:

What processes are used by designers?

It can be asked in a number of different ways with emphasis on various aspects of design processes. For example,

Is one process better than another, constituting 'right' and 'wrong' ways to design?

Why are some processes favourable over others?

Do different processes lead to different qualities of results?

The last few decades have seen a significant amount of research devoted to developing design theories with the ultimate aims at clarifying the human ability of designing in a scientific way, and at the same time, producing the practical knowledge about design methodology. Such knowledge is believed to be useful and essential to construct computer aided design systems.

As one of the most complex man-made artefacts, computer software is very difficult to design. There are many factors that affect designs and many stakeholders, i.e. people who participate in the design process, play various different roles in the design processes and influence the design of software. The questions that researchers in the area of design theory have been searching for answers to are also questions that computer scientists are looking for answers to in the context of software development. In fact, software design shares many characteristics with designs in other fields. As McPhee pointed out [2], much can be learned from the philosophical and methodological studies of design in general. This chapter is only a brief review of the basic concepts of design theory.

1.2 CHARACTERISTICS OF DESIGN ACTIVITIES

Let's first have a look at how design theory characterises design activities in the most general sense.

1.2.1 The input and start point of designs

Many design researchers believe in the aphorism 'necessity is the mother of invention'. It is considered as one of the basic characteristics of design that design can only be undertaken intentionally. Lawson [3] and Dasgupta [4] pointed out that a real or perceived need forms the basis for the definition of design projects. A need acts as the initial motivational force that provides the basis for starting design work. Willem [5, 6] explicitly expressed that the universal feature of design is simply the intentional devising of a plan or prototype for something new. The need or intention forms the first basic elements of all designs, i.e. the problem to be solved. In software design, the need or intention is usually explicitly or implicitly specified as users' requirements. Without users' requirements, there will be no software design.

1.2.2 The outcome and results of designs

Many designers believe that the output or product of a design is a symbolic representation of an artefact for implementation. For example, Booker (1964) regards design as simulating what we want to make (or do) before we make (or do) it as many times as may be necessary to feel confident in the final result. Dasgupta [4] expressed that design is essentially 'the formation of a prescription or model for an unfinished work in advance of its embodiment'. Design representation serves as the basis to conceptualise and compare various design decisions. This is very true in software design. Computer scientists and software engineers learned this lesson mostly from practical experiences that neglected design stage can only cause problems at later stages of implementation and so on.

However, the true output of design is more than just a plan or symbolic representation. MacLean et al. [7] pointed out that, the final output of a design also include what they call 'design space', which is a body of knowledge about the artefact, its environment, its intended use, and the decisions that went into creating the design. Designers must consider the representations of this kind of meta-knowledge about how they arrived at a particular design. Recently such meta-knowledge about software designs has been collected and studied systematically.

Two forms of systematic studies of such knowledge emerged in the literature of software design. One is about software architecture and the other is design patterns of object oriented systems. These types of knowledge form the main contents of this book.

1.2.3 Transformation of data

A basic feature of design that almost all design researchers accept implicitly or explicitly is the transformational nature of design. For example, Dasgupta [4] noted that need acts as a seed that design transforms into a form that is eventually used to guide the implementation of an artefact, plan or process. Simon [8] wrote that design is the restructuring of a current situation to achieve some preferred situation. Willem [5, 6] preferred to use the term 'development' to describe the transformation that occurs during design. Page [9] regarded design as an 'imaginative jump from present facts to future possibilities'.

1.2.4 Generation of new ideas

The requisite of the generation of new ideas during design processes is another commonly cited characteristic of design. Reswick defined design as a creative activity – it involves bringing in something new and useful that has not existed previously. However, creativity remains an elusive subject of design researches and still beyond science's firm grasp. The precise manner in which new ideas are generated still cannot be codified. Some researchers, such as Freeman [10], have postulated that idea generation is not entirely a haphazard activity. He believed that two styles of idea generation exist: abstraction and elaboration. Abstraction is used to make generalisations while elaboration attempts to develop into great detail the specifics of a design. In fact, these two styles of idea generation play a significant role in software design methodology.

1.2.5 Problem solving and decision making

Design methodologists tend to characterise design as a type of problem solving or decision making activity. For example, Asimow defined design as decision making, in the face of uncertainty, with high penalties for error. For many scientists and engineers, design invariably involves the application of some sort of logical analysis on the problem. Others, including Willem, believe that various design problem solutions are not necessarily connected through logic to their initial problem state. Design problems are often described as 'ill-structured' problems because of their complexity and the difficulties in determining their associated constraints and requirements. Freeman [10] preferred to use a decision-making analogy to view design problem solving. He characterised design as a series of decisions between various design alternatives. Each alternative is determined by the current state of abstractions, elaborations, operational statements and other known and unknown factors. Both design-as-problem-solving and design-as-decision-making views characterise design as goal directed activity and design process as navigation in a design configuration space.

1.2.6   Satisfying and discovering constraints

An initial need not only determines the problem to be solved, but also imposes the most basic constraints on the solution. In general, more constraints are often discovered during the design work itself. Many researchers agree that a major part of designing involves discovery and satisfaction of constraints on the eventual form of the design. Such constraints apply both to the designed artefacts and to the processes and participants involved in the design activity. For example, Mostow [11] regarded design as an activity with the goal of creating an artefact description that satisfies constraints derived from functional and performance specifications of the artefact, limitations of the medium and process by which the artefact is rendered or produced, and aesthetic criteria on the form of the artefact. For Alexander [12], design is 'finding the right physical components of a physical structure'. In the context of architectural design, Lawson [3] presents design problems as the assembling of constraints.

1.2.7   Evolution and optimisation in a solution space of diversity

As consequences of the complexity of design problems, diversity presents in almost all design solutions. Diversity often leads to uncertainty, because the knowledge that there are many other solutions to the same design problem causes designers to question the optimality of their initial solution. Thus, they test, evaluate and modify their design. Designers compensate for weaknesses exposed during testing and evaluation. They redesign as necessary until they are satisfied with their design. Therefore, design processes often demonstrate an evolution process. The evolution of a design is often closely related to the consolidation of the constraints and requirements applied in a particular design situation. Design requirements are often imprecise and incomplete. The consequences of a design decision often cannot be forecast with complete accuracy. Hence, design solutions evolve in tandem with known problem constraints and requirements. Eventually, a successful design process includes a convergence of requirements, constraints, and knowledge about the design and its effects on the implementation environment.

1.3   ESSENTIAL ELEMENTS OF DESIGNS

Having studied the characteristics of design processes, now let's examine the plan facet of design and identify the basic elements of designs. We will look to the designs made by a mastermind of designs, Thomas Edison, as our examples. Figure 1.1 is the one of Edison's USA patents of electric lights [13].

Notice that, the design presented in the document is not the kind of electric lights that we are using nowadays. It can be considered as one of Edison's designs of electric lights at an early stage of a long evolutionary design process. Although the design was not presented as a complete engineering design document due to the nature of the document, it still contained the basic components of all engineering designs. These components are discussed below.

1.3.1   Statement of design problem and objectives

The objective of a design is the problem to be solved and the goal to achieve. For example, in Edison's patent, it was stated that the design was about electric lights.

Design problems are often described as ill-structured [14] or 'wicked' [15] in contrast to well-structured or well defined problems such as chess-playing or crossword puzzles. Well defined problems have a clear goal, often one correct answer, and specific rules or known ways of proceeding that will generate an answer. The characteristics of ill-structured or wicked problems can be summarised as follows.

(a) No definitive formulation of the problem.

When a design problem is initially set, the goals are usually vague and many constraints and criteria are unknown. The context of the problem is often complex and poorly understood. In the example of Edison's design of electric lights, the goal of designing an electric light was obviously vague and the context was unclear. Understanding such a design problem is bound up with the ideas that we may have about solving it. This may lead to certain temporal formulations of the problem. For example, in the course of problem solving, Edison made a temporal formulation of the problem by assuming that an electric light was an apparatus that produces electric light *'by coil or strip of platinum or other metal that requires a high temperature to melt, the electric current rendering the same incandescent'*. This led to the problem that *'there is danger of the metal melting and destroying*

BEST AVAILABLE COPY

UNITED STATES PATENT OFFICE.

THOMAS A. EDISON, OF MENLO PARK, NEW JERSEY.

IMPROVEMENT IN ELECTRIC LIGHTS.

Specification forming part of Letters Patent No. **214,636**, dated April 22, 1879; application filed
October 14, 1878.

CASE 156.

To all whom it may concern:

Be it known that I, THOMAS A. EDISON, of Menlo Park, in the State of New Jersey, have invented an Improvement in Electric Lights, of which the following is a specification.

Electric lights have been produced by a coil or strip of platina or other metal that requires a high temperature to melt, the electric current rendering the same incandescent. In all such lights there is danger of the metal melting and destroying the apparatus, and breaking the continuity of the circuit.

My improvement is made for regulating the electric current passing through such incandescent conductor automatically, and preventing its temperature rising to the melting-point, thus producing a reliable electric light by rendering conducting substances incandescent by passing an electric current through them.

In my apparatus the heat evolved or developed is made to regulate the electric current, so that the heat cannot become too intense, because the current is lessened by the effect of the heat when certain temperatures are reached, thereby preventing injury to the incandescent substance, by keeping the heat at all times below the melting-point of the incandescent substance.

Various devices for carrying my improvement into practice may be employed, and I have tested a large number. I however have shown in the drawings my improvement in a convenient form, and contemplate obtaining separate patents hereafter for other and various details of construction, and I state my present invention to relate, broadly, to the combination, with an electric light produced by incandescence, of an automatic thermal regulator for the electric current.

Figure 1 represents the electric-light apparatus in the form in which the thermal regulator acts by the heating effect of the current itself, and Fig. 2 illustrates the same invention when the radiated heat from the incandescent conductor operates the thermal regulator.

The incandescent metal is to be platinum, rhodium, iridium, titanium, or any other suit-

able conductor having a high fusing-point, and the same is used in the form of a wire or thin plate or leaf.

I have shown the platinum wire a as a double spiral, the two ends terminating upon the posts b c, to which the conductors d e are connected. The double spiral a is free to expand or contract by the heat, as both ends are below the spiral.

A circuit-closing lever, f, is introduced in the electric circuit, the points of contact being at i, and there is a platinum or similar wire, k, connected from the lever f to the head-piece or other support l.

The current from a magneto-electric machine, a battery, or any other source of electric energy, is connected to the binding-posts n o, and when contact at i is broken the current passes from o through lever f, wire k, support l, wire e, post c, platina coil a, post b, and wire d, or metallic connection, to binding-screw n. In this instance the wire k, being small, is acted upon by the electric current and heated, and by its expansion the lever f is allowed to close upon i and short-circuit the current.

The contact-point i is movable, and it is adjusted so that the shunt will not be closed until the temperature of the apparatus arrives at the desired height, and, by diverting a portion or the whole of the current, the temperature of the incandescent conductor is maintained in such a manner that there will be no risk of the apparatus being injured by excessive heat or the conductor fused.

If the wire k is small, so as to be heated by the electricity itself, it may be placed in any convenient position relatively to the light; but if such wire is heated by radiation from the electric light, then it should be adjacent to the incandescent material.

In all instances, the expansion or contraction of a suitable material under changes of temperature forms a thermostatic current-regulator that operates automatically, to prevent injury to the apparatus and to the body heated by the current.

In Fig. 2 the current does not pass through the wire k, and the short-circuiting lever is

---

2   214,636

operated by the radiated heat expanding the wire k. This in practice does not operate as rapidly as the device shown in Fig. 1.

The electric light may be surrounded by a glass tube or any other suitable device, such as two concentric glass tubes with the intervening space filled with alum-water or other bad conductor of heat, the object being to retain the heat of the incandescent metal and prevent loss by radiation, thus requiring less current to supply the loss by radiation.

I am aware that the electric current has been used to produce heat, and that such heat has been employed to vary the relative position of the light-giving electrodes and the length of the intervening arc. In my light there is no electric arc.

I claim as my invention—

1. In combination with an electric light having a continuous incandescent conductor, a thermostatic circuit-regulator, substantially as set forth.

2. In combination with an electric light, a thermostatically-operated shunt, substantially as set forth.

Signed by me this 5th day of October, A. D. 1878.

THOMAS A. EDISON.

Witnesses:
  ALFRID SWANSON,
  STOCKTON L. GRIFFIN.

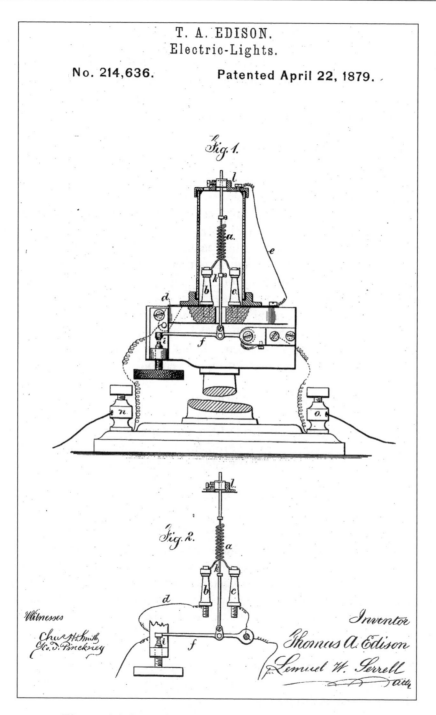

Figure 1.1 One of Edison's designs of electric lights

the apparatus, and breaking the continuity of the circuit'. However, as often occurs in all design processes, temporal formulations of design problems are unstable and can change as more information becomes available. Notice that, Edison's design of electric light presented in this patent is not that commonly used nowadays. Moreover, problem formulations are commonly inconsistent. Many conflicts and inconsistency must be resolved in the solution.

(b) No definitive solution to the problem.

Solutions to a design problem are often not true or false, but good or bad. Different solutions can be equally valid responses to the initial problem. There is often no objective criterion for the evaluation of a solution. However, solutions are assessed as good or bad, appropriate or inappropriate. For example, can we say Edison's design of electric lights presented in this patent is correct or incorrect? Instead, we might be able to say that this design is not as good as the design presented in Figure 1.3, which is now commonly in everyday use. Moreover, there is often no best solution. Essentially, this implies that there is a lack of any criteria that can be used as a 'stopping rule' to establish when the solution to a problem has been found such that any further work will not be able to improve upon it. No wonder why so many different types of electric lights have be designed, manufactured, marketed and used nowadays since Edison's invention.

(c) No definitive way of solving the problem.

There are no proven methods and rules that can definitely generate a solution to a design problem. Even a fairly precise problem statement gives no indication what a solution must be. Yet, solutions and problems influence each other in a 'wicked' way. A wicked problem can often be considered to be a symptom of another problem. Resolving a discrepancy or inconsistency in a design may pose another problem in its turn. The formulation of a problem often depends on the way of solving it. Many assumptions about the problem and specific areas of uncertainty can be exposed only by proposing solution concepts. Many constraints and criteria emerge as a result of evaluating solution proposals. Sub-solutions of the design problem can be found to be inter-connected with each other in ways that form a pernicious circular structure to the problem. For example, a sub-solution that resolves a particular sub-problem may create irreconcilable conflict with other sub-problems.

The ill-structured and wicked problem of design is the main reason why design is difficult. In Chapter 3, we will have a closer look at the particular reasons why software design is difficult.

1.3.2 Constraints

The objectives of a design often have to be achieved within certain constraints. These constraints define the solution space of the design problem. For the electric light problem, the most significant constraints are that the power must be electricity and it must be able to provide light continuously for a practically acceptable length of time. There are also other physical constraints, for example, the fusing-point of the metal used for the coil. Some of the constraints are explicitly mentioned in the patent document, and many others left as implicit. Some constraints are discovered and/or introduced by the designer during the course of design. In general, constraints can be classified along the following three dimensions according to Lawson [3].

(a) The generator of the constraint.

Constraints can be generated by the eventual users of the artefact, by the designers themselves, by legislators (e.g. safety related constraints), and by the design clients (i.e. the people who have commissioned or sponsored the design and who may or may not be eventual users of the artefact).

(b) The domain of the constraint.

According to Lawson, constraints fall into two domains, external and internal. External constraints are imposed by the factors not under the designer's control, while internal constraints give the designer at least some ability to control them.

(c) The function of the constraint.

Lawson's third dimension, constraint function, relates to the rationales behind the imposition of each of the constraints. Constraints can exist for reasons relating to symbolism and social norms, formal intentions of the designer, practical implications brought by the implementation technologies, and 'radical' reasons that deal with the primary purpose of the artefact.

1.3.3 Description of product

The main result of the design activity must be presented in the form of a description of the designed product. In this example, the product is described by the diagrams and in the text as well. The product of Edison's patent is an *automatic thermal regulator* for the electric current that prevents the melting and destroying of the apparatus. In addition to the description of the structure of the apparatus, there are also descriptions of the materials used to make the various parts of the apparatus and how the apparatus works.

Notice that Edison used two diagrams to indicate two different states of the apparatus. In more complicated products, engineers often find that it is too complicated to use only one diagram to describe the structure and states of a system. Therefore, a number of different diagrams or drawings may be used to give details of various parts of the system. Sometimes, different notations may be used to specify different aspects of the system. This is a common practice in all engineering designs. For example, Leonardo Da Vinci, a great artist and inventor in the 15th to 16th century, often produced a number of drawings for one design of machinery. As shown in Figure 1.2a, Leonardo presented his design of a crossbow by a drawing that shows its overall structure and several drawings of the critical parts of the crossbow. Similarly, Figure 1.2b is a design of a wing as a part of Leonardo's flying machine dated to between 1486 and 1490. On the lower right corner of the drawing shows how the wings are to be connected and operated. The main part of the drawing gives more details of the design of the wing itself. In software engineering, software designs are also represented in a number of interrelated diagrams and with text explanations. We will see some examples later in the book.

Representing a complicated design in a number of different levels of abstraction and with different details is, in fact, an important principle of the representation of engineering designs. It is recognised in software engineering as *structural* or *hierarchical representation*.

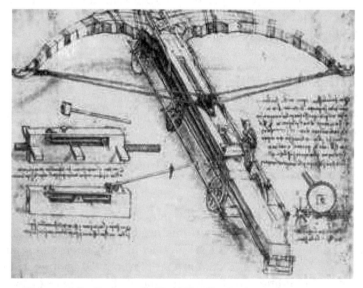

Figure 1.2a Leonardo Da Vinci's design of crossbow

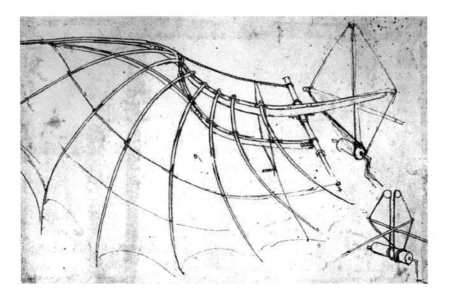

Figure 1.2b Leonardo Da Vinci's design of a flying machine

Using a number of diagrams to represent a complicated design is also related to another important principle of design, which is called *multiple views* in software engineering. Because the design and production of a system may involve many people of different backgrounds who play different roles in the course, the design should be presented to each person only with the information that they are concerned with and in the way that is suitable for their background and is convenient for them to work on. Therefore, different notations should be used to describe different aspects of a design. Such descriptions of one system in various notations form a set of models of the system. Each model presents a view of the system. These views must be consistent with each other.

1.3.4 Rationale

Engineering designs must be based on scientific principles and technical information. The rationale underlying a design justifies the design by applying such scientific and technological knowledge to show how the design problem is actually solved, or at least why we can predict that the design problem will be solved by the design. Edison gave a very clear expression of the rationale underlying this design. In particular, the automatic thermal regulator is deployed to keep the heat 'at all times below the melting-point of the incandescent substance'.

Since the document is only a partial result of an early stage of Edison's design of electric lights, there are a few important elements missing from the document.

These elements were presented in Edison's other patent documents. For example, the following elements can be found.

1.3.5 Plan of production

As an engineering design, we not only require to know whether a design can solve a problem, but also we must know the design is practical. One of the most fundamental questions related to the practicality of a design is how to bring about the design. In this case, it is the problem of the manufacture of light bulbs. Edison addressed this problem and obtained a number of his patents, which include the manufacture of Carbon filament, etc. Figure 1.3 shows the diagram in a patent by Edison in 1889 about how to manufacture electric lights[2] [16]. Sometimes, how to bring about a design is a common knowledge when the product is clearly described. However, engineers often found it is one of the most challenging problems of design.

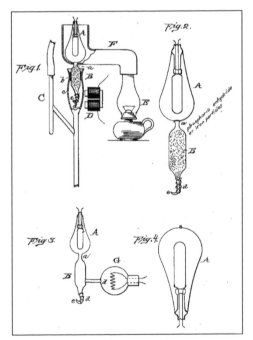

Figure 1.3 Manufacture of electric lights as patented by Edison

---

[2] Notice that the electric light is not the same as that in Figure 1.1.

1.3.6 Description of usage

There are always certain conditions under which a product can be used safely and effectively so that the objectives of the design can be achieved. How a product is to be used is sometimes not a trivial problem. Instead, it can be as hard as, sometimes even more difficult, to solve than the problem of designing the product itself. It may appear in the form of designing a system of which the product is only a part. Figure 1.4 shows the system of electric light as designed by Edison in one of his patents [17].

These elements of designs that we found in Edison's designs of electric lights appear in all designs including the designs of software systems although they may appear in different forms.

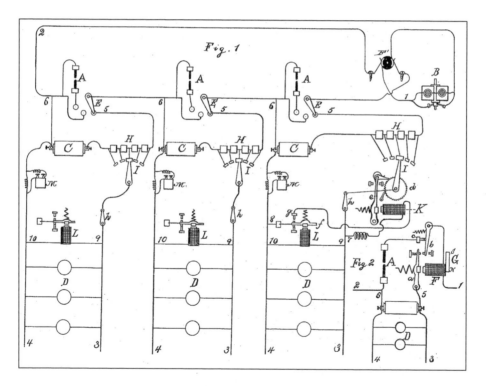

Figure 1.4 System of electric lights as patented by Edison

1.4   THE FACTORS THAT AFFECT DESIGNS

In search of the factors that affect design processes and outcomes and the analysis of their interrelationships, Mayall proposed a set of axioms as the principles of designs [18]. Although different types of product may have different features and their design processes may involve different domain-specific activities, Mayall's axioms present a set of general laws of design that characterise the nature of design. The following looks at these general laws and explains them in the context of software design.

(1) *The Principle of Totality*: All design requirements are always interrelated and must always be treated as such throughout a design task.

This axiom states that design requirements are the most important factor that affects the whole design process. Moreover, the elements of design requirements are interrelated and should be treated as a whole during design.

This axiom is very much true in software design. The relationships between software requirements vary significantly. Sometimes, users' requirements conflict one to another. It has been widely recognised that conflict resolution and requirements prioritisation must be considered as an essential part of requirements analysis in software development. The axiom also tells us that design decisions must be made on the basis of a deep understanding of the interrelationships between the requirements.

(2) *The Principle of Time*: The features and characteristics of all products change as time passes.

This axiom states that time is an important factor that affects designs. This nature of design has been well demonstrated in software designs. For example, 20 years ago, a program that interacts with the user through command line input/output may be considered as user-friendly, if it gives prompts for user's input and displays outputs in the form of dialogues. Now, with the wide spread of graphic user interfaces, such computer-human interaction can hardly be considered as user-friendly. A program that uses 10 mega-bites of memory space would be considered as requiring too much resource and impractical 20 years ago, but nowadays a student dissertation project would normally take more than that size of memory space. Therefore, a design cannot be evaluated without taking into consideration of the times when the design was made and when the evaluation was made.

(3) *The Principle of Value*: The characteristics of all products have different relative values depending upon the different circumstances and times in which they may be used.

This axiom states that the relative value of a product is an important issue that must be taken into consideration in the design. It further states that the value depends on the circumstances and time when the product is used. It is not fixed. A good software design made ten years ago is probably out of date and less satisfactory now because users' requirements have changed and the hardware and software platforms to implement and execute the software have also changed. Features that were considered desirable years ago may have become less important, unnecessary even harmful, while new features become the most important. Different users may value the same product differently. Even the same user may value the same product differently upon different circumstances such as in different use purposes. Designers should be aware of the user types and their purposes of use and to apply this knowledge in the design of the software. Adaptability for a wide range of user types should be considered.

(4) *The Principle of Resources*: The design, manufacture and life of all products and systems depend upon the materials, tools and skills upon which we can call.

This axiom states that the resources that are available for the design, manufacture and operation of the product are important factors that design must take into consideration. Such resources include tools, skills and materials. Software development, operation and maintenance demand a large amount of resources, which include the following types: (a) *development tools*, such as programming languages and compilers, CASE tools including configuration management and testing tools, etc. (b) *run time support systems*, including software and hardware platforms, other system software such as database management systems, network protocols, etc. (c) *human resource*, which is perhaps the most important among all resources of software development, (d) *application domain-specific tools and equipment*, especially in the development of embedded systems.

(5) *The Principle of Synthesis*: All features of a product must combine to satisfy all the characteristics we expect it to possess with an acceptable relative importance for as long as we wish, bearing in mind the resources available to make and use it.

This axiom states that features, or functions, of a product constitute a factor that affects design as the objective of design. They combine together to satisfy the requirements. In software engineering, a good design must take all functional and non-functional requirements and their relationships into account. In software design practice, it is almost inevitable to make trade-offs between desirable features and functions. Such trade-offs must be based on a deep understanding of the users' requirements as a whole and bear in mind the constraints on the resource available. In the next chapter, we will examine in detail the quality attributes of software systems and software development processes. We will see that certain quality attributes may affect other quality attributes in a negative way.

(6) *The Principle of Iteration*: Design requires processes of evaluation that begin with the first intentions to explore the need for a product or system. These processes continue throughout all subsequent design and development stages to the user himself, whose reactions will often cause the iterative process to continue with a new product or system.

This principle states the importance of design process. It emphasises the importance of evaluation of design and users' feedback, which is no exception to software design. In fact, being perhaps the most complicated artefacts that human beings have ever designed and built, software systems are difficult to design, evaluate and validate. Software development practices indicate that errors made during design stage are difficult even impossible to rectify at later stages during implementation and maintenance. As a consequence of evaluation and validation, also for many other reasons, designs have to be changed to correct errors and to improve quality. Such changes often need to go through many loops of evaluation-modification iteration to reach a satisfactory status.

(7) *The Principle of Change*: Design is a process of change, an activity undertaken not only to meet changing circumstance, but also to bring about changes to those circumstances by the nature of the product it creates.

This axiom states that the consequence of design is to bring about changes. The application of computers has significantly changed the way we work and live, and brought the human civilisation to the so-called information age. Information systems can be classified into three types according to the changes that they bring about. An information system is *automational*, if it automates certain activities that were originally carried out by human beings. It is called *informative*, if it generates information that was not available before. It is called *transformational*, if it changes the way that business or certain tasks were carried out within the organisation. The design of a software system must take into consideration about how the software is to be used. We need to consider not only how the design fits into the way that we are working and living, but also how it changes the way that we will work and live as the consequence of using the system. Software designers must be aware of their responsibility. On the other hand, the changed world raises new requirements for software designers. This requires new designs of software systems as well as modifications on existing systems. An important quality issue of software designs is modifiability, which means whether it is easy to make modifications.

(8) *The Principle of Relationships*: Design work cannot be undertaken effectively without established working relationships with all those activities concerned with the conception, manufacture and marketing of products and, importantly, with the prospective user, together with all the services he may call upon to assist his judgement and protect his interests.

Of course, the people involved in the design process are a very important factor that affects design. What's important is not only the individuals involved in design, but also the working relationships between them. Software design methodologies have also identified various stakeholders who may contribute to software design in various ways. Typically, in addition to software designers, other stakeholders involved in software design include:

- *Customers:* who purchase the software

- *Users:* who use the software and are responsible for executing the software

- *System administrator:* who is responsible for managing the data repositories used by the systems

- *Project managers:* who manage the software development process

- *Developers*: who are responsible for developing and/or modifying the runtime functions of the system. Developers can be further divided into a number of sub-types of stakeholders, such as requirements analysts, designers, programmers, testers, etc.

- *Requirements analysts:* who analyse, specify and approve the requirements of the system which is the basis of design

- *Designers*: who design the software system at architectural level or at detail level. In particular, designers of software architectures are often call software architects

- *Programmers:* who implement the software according to the design

- *Testers:* who review and/or inspect various development documents and test the software product after implementation

- *Auditors:* who audit the development activity

- *Support technicians:* who provide technical supports, such as providing and maintaining software development and design tools.

(9) *The Principle of Competence*: Design competence is the ability to create a synthesis of features that achieves all desired characteristics in terms of their required life and relative value, using available effective information about this synthesis to those who will turn it into products or systems.

This axiom states that an important factor that affects design is the competence of the designer. In the context of software design, this principle reads that design competence is the ability to design a software system that satisfies all requirements including functional and non-functional requirements and to effectively document the design so that the software can be implemented according to the design.

(10) *The Principle of Service*: Design must satisfy everybody, and not just those for whom its products are directly intended.

This axiom states that service must also be considered in design. In the context of software design, a good design should not only satisfy the requirements of the intended usage of the system, but should also satisfy other stakeholders. For example, it must be easy to maintain, easy to reuse, easy to transport to other operation environments and to be inter-operable to other software systems, etc.

SUMMARY

There are two facets of the concept of design. Firstly, a design is a *plan* to bring about a man-made product. Such a plan must achieve a prescribed goal and satisfy certain constraints. Secondly, it is a *process* of the creative development of such a plan. During this process, the designer must use related scientific principles, technical information and imagination to discover constraints and to solve the design problem. Therefore, we can define engineering design as follows.

Engineering design is the use of scientific principles and technical information in the creative development of a plan to bring about a man-made product to achieve a prescribed goal with certain specified constraints. The consequence of the implementation of the design will bring changes to the environment, while the environment of the designer influences the design itself. Software design is a branch of engineering design where the product to bring about is software.

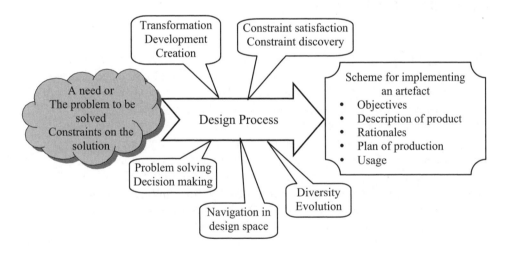

Figure 1.5 Basic concepts of design

As depicted in Figure 1.5, design activities have the following characteristics. Design starts with a need and requires intention. It results in a scheme for implementing an artefact. It involves transformations and the generation of new ideas is fundamental to all designs. Design is goal directed problem solving and decision making. It must satisfy the constraints and the requirements. The design process is also a constraint discovery process. Design is to achieve optimality in a solution space of diversity; hence, it is often an evolutionary process.

An engineering design should contain at least five basic elements: (a) the objectives of the design, (b) a description of the designed product, (c) the rationale of the design, (d) a plan of the production, and finally, (e) the designated usage of the product.

There are a number of factors that effect design processes and their outcomes. These factors include (a) the requirements to be satisfied by the design, (b) the time design was made and evaluated, (c) the value of the product, (d) the resource available to the design, manufacture and use of the product, (e) the features, or functions, of the product, (f) the process of design, (g) the consequence of design, i.e. the change to be brought about, (h) the people involved in the design process and their working relationships, (i) the competence of the designer, (j) the service of the designed products. These factors interrelate with each other as stated in the axioms of design proposed by Mayall.

FURTHER READING

There are a number of books on design methodology, most of which illustrate the theory with examples of designs of architectures, physical articles and machinery. For example, Jones' book *Design Methods: Seeds of Human Future* [1] is one of the best-known. The book *Developments of Design Methodology* [19] edited by Cross and published in 1984 collected a number of papers on design methodology that represent the milestones in the development of design methodology into an independent scientific discipline. Many of the authors of the papers collected in the book have been referred to in this chapter. The current state of art in the research on design methodology is well represented by the publications in the Design Research Society's quarterly journal *Design Studies*, which is published by Elsevier Science and Technology in London. More details about the journal including table of contents in each issue can be found at the website of the journal at the URL: http://www.drs.org.uk/. The research on software design has evolved rapidly over the past few decades. Most of the earliest work on the subject is collected in the *Tutorial on Software Design Techniques* [20] edited by Freeman and Wasserman and published by IEEE in 1980. Since then, significant progress has been made.

EXERCISES

(1–1) Discuss whether an activity can be considered as a design activity if it has no fixed goals or objectives to achieve.

(1–2) Discuss why the output of design is a symbolic representation of an artefact for implementation rather than a real product.

(1–3) Discuss whether code in a high level programming language is an appropriate form to represent the results of software design.

(1–4) Regarding design as a process of transformation, discuss what is transformed in software design.

(1–5) Discuss why design is a creative activity.

(1–6) Discuss why design problems are often said to be ill-structured. Give an example of an ill-structured design problem.

(1–7) Discuss why decision making in design process often faces uncertainty.

(1–8) Consider the following constraints imposed on the design of a software system. Apply Lawson's theory of constraints to analyse these constraints and find out the three dimensions of each constraint.

  (a) The software is to be executed on a PDA (Personal Data Assistance);

  (b) The output of the software must be displayed on the screen of the size $3'' \times 2''$;

  (c) The software should be easy to operate through a small keypad that has character buttons and some functional buttons;

  (d) The software can only be used if the user subscribes to a specific online service of the client's company;

  (e) The software will be implemented using the C language.

(1–9) Discuss why testing and evaluation of designs are important.

(1–10) Assume that you want to make a bookshelf to put in your room.

(i) Make a design of the bookshelf, and record the activities that you perform during the design process.

(ii) Answer the following questions.

(a) What are the objectives of the design? How do they interrelate to each other?

(b) What are the constraints on the design at the beginning? Do you discover any constraints during the course of design?

(c) What are the stakeholders involved in the design? (*Hint: a person involved in a design may play different roles. In such cases, the person should be considered as different stakeholders.*)

(d) What is the designed product? How do you describe it?

(e) What is your plan of making the bookshelf? How do you describe the plan?

(f) What are the design decisions you made during the design and what are your rationales of the specific design?

(g) What are the normal use conditions of the bookshelf? Are the conditions the same as the condition in which the bookshelf will be used? What are the consequences if any of the conditions is not satisfied?

(h) What are the changes that the bookshelf will bring to you?

(1–11) Design a software system and present your design in a document.

(i) Does your document contain all the elements discussed in section 1.3?

(ii) Replace the term 'bookshelf' in the questions (a)–(h) of exercise (1–10) with the software that you design. Then, find their answers from the design document.

(ii) Discuss the consequences if one element is missing from the document.

(1–12) Give an example of a software system that was considered as a good design several years ago, but now it is considered as out of date. Discuss the reasons why it happened by referring to Mayall's axioms.

(1–13) Give an example of a software system that was considered as a bad design several years ago, but now has become widely used and considered as a good design. Discuss the reasons why it happened by referring to Mayall's axioms.

(1–14) Give an example of information system for each type of automational, informative, and transformational information systems.

(1–15) A hospital would like to develop an online patient information system. Discuss the stakeholders who might be involved in the development of the system.

(1–16) Use the record of the design process that you made in answering question (1–10) to examine and explain Mayall's axiom of designs.

REFERENCES

1   Jones, C. J., *Design Methods: Seeds of Human Futures,* John Wiley & Sons, 1970.

2   McPhee, K. , *Design Theory and Software Design*, Technical Report TR 96-26, October 1996, Department of Computing Science, The University of Alberta, Canada, 1996.

3   Lawson, B., *How Designers Think*, The Architectural Press Ltd., London, 1980.

4   Dasgupta, S. , The structure of design processes, in *Advances in Computers*, Yovits, M. C., Ed., Academic Press, 1989, pp1–67.

5   Willem, R. A. , Design and science, *Design Studies*, Vol. 11, No. 1, pp43–47, 1990.

6   Willem, R. A. , Varieties of design, *Design Studies*, Vol. 12, No. 3, pp132–136, 1991.

7   MacLean, A. , Bellotti, V. and Young, R., What rationale is there in design?, in *Human-Computer Interaction – INTERACT'90*, 1990, pp207–212.

8   Simon, H. A. , The structure of ill-structured problems, *Artificial Intelligence*, Vol. 4, pp181–200, 1973.

9   *Building for People*, 1965 Conference Report, UK Ministry of Public Building and Works, London, 1965.

10 Freeman, P. , The nature of design, in *Tutorial on Software Design Techniques*, Freeman, P. and Wasserman, A. I. Eds, IEEE, 1980, pp46–53.

11 Mostow, J. , Toward better models of design process, *AI Magazine*, Vol. 6, No. 1, pp44–57, Spring, 1985.

12 Alexander, C., *Notes on the Synthesis of Form*, Harvard University Press, Cambridge, Mass., 1964.

13 Edison, T. A., Improvement in electric lights, United States Patent Office, No. 214,636, April 22, 1879.

14 Simon, H. A., The structure of ill-structured problems, in *Developments of Design Methodology*, Cross, N. (Ed.), pp145–166, Wiley, 1984.

15 Rittel, H. J. and Webber, M. M., Planning problems are wicked problems, in *Developments in Design Methodology*, Cross, N. (ed.), pp135–144, Wiley, 1984.

16 Edison, T. A., Manufacture of incandescent electric lights, United States Patent Office, No. 411,019, Sept. 17, 1889.

17 Edison, T. A., System of electric lighting, United States Patent Office, No. 446,666, Feb. 17, 1891.

18 Mayall, W. H., *Principles in Design*, Design Council, London, 1979.

19 Cross, N. (Ed.), *Developments of Design Methodology*, Wiley, 1984.

20 Freeman, P. and Wasserman, A. I. (Eds.), *Tutorial on Software Design Techniques*, IEEE, 1980.

2 Design Quality

This chapter addresses the question of what constitute a good design. As discussed in Chapter 1, a design is essentially a plan to bring about a man-made artefact. Therefore, there are two facets of the quality of a design. The first is the quality related to the product it brings about. The second is the quality related to the process of bringing about the product. Of course, these two facets are closely related. The objectives of the chapter are:

- To understand the quality of software systems;

- To understand how design affects software quality;

- To understand the quality attributes of software design.

The chapter is organised as follows. In section 2.1, we first briefly review the theories about software quality. In section 2.2, we discuss the impact of design on software quality. In section 2.3, we discuss the quality attributes of software design.

2.1   SOFTWARE QUALITY MODELS

Quality is one of the most elusive concepts that one may have. Different people may have different views on what is quality and how to measure the quality of a product or service. Even the same people may have different views on quality from time to time. According to the general theory of quality management, the complex and multifaceted concept can be described from five different views [1]. The *transcendental* view sees quality as something that can be recognised but not defined. It is the excellence of the product or service. From a *user's* point of view, quality is 'fitness for purpose'. This view of quality evaluates the product or service according to whether it meets the user's needs. It, therefore, can be highly personal. The *value-based* view of quality is concerned with the ability to provide what the customer requires at a price that they can afford. Therefore, quality depends on the amount that a customer is willing to pay for it. From the *manufacturing* point of view, the quality of a product is the conformance to specification. It see quality as whether it is constructed 'right the first time', therefore, the costs associated with rework during development and after delivery can be avoided. It focuses on the development and construction process and leads to quality assessment that is virtually independent of the product itself. In contrast, the *product* view sees the quality of a product as tied to inherent characteristics of the product. It looks inside of the product. Therefore, quality can be measured by a number of quality attributes or inherent characteristics of the product. Ideally, these quality attributes should reflect users' views of quality and reflect the value of the product and the quality of manufacturing. As software designers, we take the product view of quality to study what quality attributes the software should have. The questions are: What are software quality attributes? How are they interrelated? Proposals to answer these questions have been advanced as software quality models.

2.1.1   Hierarchical models

There are a great number of quality attributes identified for software products. These quality attributes are often classified into a hierarchical structure to highlight the relationship between them. For example, McCall [2] divided software quality attributes into 3 groups as shown in Figure 2.1. Each group represents the quality with respect to one aspect of the software system while the attributes in the group contribute to that aspect. Each quality attribute is defined by a question so that the quality of the software system can be assessed by answering the question.

Similar models of software quality include Boehm's model [3] and the ISO 9126 software quality model [4]; also see exercise (2–1). Such a hierarchical model has the advantage of simplicity. However, the relationships between quality attributes are more complicated than hierarchical models can describe. It cannot express negative relationships, which means if a software system is good on one attribute, then it will inevitably be bad on another attribute. For example, if a program has a fault-tolerant property, its efficiency will probably suffer.

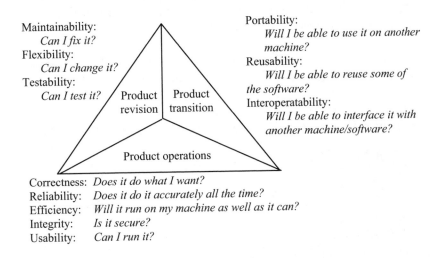

Figure 2.1 McCall's model of software quality

2.1.2   Relational models

The shortcomings of hierarchical models were addressed by Perry [5]. Perry's model contains three types of relationship between the quality attributes. The *direct* relationship between two quality attributes means that if a software system is good at one attribute it should also be good at the other attribute. The *inverse* relationship means that a software system that is good at one attribute will not be good at the other attribute. The *neutral* relationship means that the two attributes are normally independent of each other. Perry analysed 12 pairs of quality attributes for their relationships, see Figure 2.2. The following are some examples.

- *Integrity vs. efficiency* (inverse): The control of data access will need additional code, leading to a longer runtime and more storage requirement.

- *Usability vs. efficiency* (inverse): Improvement of HCI will need more code and data, hence the system will be less efficient.

- *Maintainability and testability vs. efficiency* (inverse): Compact and optimised code is not easy to maintain and test, and well-commented code is less efficient.

- *Flexibility, reusability vs. integrity* (inverse): Flexible data structures required for flexible and reusable software increase the data security problem.

- *Flexibility and reusability vs. maintainability* (direct): Maintainable code arises from the code that is well structured; meantime, well-structured maintainable code is easy to reuse in other programs.

- *Portability vs. reusability* (direct): Portable code is likely to be easily used in other environments. The code is likely well-structured and easier to be reused.

- *Correctness vs. efficiency* (neutral): The correctness of code has no relation with its efficiency. Correct code may be efficient or inefficient in operation.

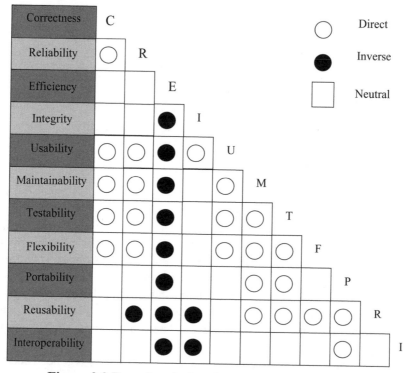

Figure 2.2 Perry's relational model of software quality

Perry's model is a relational model in which stereotypes of relations between quality attributes are defined and represented. Perry's model is very useful. However, it still suffers from two shortcomings. The first is that his analysis is based on 'common sense' and lack of hard evidence. In fact, the relationship between quality attributes can be much more complicated and often application-dependent. The second is the assumption that the relationships are commutative.

In a study of software quality in six big organisations, Gillies developed six hierarchical quality models, in terms of the criteria used by both users and developers of software[6]. Gillies also gave a relational model, illustrated in Figure 2.3. As many as 16 pairs of quality attributes appeared in his model. His studies demonstrated that the relationships were often not commutative, which means although attribute A may reinforce attribute B, attribute B may not reinforce attribute A. Gillies claimed that his relational model was not project dependent.

Criteria	R	E	I	S	U	F	EI	P	U	A	T	T	A	U	C
Reliability	O	+	+	O	O	O	O	O	O	O	O	O	O	O	O
Efficiency	O	–	–	–	–	–	–	–	O	–	+	–	–	O	–
Integrity	+	–	+	+	O	–	–	+	+	–	O	O	–	O	+
Security	+	–	+	+	O	–	–	+	+	–	O	O	–	O	–
Understandability	O	–	O	O	+	O	O	O	O	–	–	O	O	O	O
Flexibility	O	–	O	O	+	O	O	O	O	–	–	O	–	O	–
Ease of interfacing	O	O	+	+	+	+	+	+	–	–	O	O	O	O	O
Portability	O	–	O	O	O	+	+	O	O	–	O	O	O	O	–
User consultation	O	O	+	O	+	O	O	O	O	–	O	O	O	O	O
Accuracy	+	O	+	+	+	O	O	O	+	–	O	O	O	O	O
Timeliness	–	O	–	–	O	–	–	–	–	–	–	–	–	O	–
Time to use	+	+	O	O	–	–	–	O	O	O	+	+	–	O	–
Appeal	+	+	O	+	+	+	+	+	+	+	+	+	+	+	+
User flexibility	O	–	O	O	O	+	O	+	+	+	O	–	O	O	O
Cost/benefit	+	+	+	+	+	+	O	O	+	+	+	+	O	+	+
User friendliness	+	O	O	O	O	O	O	O	+	O	–	O	+	+	O

O   no relationship or that the relationship is heavily context-dependent.
+   direct
–   inverse

Figure 2.3 Gillies' relational model of software quality criteria

Relational models improved hierarchical models by providing more types of relationships between quality attributes. However, the relationships are simplified to be binary and stereotypes. Both hierarchical models and relational models discussed above are generic models. They are claimed to be applicable to all software systems. Therefore, they ignored the issues related to the specific features and application domains. For example, there is no weight associated to the quality attributes to express their relative importance. As discussed in Chapter 1, in general, quality attributes are not always of equal importance. This is equally true for software systems. For example, for the software that controls a nuclear power station, safety[1] is perhaps the most important quality attribute, while, for a word processor, it is not an issue at all. Moreover, the importance of a quality attribute in assessing a particular software system may change as time passes. The value of a quality attribute for a given system can also change. Therefore, a good design made ten years ago can become less satisfactory now and might be regarded as out of date. Such phenomena are not unique for software designs. In fact, they are more general for all types of designs as stated in Mayall's axioms [7]; see also Chapter 1. These properties of software quality are not represented in the quality models discussed in this section.

[1] Software safety is a quality attribute that the software should never cause harm to human lives or severe damage to the environment.

2.2 THE EFFECT OF DESIGN ON SOFTWARE QUALITY

Software quality must be addressed during the whole process of software development. However, design is of particular importance in developing quality software for two reasons. First, design is the first stage in software system creation in which quality requirements can begin to be addressed. Errors made at this stage can be costly, even impossible, to be rectified. Second, as we will see below, design decisions have significant effects on the quality of the final product. Of course, design has many different aspects. Software design tasks can be divided into several interrelated subtasks such as architectural design, interface design and detail design including algorithm and data structure design.[2] Architecture design determines how a software system is decomposed into components and how these components are interconnected. Interface design determines how the software interacts with its environment, such as human computer interactions (HCI). Detail design determines the details of the implementation, such as the algorithms and data structures for implementing each functionality and component, and the programming language for coding. Different quality attributes manifest themselves differently during various phases. The following discusses how architecture design, interface design and detailed design affect the key quality attributes of software.

2.2.1 Efficiency

Efficiency refers to the responsiveness of the system, i.e. the time required to respond to stimuli (events), or the number of events processed in some interval of time. The time to process a sequence of events can be divided into three parts.

First, time is needed to communicate between different software components that collaborate to process an event. The structure of a software system determines how much time is required by the communication between components in terms of the amount of communications required and the means of communications and interactions between components. The amount of communication depends on how functions of a software system are grouped into components. A bad design would result in a large amount of communication between components; while a good design can keep communications within components hence avoid unnecessary communications between components. The means of communication depends on the nature of components. For example, if a component is a procedure,

---

[2] Software design processes will be discussed in more detail in Chapter 3.

communication with the component must be through a procedure call. If the component is a process, the communication must be through messages between processes. The time required for a communication between components also depends on how components are distributed on the network. If the components reside on different computing elements, such as on different computers in a distributed system, the communication between these components has to go through a communication network, which takes much longer than communications between two components that reside on the same computer. However, even if the components are on the same computer, the amount of time required for interaction by subroutine invocations, message passing between processes, or other communication mechanisms still takes much longer than straight line codes and shared memory. In general, communication tends to be a performance driver, which makes efficiency largely a function of architecture.

Second, the computation times that components executed may have overlaps or gaps between them, i.e. the executions can be in parallel and time is required to synchronise their executions. Architectural design also determines how much parallel execution can be achieved and how long parallel processes have to spend on synchronisation and mutual exclusion. A good division and grouping of functionality into components and distribution of components on different computing processors would maximise components' parallel executions and minimise time spent on synchronisation and waiting for each other. Therefore, architectural design plays a key role in determining the performance of the software.

Third, the times are needed for each component to complete its computation. Once given an architectural design, the performance depends on the choice of algorithms and data structures to implement selected functionality assigned to the components. It also depends on how the algorithms are coded, e.g. in a particular programming language. The selection of algorithms, data structures and programming language is an issue of detailed design, while the coding is an implementation issue.

Interface design determines how the users interact with the software system and decides which graphical user interface package is used or the functionality of the package. The efficiency of the human–computer interaction process and the efficiency of the GUI package all have effects on the efficiency of the system, although such effect is normally less significant than architecture design and algorithm and data structure designs.

2.2.2 Correctness and reliability

Correctness is the property that software implements the specified users' requirements. It is impossible that a design at any level that does not correctly implement the specified requirements would lead to a correct implementation. Reliability can be defined as the probability that a system performs user required functionality correctly at a specified environment in a given period of time. Although reliability can be measured in a number of different ways, such as the mean time between failures, the probability of failure on demand, availability and so on, reliability largely depends on the amount of faults (i.e. defects) in the software system. Such faults can be faults at architectural structure, errors in algorithm and data structure design, flaws in coding and implementation. A good architectural design naturally decomposes a complicated design problem into simpler sub-problems and provides an understandable solution of the original problem. This can reduce the probability of errors made at lower level design and implementation. Well-structured designs also help on testability so that errors in design and implementation can be tested and fixed. Software fault-tolerant features can also be introduced in architecture design to detect failures and to recover from failures at run-time, hence improve the reliability of the system.

Interface design plays a major role in human–computer interaction. It has been recognised that human operation errors constitute a large proportion of system failures. Good HCI designs can prevent invalid input and misinterpretation of output; hence, they can significantly reduce the probability of system failures caused by human operation errors.

Detailed design such as algorithm and data structure design affect the simplicity of the coding. The choice of programming language determines whether algorithms and data structures can be naturally and easily coded. The choice of programming language, algorithm and data structure etc. should also take into consideration the programmer's experience. Such factors have great impact on the probability that the programmer correctly implements the designs.

2.2.3 Portability

Portability is the property of a software system that can be easily transported from one hardware/software platform to another, for example, from a PC/Windows environment to a Sun/Unix environment or a Macintosh environment. Moving from one environment to another usually requires replacing the part of the code that depends on the facilities provided by the environment, such as system calls. A well structured design should group environment dependent code into a small number of components so that the change on the code to move to another environment can be achieved by replacing such components with new ones rather than rewrite the whole system.

At detail design level, the design of algorithms and data structures should not heavily depend on the platform specific feature so that portability can be obtained.

As for interface design, if an interface is heavily dependent on the environment specific features, the moving from one environment to another will be difficult. With the standardisation of graphic user interface supporting packages and their availability in various environments, interface designs are more or less environment independent. However, even if an interface is represented in an environment independent standard format such as in HTML, different web browsers may give different results and cause problems in using the same software in different environments.

2.2.4 Maintainability

Maintainability refers to the easiness of maintaining a software system. There are two types of software maintenance operations. One is the modification of the software system for correction of bugs that are found during the operation. Such modifications are called corrective maintenance. The second is the modification of the system due to environment changes, such as the upgrade of the system software, e.g. the operating system and the database management system. Such modifications are usually called adaptive maintenance. Both types of maintenance operations require software engineers who understand how the software system works so that bugs can be fixed and changes in the environment can be adapted. Well-structured design helps software engineers to understand the system. Hence, architectural design plays an important role in maintenance, while maintainability is less heavily dependent on detail design and interface design.

2.2.5 Reusability

Reusability is the property of a software system that its components can be easily reused in the development of other software systems.[3] Reusability depends on the generality of the components in a given application domain and the extent to which the components are parameterised and configurable. Architecture design is obviously of significant importance because it determines how the functionality of

---

[3] Reuse can be defined in a more general sense for all types of software artefacts, such as the reuse of a design, reuse of a test plan, etc.

a software system is decomposed into components and how they are inter-connected. If such architecture can be used in a series of applications in a particular domain, and the components can be developed for reuse again and again, productivity can be significantly improved. This idea of reuse has been proposed and further developed into component-based software development and software production lines; see, for example, [8]. Detailed design in terms of algorithm and data structure design also play a role in reusability in the way that they determine how easily the components can be parameterised and the way to configure the components. However, they are less influential to reusability. Interface design contributes to the reusability in a minor way in that it determines how reusable the interface is.

2.2.6 Interoperability

Interoperability is the property of how easy a software system can be used with other software systems. For example, the interoperation of a word processor with an image processing system requires that the result of one software system, such as image processing of a photo, can be used in another so that a document can contain both text and image contents. Interoperability mostly depends on the interface between a software system and its environment. It requires that the implementation of the software follow certain standard interface and coding conventions. Architecture design and algorithm and data structure design have little to do with interoperability.

The discussion made above on the effects of design on software quality demonstrates that design is critical to many of the quality attributes of software systems, and these qualities should be designed in and evaluated at the design phase. However, some quality attributes are not sensitive to certain levels of design. It would not be fruitful attempting to achieve qualities on these aspects via design or to analyse a design for its quality on such aspects. It should be noticed that the above discussion is not conclusive because it may be not true for all software systems.

In terms of different levels of design, algorithms and data structures are crucial to the correctness of the implementation of the functionalities of a software system. The structural issues include the division of functions into components, the interfaces between the components and the distribution of software components onto physical computational resources. These issues are crucial to almost all software quality attributes. This is especially true of efficiency, reusability, portability, interoperability, maintainability, and reliability, etc. Interface between a software system and its environment, including the hardware and software platform that it executes on, is crucial to the portability. Human computer interaction design is crucial to the usability of the system and may have a significant impact on human errors in the use of the system; see exercise (2–5).

2.3 QUALITY ATTRIBUTES OF SOFTWARE DESIGN

Having discussed what software quality means and how design affects software quality, we can now answer the question – what constitutes a good design. A simple answer to this question is that a good design should be able to bring about a good software system and lead to a quality development process for bringing about the product. However, such an answer provides little direct guidance to our software design activities. Therefore, we will apply the general theory of quality again and take the product view to software design quality, i.e. the quality of a software design is the totality of its quality attributes. Among many software design quality attributes, some are believed to be more important than the others. In the literature of software design methodology, different authors have proposed different sets of quality attributes that are considered as most desirable.

2.3.1 Witt, Baker and Merritt's design objectives

Witt, Baker and Merritt regarded the following properties as design 'objectives' [9]. Most of these properties can be considered as quality attributes of software designs.

(1) *Modularity*: The design should be composed of replaceable, self-contained assemblies of elementary parts, thereby aiding both the initial development and the later maintenance.

(2) *Portability*: Individual parts of the design, as well as the design as a whole, should be capable of reuse in different environments. The designed product should be able to be moved unchanged from test environments to operational environments and from one operational environment to another.

(3) *Malleability*: The design should facilitate adaptation to changing end-user requirements, for example, changes based on new problems in the end users' world, the discovery of a need for information not previously anticipated or included in the original specifications. This property is also widely known as *flexibility* or *modifiability*.

(4) *Conceptual integrity*: The design should exhibit harmony, symmetry and predictability. The system should appear to reflect the mind of a single person, and to faithfully adhere to a single concept. There should be no surprises for its users or its maintainers; knowledge gained in one use or change should be immediately transferable to the next.

These objectives are properties of software design. As discussed in the previous sub-section, designs that have these properties relatively easily achieve many software quality attributes.

Witt, Baker and Merritt also expressed a design objective called *intellectual control*, i.e. the design process should be under intellectual control. An evolving design is under intellectual control if, despite its complexity, it is deeply understood by those responsible for its correctness; they have mastery of its form and content. Managers may understand cost and schedules; but those responsible for the design itself must understand the manner in which the parts interrelate, the rationale and criticality of design choices, and effect of the proposed change. This property is neither a quality attribute of the designed product, nor a quality attribute of the plan for bringing about the product. Instead, it is a quality attribute of the design process itself. We, therefore, consider intellectual control as a good guideline for how to make a good design, rather than a measurement of what is a good design.

It is worth noting that *correctness* is not even mentioned in Witt, Baker and Merritt's design objectives, perhaps because it is too obvious to require a software design that correctly solves the problem that the users require.

2.3.2   Parnas and Weiss's requirements of good designs

In the literature of software design, emphasis has almost always been put on the product facet of designs. For example, Parnas and Weiss identified the following eight requirements for good designs [10]. These requirements are also quality attributes of software designs.

(5)   *Well structured*: The design should be consistent with chosen design principles, such as information hiding, to organise the structure of the design.

(6)   *Simple*: The design should be 'as simple as possible, but no simpler'.

(7)   *Efficient*: The functions provided by the design should be computable by using the available resources.

(8)   *Adequate*: The design should meet the stated requirements.

(9)   *Flexible*: The design should be able to accommodate likely changes in the requirements, however these might arise.

(10) *Practical*: Each module in the design should provide the required facilities, neither more nor less.

(11) *Implementable*: The functions offered by the design should be theoretically computable with the information available and achievable using currently available software and hardware technology.

(12) *Standardised*: The design should be represented using standard or well-defined and familiar notation for any documentation.

Among these requirements, only one is directly related to the quality of development process as design specified. It is the requirement of implementability. This process facet of software design is studied under different subject titles such as software process models, risk management, configuration management, and economics of software development. They focus on a specific aspect and/or to extend to a wider scope to cover the whole development process. However, software designers should not forget the process facet. It is briefly discussed in the next sub-section.

2.3.3 Quality of development process

While product-oriented quality attributes are defined in terms of the designed product and its model, process-oriented quality attributes are defined in terms of the process of developing the product. They measure the quality of design according to the development process. The following are some examples of process-oriented quality attributes of software design.

(13) *Feasibility*: The designed process of bringing about the product should be executable.

(14) *Simplicity*: The production (i.e. the development) of the designed software should be as simple and straightforward as possible without unnecessary complication.

(15) *Manageability*: The development process should be easy to manage, for example enable managers to check the progress against the schedule.

(16) *Quality product*: The designed development process should lead to a software system of required quality.

(17) *Reliability*: The designed development process should with high probability be successful rather than fail to achieve its goal.

(18) *Productivity*: Following the designed development process, software engineers should be able to work productively.

(19) *Time to market*: Following the designed process, the software is developed within the required time to market.

(20) *Risk*: The development process should have a minimal risk, i.e. the lowest probability of failure and the minimal consequences if it fails.

(21) *Resourcefulness*: The designed process should use resources economically and with the minimal cost.

(22) *Technical requirements*: It refers to the degree and extent to which the designed process relies on expensive equipment and tools and requires intensive training to obtain required technical skills for the people to develop the system.

(23) *Material requirements*: It refers to the amount of expensive materials or other resources, such as data, to be used in the development of the software.

(24) *Legitimacy*: The development process and the product should be allowable according to law and conformant to applicable standards and regulations.

(25) *Environment friendliness*: The development process should cause minimal harm to the environment, such as pollution.

Many factors affect this type of design quality attribute, for example, the capability of the organisation and persons to execute the development process, the limitations on resource and time, availability of tools and supporting hardware and software, etc. Notice that, Mayall's principles of design discussed in the previous chapter apply very well to software design.

SUMMARY

Among many quality attributes of software designs, the most important one is the quality of the product, i.e. the designed software system should meet the required quality. Two types of software quality model have been proposed in the literature, hierarchical models and the relational models. The most important quality attributes of software systems include correctness, reliability, efficiency, integrity, usability, portability, reusability, inter-operability, maintainability, flexibility, testability, modularity, etc. The quality of a software system is the totality of all quality attributes. Different software applications may impose different importance on different quality attributes. The importance of a quality attribute may change as time goes by and when viewed by different people.

While design affects most software quality attributes, some quality attributes are not only sensitive to design, but also rely on other development activities.

Software design quality attributes can be classified into two types.

(1) *Product-oriented quality attributes are related to the software system to be developed.* Among many such quality attributes, there are modularity, portability, malleability (or modifiability, or flexibility) and conceptual integrity as Witt, Baker and Merritt stated as design objectives. Software designs are also required to be well structured, feasible (or implementable), simple, efficient, practical, standardised, correct (or adequate), etc. as Parnas and Weiss stated as design requirements. A quality design must take all of these into consideration.

(2) *Process-oriented quality attributes are related to the process of developing the software.* Among many development quality attributes, there are feasibility, productivity, time to market, risk, cost, resourcefulness, simplicity of production, etc. Such quality attributes affect the process of software development.

FURTHER READING

Details of the quality models, such as McCall's, Boehm's, ISO and Perry's models can be found in references [2], [3], [4] and [5], respectively. Gillies' textbook on *Software Quality: Theory and Management* (2nd Edition) published in 1997 [6] gives a good introduction to the concept of quality, various software quality models and their uses in quality assurances in software development. More recent development in the study of software quality can be found in *IEEE Software*'s special issue on software quality in Volume 13 Number 1 published in January 1996. The magazine is also where issues related to software quality are often discussed and research results reported. *IEEE Transactions on Software Engineering*, the journal of *Information and Software Technology*, and the *Journal of Systems and Software* are among the top journals in which research papers on software quality are published.

EXERCISES

(2–1) The ISO standard ISO 9126 *Information Technology – Software Product Evaluation – Quality Characteristics and Guidelines for Their Use* [4] defines a hierarchical model of software quality with 6 top-level quality characteristics and suggested to each top-level quality characteristic a set of quality attributes; see diagram in Figure 2.4.

(i) Find out the definitions of the software quality attributes.

(ii) Discuss where to put each quality attribute in McCall's model.

(2–2) Consider the design of the bookshelf that you made in exercise (1–10).

(i) How do you evaluate the design?

(ii) What are the properties of your design that are related to its quality?

(2–3) Discuss the most important quality attributes of a B2C e-commerce system.

(2–4) *Robustness* is a property of a computing system (especially distributed systems) that the system can still provide the required service (although often suffer from a lower performance and/or possibly the losts of some services) when certain hardware/software elements fail. Discuss how architectural design, detail design and interface design affect robustness.

(2–5) Discuss the effects of architectural designs on the following software quality attributes.

(a) testability, (b) usability, (c) integrity, (d) security.

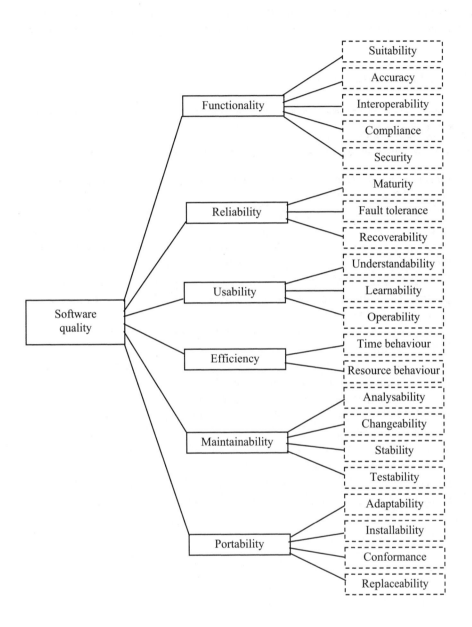

Figure 2.4 ISO 9126 software quality model

(2–6) Consider software design as a product of software design process. Using the quality attributes given in section 2.3, build a hierarchical model and a relational model of software design quality, respectively.

(2-7) Search for the literature of standards of computer science and information technology, and find the definitions of the following terms used in the context of software:

(a) fault, (b) failure, (c) error.

REFERENCES

1   Garvin, D., What does product quality mean? *Sloan Management Review*, Vol. 4, 1984.
2   McCall, J. A. *et al.*, Concepts and definitions of software quality, Factors in Software Quality, *NTIS*, Vol. 1, 1977
3   Boehm, B. *et al.*, *Characteristics of software quality*, North-Holland, New York, 1978.
4   ISO, ISO 9126: *Information Technology – Software Product Evaluation – Quality Characteristics and Guide Lines for Their Use*, ISO/IEC IS 9126, Geneva, Switzerland.
5   Perry, W., *Effective Methods of EDP Quality Assurance*, 2nd edition, Prentice-Hall, 1987.
6   Gillies, A., *Software Quality: Theory and Management*, Second Edition, International Thomson Computer Press, 1997.
7   Mayall, W. H., *Principles in Design*, Design Council, London, 1979.
8   Bosch, J., *Design and Use of Software Architectures – Adopting and Evolving a Product-Line Approach*, ACM Press and Addison Wesley, 2000.
9   Witt, B., Baker, T. and Merritt, E., *Software Architecture and Design*, Van Nostrand Reinhold, New York, 1994.
10   Parnas, D. L. and Weiss, D. M., Active design reviews: principles and practices, *Journal of Systems and Software*, Vol. 7, p259, 1987.

3 Design Principles

In this chapter, we discuss how to make good designs at three levels of abstraction. At the lowest level, there are rules that guide software design activities. At the middle level are design strategies, which link design activities together to form well-organised design processes. At the highest abstraction level is software design methodology, which is the study of design methods. The objectives of the chapter are:

- To understand the causes of difficulties in software design and the vehicles to overcome the difficulties;

- To understand various strategies to solve software design problems;

- To understand the basic structure of software design methodologies.

The chapter is organised as follows. In section 3.1, we discuss the causes of difficulties in software design and the vehicles to overcome them. In section 3.2, we discuss the process of software design and various strategies of software design. In section 3.3, we give a brief introduction to the structure of software design methods and present a brief overview of software design methodology.

3.1 BASIC RULES OF SOFTWARE DESIGN

3.1.1 Causes of difficulties

Software development is complicated and difficult. Design is one of the most difficult tasks in software development. Before we start to search for methods that allow us to make good designs of software systems, we need to understand why software development is difficult.

As discussed in Chapter 1, all designers face difficulties. The question is whether or not there are specific reasons that make software design even more difficult in additional to the general reasons. In the paper *No Silver Bullet: Essence and Accidents of Software Engineering* [1], Fred Brooks pointed out some of the principal causes of the difficulties of software development. These causes are classified into two types: the essence and the accidents. Essences are the difficulties inherent in the nature of software. They are irreducible, will not disappear and cannot be solved through technical solutions. Accidents are difficulties that today attend its production but are not inherent. Brooks' four essences of difficulties of software development are the following.

(a) Complexity

Complexity is an essential property of software. Software entities are complex in terms of the sizes of their state spaces and the way these states are interrelated one to another. This makes conceiving, describing, and testing software hard. Digital computers are more complex than most things that people build. They have large numbers of states. Software systems have orders of magnitude more states than computers do. Software entities are also complex in terms of the numbers of their elements and the way they interact with each other. Elements in a software entity are not repetitions of the same because if two parts are similar, we make them a subroutine or procedure. Therefore, elements in a software entity are all essentially different from each other. A scale up of a software entity, therefore, is not merely increasing the repeated occurrences of same elements or enlarging the elements in sizes. It is necessarily the increase of the number of different elements. These elements in a software entity interact with each other nonlinearly in most cases, e.g. the state space of the whole system is often a nonlinear function of the state spaces of the elements.

The complexity of software and its nonlinear increase with size is the main cause of many difficulties in software development. The complexity of the problem to be solved by software causes difficulty in communication between users and developers, which leads to errors in requirements elicitation and specifications, and consequently, developing wrong software. It also causes difficulty in communication among development team members, which leads to product flaws, cost overrun, schedule delay, etc. The complexity of the state space causes some difficulty in understanding the behaviour of the program, even in enumerating the states, and from that comes the unreliability. The complexity of the functions provided by software causes the complexity in the invocation of these functions, which makes software hard to use. The complexity of the structure of software systems makes modifications of software difficult; hence software is hard to extend with new functions, to transport to new environment and to fix faults in the code or design, even to find the faults in the software. Complexity not only causes these technical problems, but also management problems as well. For example, it makes overview of the software difficult, hence impeding conceptual integrity. It creates a tremendous learning and understanding burden that makes personnel turnover a disaster.

(b) Conformity

Software is expected to conform to the standards imposed by other components, such as hardware, or by external bodies, or by existing software. As Brooks pointed out, scientists and engineers of other disciplines also face complexity. The complexities that the software engineer faces is different from that others face because of the origin of complexity. In natural sciences, scientists, such as Einstein, firmly believed that there are unified principles that provide simplified explanations of nature. For example, some believe God is not capricious or arbitrary; some believe in evolution. However, no such faith comforts the software engineer. Much of the complexity that a software engineer must master is arbitrary, forced without rhyme or reason by the many human institutions and systems to which the interface of the software system must conform. This complexity cannot be simplified by any redesign of the software alone.

(c) Changeability

Software suffers constant need for change. Of course, almost all man-made artefacts are subject to changes. For example, certain models of cars are sometimes called-back; computers are made field changes; buildings have extensions and rearrangement of rooms, and so on. They are also superseded by later models that copy the basic designs with some modifications. However, the frequency of such changes is no comparison to that of the modifications made on released software. The reason is, in part, because the software of a system embodies the function of the system that feels most of the pressure of change. In part, it is because software is perceived to be easy to change. To some extent, it is true that software is 'pure thought-stuff', infinitely malleable. In fact, the sole purpose of program in a programmable general purpose digital computer is to enable the flexibility that special purpose computers cannot achieve. The most fundamental reason for why software is constantly under the pressure of change is because software and computers collectively bring profound changes to our life towards the age of information. Such changes in turn request more changes on the software. In Brooks' words, the software product is embedded in a cultural matrix of applications, users, laws, and machine vehicles. These all change continually partly because of the uses of computer and its software, and their changes inexorably force change upon the software product.

(d) Invisibility

Different from almost all other man-made artefacts, software is invisible. Existing methods of visualisation and representation of the structure and behaviour of other man-made artefacts mostly rely on models in the form of drawings, cardboard models, etc. Such models catch the geometric reality in a geometric abstraction and naturally link geometric structures to the dynamic behaviour as well as other properties of the system. For example, the floor plan of a building helps architect and client evaluate spaces, traffic flows and views. Contradictions and omissions become obvious. Scale drawings of mechanical parts and stick-figure models of molecules serve the same purpose. However, models based on geometric abstraction are hardly applicable to software due to its invisibility. The representations that are used to describe software inherently lack the kind of visual links that can provide an easily grasped relationship between the representation and the system. This lack not only impedes the process of design within one mind, it severely hinders communication among minds. As discussed in Chapter 1, communication is one of the most important factors that affect design process and its outcomes.

These essences of software do not only cause problems in the creation of software designs, but also often lead to errors in software designs. According to Parnas and Weiss [2], such errors can be classified into 4 types: inconsistency, ambiguity, inefficiency and inflexibility. Obviously, inefficiency and inflexibility are poor qualities of software design. In general, a common error of software design is it is unable to achieve the required software quality in design, which can be any of the quality attributes discussed in the previous chapter. Therefore, adding incorrectness as an obvious design error, which is by no means less common than other types of design errors, we can classify design errors into the following four types.

(1) *Incorrectness*. The design does meet the users' requirements on its functionality and features. Such an error may appear in the form of

misinterpretation of users' requirements, or simply the omission of users' requirements.

(2) *Inconsistency*. Inconsistency is where a design does not work. For example, if two design statements make conflicting assumptions about the functionality of a component or the meaning of a data item, the design simply does not work.

(3) *Ambiguity*. Ambiguity occurs when the design specification may be interpreted in several different ways, or it is not clear enough. Ambiguity causes errors in the implementation of the design due to inconsistent interpretations made in the implementation process.

(4) *Inferiority*. The design does not address quality requirements adequately. Consequently, the designed software is of poor quality with respect to users' quality requirements. Typical inferior quality problems include inefficiency and inflexibility, etc. *Inflexibility* causes the designed software to be difficult to change. *Inefficiency* is where a design imposes a barrier to efficient implementation of the design.

In the previous section, we have discussed in detail about how a design affects various software quality attributes. In many cases, software quality problems can be a result of design flaws. For example, consider software efficiency. Assume that a component A of a software system only needs the data about the latitude of a location from another component B, but component A can only request both latitude and longitude of the location from component B at the same time. The design of component B and the interface between components A and B causes inefficiency due to the unnecessary computation of longitude in component B and the unnecessary transfer of longitude data from component B to A.

3.1.2   Vehicles to overcome difficulties

In the research on software design methodology, computer scientists not only developed a set of principles of design as rules to guide design activities, but also investigated why such rules can lead to good designs. In the book *Software Architecture and Design* [3], Witt, Baker and Merritt listed four primitive statements as the bases for the reasons why a principle can lead to good designs. These statements were called axioms[1] because they believe that the truth of these statements was self-evident.

---

[1]   These axioms are referred to as WBM axioms in the sequel.

(1) *The Axiom of Separation of Concerns:* A complex problem can best be solved by initially devising an intermediate solution expressed in terms of simpler independent problems.

There are three key points implicit in the statement.

- The simpler problems that we identify must collectively solve the original problem.

- The simpler problems must be independent. Indeed, a division into parts with significant inter-dependencies may complicate rather than simplify the original problem.

- Simplification comes with the devising of the intermediate solution, and the identification of the component parts. The solutions of the simpler problems must still be addressed, but that concern is separate from the simplification step.

(2) *The Axiom of Comprehension*: The mind cannot easily manipulate more than about seven things at a time.

This axiom is widely known as the *Rule of Seven Plus or Minus Two*. It is derived from the discovery in the 1950s that humans have a limitation on short-term memory; we can keep only about seven (plus or minus two) random numbers in our head [6]. Although it is not clear to what extent the discovery applies to software design, the general assertion seems self-evident that we humans are overwhelmed when given a large number of independent units of information.

(3) *The Axiom of Translation*: Design correctness is unaffected by movement between equivalent contexts.

A correct design that meets its interface and behaviour specifications in one environment will continue to meet its specifications despite a change in environment, provided that the new environment provides equivalent services. For example, if a new version of an operating system replaces an old version, and if it promises to initiate our application program, and to provide the same services when we call for them, then, our application program will produce the same results as before. Similarly, during system development, a program can be executed in a testbed to evaluate its performance and storage utilisation. When the program is executed in its real operational environment, we can expect that its performance is close to the results produced by test cases provided that the testbed accurately represents the real environment.

(4) *The Axiom of Transformation*: Design correctness is unaffected by replacement of equivalent components.

Suppose that we have a design with several components that meet their interface and behaviour specifications. The axiom asserts that the overall design will continue to meet its specifications despite a replacement of one of its components with a different design, provided that the replacement satisfies the interface and behaviour specifications of the original component.

An implication of the axiom is that a high-level design unit may make references to low-level unit specifications, but how those specifications are satisfied is immaterial ('transparent') to the high level design. This property is known as *referential transparency*.

What these axioms tell us is one simple message that separation of concern and abstraction as two major vehicles to deal with complexity are necessary and applicable in software design.

3.1.3 Basic rules of software design

Now, the question is how to use these tools effectively. Witt, Baker and Merritt proposed five principles of design corresponding to the design objectives that we discussed in section 2.3.1. Each principle aims to achieve one design objective. These principles form the basic rules of software design.

(1) *The principle of modular designs*: Modularity can be achieved by dividing large aggregates of components into units having *loose inter-unit coupling* and *high internal cohesion*, by abstracting each unit's behaviour so that its collective purpose can be known, by recording each unit's interface so that it can be employed, and by hiding its design so that it can be changed.

(2) *The principle of portable designs*: Portability can be achieved by employing abstract context interfaces.

(3) *The principle of malleable designs*: Malleability can be achieved with designs that model the end-user's view of the external environment.

(4) *The principle of conceptual integrity*: Conceptual integrity can be achieved by uniform application of a limited number of design forms.

(5) *The principle of intellectual control*: Intellectual control can be achieved by recording designs (after developing a design strategy) as hierarchies of increasingly detailed abstractions.

Besides these principles, we add one more to address the difficulties in software design caused by invisibility. It is stated in the style of Witt, Baker and Merritt's principles as follows.

(6) *The Principle of visualisation*: Visibility can be achieved (or partially achieved) by representing designs in visual notations such as diagrams, pictures and figures, etc. to express the characteristics of the behaviour of system components and the relationships between the components.

In fact, almost all well-established software design methods employ diagrams to represent software designs. Existing visual notations include data flow diagrams, entity-relationship diagrams, state transition diagrams, the Jackson structure diagram (also called entity life-history diagram), state chart, Petri nets, structure chart, structure graph, and so on. In object oriented analysis and design methods, a large variety of diagrams are used, including class diagrams, object diagrams, sequence diagrams, interaction diagrams, component diagrams, deployment diagrams, etc. In this book, we will use software architecture diagrams to describe and analyse software architecture designs.

3.2 DESIGN PROCESSES

A wide range of activities are involved in software design. Each activity consists of at least four aspects: the action carried out in the activity, the participants, the input information, and the output or the result of the action. There are also other aspects of activities, such as the conditions and constraints on which the activity to be carried out. A process model describes the activities involved in the design process and the interrelationships between the activities. We will first look at a generic process model that applies to the design of all kind of products. We will then look at process models for software development and focus on the design of software systems.

3.2.1 The context of design in software development process

Software design is a part of software development process. To understand the input and output of software design and the context of design activities, we must put software design in a wider context of the process of software development.

3.2.1.1 In the context of V model

Figure 3.1 is the 'V' model of software development, which is an industrial standard version of a 'waterfall' model. It shows clearly that:

- *The input of software design*: It includes functional specification and non-functional requirements as the result of requirements analysis and functional specification phases.

- *The output of software design*: It includes the design specification that describes software architecture and module design which describes the design of the components in the software. These outputs are used for programmers to implement modules, for testers to perform unit and integration tests.

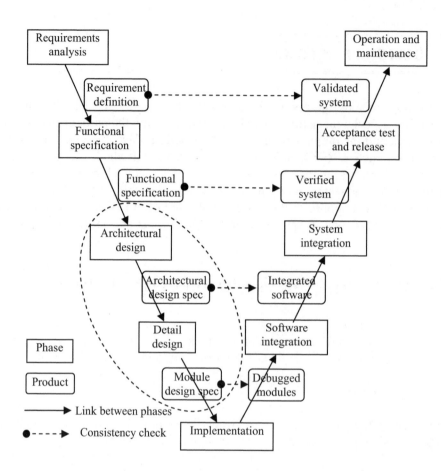

Figure 3.1 The 'V' model of software development process

3.2.1.2   In the context of spiral model

Figure 3.2 gives the spiral model of software development life-cycle. Each stage in the spiral model involves the following activities.

- The *objectives* of the stage are identified;

- The *options* and *constraints* are listed and explored;

- The *risks* involved in choosing between these options are evaluated;

- A *plan* for how to proceed to the next stage is determined, which may require the development of a prototype, or may more closely approximate to a traditional waterfall step, according to the conclusions of risk analysis.

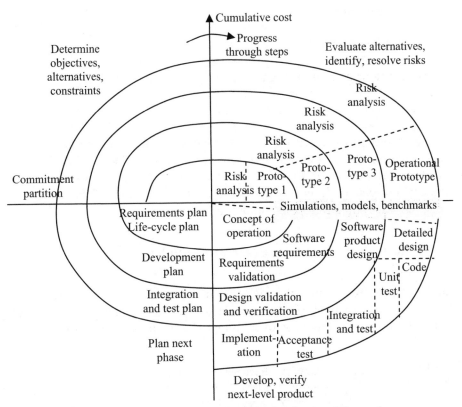

Figure 3.2 The spiral model of software life-cycle

The spiral model clearly shows the role of design validation and verification in the process and the role of models, simulations and prototypes in software design.

3.2.1.3 Two stages of software design

Both 'V' model and spiral model divide the design process into two phases, *architectural design* and *detailed design*. Architectural design addresses the structural issue in software design, which includes:

- the organisation of a system as a composition of components;

- the assignment of functionality to components;

- the global control structures;

- the protocols for communication, synchronisation, and data access;

- physical distribution;

- scaling and performance;

- the dimensions of evolution; and

- the selection among design alternatives.

Detailed design is concerned with the data structures and the algorithms to implement the functions of each component in the system. Detailed design issues also include the details of the user interface, input/output formats, and other implementation-related design issues such as the selection of implementation language, libraries and development tools, and so on.

3.2.2 Generic design process: descriptive models

A generic design process model is depicted in Figure 3.3, which is based on the model in Budgen's textbook on software design [4], but extended with producing multiple solutions and comparison of solutions. It also applies to software design.

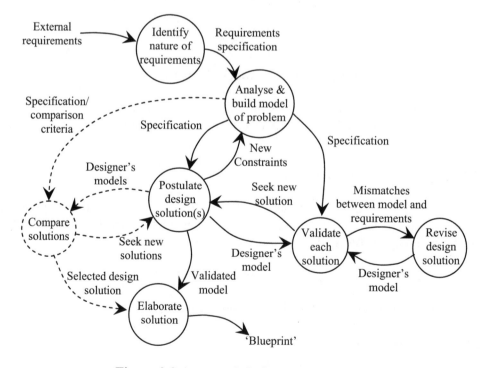

Figure 3.3 A general design process model

This model shows that the key activities in the design process include:

- Postulating a number of solutions

- Building a model of each solution

- Evaluating the models against the original requirements

- Comparing the validated solutions and select one for further development

- Elaborating the model to produce a detailed specification of the solution in the form of 'blueprint'.

There are three key points in this process model that are worth noting. Firstly, it emphasises the iterations of design activities. There are two main cycles in this process model. The first is the iteration for developing a solution. During the development of solutions, new constraints may be discovered, and consequently, new solutions can be postulated. This process may also involve the second iteration, i.e. the postulation, evaluation and revision process. Evaluation plays a key role in design process. It decides whether a design is satisfactory with regard to the requirements. If the evaluation shows that the design satisfies all the requirements, the iteration process can stop; otherwise, the designer must go through a further round of design process. Notice that, the postulation, validation and revision of many design solutions can be performed in parallel even by different designers or design teams. Collaborations and interferences may occur between different designers or design teams.

Secondly, it emphasises the importance of model building in the process of design. Such a model can be in various different forms. It can be dynamic or static, structural or functional, abstract or concrete. The purpose of the use of the model is to evaluate the design. It is, therefore, a representation of the design.

Finally, this process model also emphasises the development of multiple solutions to the design problem, the comparisons between different solutions and the selection of an appropriate one for further elaboration and implementation. In almost all application areas such as cars, buildings, fashions, etc., we can find the existence of designs of same or very similar functionality but in different styles. It is of vital importance for a designer to understand the differences and utilities of various styles, and based on that, to create his/her own style. Notice that, it is not always necessary to make several designs for every design task. Sometimes, a designer may have a preferred style of the product. In this case, the comparison and selection become implicit. In the case when only one design is made, the comparison and selection process can be omitted. Therefore, the part depicted in dashed lines in Figure 3.3 is optional. The comparison and selection process may be performed before the validation and revision process and carried out on initial proposals of design ideas, and then the selected ones are further developed into a more complete model of solution. It can also be performed after design ideas are developed into well established and validated solutions models. In most complicated design processes, there may be several iterations of comparisons and selections are combined with evaluations and revisions.

The design process discussed above belongs to what Cross called *descriptive* process models, which identify the significance of various design activities and reflect the nature of design thinking [5].

3.2.3 Design strategies: prescriptive models

As discussed above, one of the key design activities is to build models. A number of design strategies have been advanced in the literature and used in various design methods to guide the process of building up design models. Among the well-known design strategies, are decompositional, compositional, template-based and evolutionary strategies.

(a) Decompositional methods

Decompositional methods take a top-down approach to the design process. As shown in Figure 3.4, it starts with an original description of the problem or a model of the original problem. This original problem is, then, decomposed into a number of sub-problems. These sub-problems are then solved separately. If a sub-problem is still too complicated to be solved directly, it is further decomposed until it is simple enough to be solved directly. The solutions of the sub-problems are put together to form a solution of the original problem.

A typical example of decompositional methods is stepwise refinement, which is used in structured programming. The SSADM also has a significant top-down aspect to the process model.

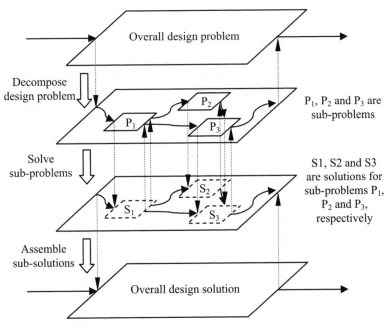

Overall design problem

Decompose design problem

P_1, P_2 and P_3 are sub-problems

Solve sub-problems

S1, S2 and S3 are solutions for sub-problems P_1, P_2 and P_3, respectively

Assemble sub-solutions

Overall design solution

Figure 3.4 Illustration of decompositional design strategy

(b) Compositional methods

As depicted in Figure 3.5, compositional strategy starts the building of a model identifying a set of particular entities or objects involved in the problem. These entities and objects are described, classified and grouped. For each group, the relationships between the entities are identified so that links between entities are established. Such groups form the components of the model. These components are further classified and grouped. The relationships between the components are identified to make larger components. This composition process continues until a complete model is built.

Typical design methods that use the compositional strategy include JSP, and object-oriented design methods.

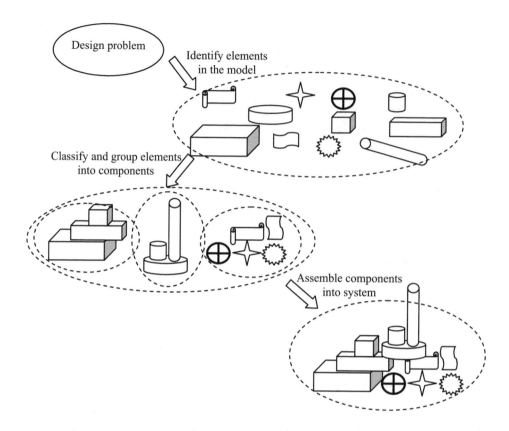

Figure 3.5 Illustration of compositional design strategy

(c) Design template and design reuse

Over many years of research and practices in software development, people find that for a certain type of problem in a certain application domain, there may be a great deal of similarities in the designs that are proved to be effective. If such similarities can be abstracted into a template of design, then once a problem is identified to be an instance of such a class of problems, the design template can be instantiated and a good design can be relatively easily obtained. The use of a design template to solve new design problems is a reuse of designs.

In recent years, a fairly large number of design templates have been recognised and described in the literature. Software architectural style is one of the ways that design templates can be described and used. In this book, we will learn the basic theory of software architecture and the application of architectural style in software design. Another successful attempt in the study of software designs in the paradigm of object orientation is called design patterns.

In the more general context of design methodologies, the studies of how design problems and design solutions are related in any particular domain have led to the theory of design space based on mathematical theories of topology. This theory has been used in the development of computer aided design tools. In this book we will give an informal introduction to theory and then apply to software architectural design.

(d) Incremental and evolutionary design strategies

Trial-and-error is perhaps the most basic approach to all designs. It involves the creation of a design and the evaluation of the design against the requirements and constraints. If some requirements and/or constraints are not satisfied, the design is modified and a new design, even new designs, created. The cycle of creation and evaluation stops until a satisfactory design is obtained. However, there is no guarantee that a satisfactory design can always be obtained. Edison's design of electric lights is a typical example of such a design process.

A systematic trial-and-error approach to design is to start with creating a design solution that only satisfies a carefully selected subset of the most important and basic requirements. This solution is evaluated against other requirements. For those requirements that are not satisfied, modifications on the design are made to meet these requirements while preserving the required properties that it has already satisfied. A typical example of software evolutionary design methods is program transformation. It starts with a formal specification of the requirements, say in a functional programming language. This specification is written in a very high level language and its correctness can be relatively easy to obtain. A series of transformations are then applied to the formal specification to derive programs that are semantically equivalent to the specification but more efficient until a satisfactory solution is obtained. Such transformations can be guaranteed for correctness when a fixed set of transformation rules are formally proved to preserve the correctness of the program. However, the efficiency gain by such a set of rules can be bounded; hence, the power of such a formal system is limited [6].

A specific form of such evolutionary design and development is based on careful analysis of the requirements to group functional requirements in such a way that some can be satisfied without affecting the others. Therefore, a design solution is first attempted to satisfy these requirements. Further designs are attempted to add more and more components to the earlier designs to satisfy more and more requirements with minimal changes to the earlier partial solutions. This approach is called *incremental* design, as illustrated in Figure 3.6.

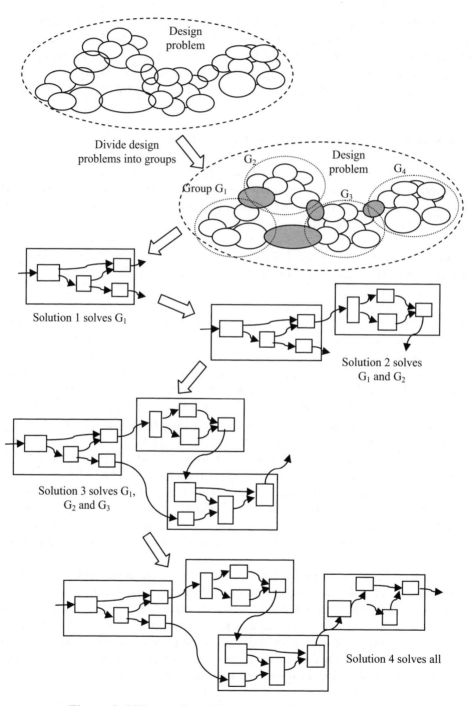

Figure 3.6 Illustration of incremental design strategy

Design strategies discussed above provide more detailed guidance to design processes, especially the generation of solutions. They can be considered as *prescriptive* design process models in Cross's terminology. A *prescriptive* process model usually offers a more algorithmic and systematic procedure of design than descriptive models. They usually emphasise the need for more analytical work before the generation of solution concepts. They are often a part of a specific design methodology.

3.3   STRUCTURE OF SOFTWARE DESIGN METHODS

Over many years of research and practices in software development, computer scientists have proposed a number of software design methods in the literature and used in software development practices. Among the most well-known design methods are:

- Jackson Structured Programming and Jackson System Development (JSP [7] & JSD [8]) methods;

- Structured methods, including SSA/SD [9, 10], SADT and SSADM;

- Object-oriented and object-based methods, including HOOD [11] and more recent developments in the UML [12] and united process [13];

- Formal methods, including model-oriented [14, 15], axiomatic and algebraic methods [16], and refinement calculus, formal proof methods, program transformation methods, etc.;

- Architecture-based design methods. In recent years, a large amount of research has been done on software design at software architectural level. A design method for software architectural design is emerging.

There is a common structure and features of these methods. In general, a design method must be based on a certain understanding of the problems to be solved by computer systems and software systems' structures and properties to represent the software designed. It should also identify a general strategy to be used by the designer and provide some guidelines on its use. Therefore, a well-established design method should consist of three basic components, as shown in Figure 3.7.

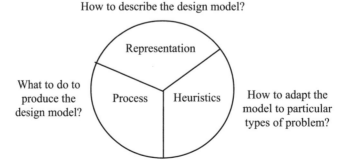

Figure 3.7 Components of a software design method

The *representation* part consists of one or more forms of notation that can be used to describe and/or model both the structure of the initial design problem and that of the intended solution, using one or more viewpoints and different levels of abstraction. It should also facilitate the analysis of the model. Such a representation is usually based on a meta-model of software structure and property, as well as the problems to be solved by the software.

The *process* part describes the procedures to follow in developing the solution and the strategies to adopt in making choices. This generally involves the designer in making a series of transformations on the different forms that comprise the representation part.

A set of *heuristics* provides guidelines on the ways in which the activities defined in the process part can be organised for specific classes of problems. These are generally based on experiences of past uses of the method with a particular problem domain, or for a particular form of structure.

As the problems to be solved by computer systems are getting more and more complicated, software design methodology is getting more and more powerful and complex as well. In addition to these basic components, tools that support a design method also significantly affect the practical uses of software design methods. Such tools are becoming an integral part of software design methods.

SUMMARY

According to Fred Brooks, the main reasons for the difficulty in software development are the complexity of the problem to be solved, the frequent change of users' requirements, the need of conformation to the standards imposed by other components of the system, and the invisibility of software system. The basic vehicles to overcome the difficulties include separation of concerns, abstraction, transformation, visualisation, etc. Design strategies include decompositional, compositional, reuse of design templates, and evolutionary designs.

A design method usually consists of three elements: (1) the notations for representing the design problems and models of the solutions; (2) the process model that consists of a sequence of design activities and the conditions for the application of the activities; (3) a set of rules for applying the method.

FURTHER READING

Many textbook books on various software design methods are available. The references to such textbooks are given in section 3.3. In addition to these textbooks that are devoted to a specific design method, Professor Budgen's textbook *Software Design* [4] is a very good introductory textbook on software design in general and contains a brief coverage of each of these design methods. Bernard Witt, Terry Baker and Everett Merritt's book *Software Architecture and Design* [3] published in 1994 has a well organised discussion about the principles of software design, which is briefly represented in section 3.1 of this chapter. However, significant progress in the research on software architecture and software architectural design has been made over the ten years since the publication of the book in 1994.

EXERCISES

(3–1) Discuss in what sense software is complex, and why software is inherently complex.

(3–2) Discuss why the complexity that software engineers face is different from that scientists in other disciplines face.

(3–3) Discuss why software is constantly under the pressure of change.

   Hint: *Refer to the literature of software evolution, such as* [17]

(3–4) Discuss how software's invisibility contributes to the difficulty of software development.

(3–5) For each type of error in software designs, discuss the consequences of such an error, and give an example.

(3–6) Discuss the following questions:

   (i) To what extent, are WBM axioms self-evident?

   (ii) Are WBM axioms equally applicable to design problems other than software design?

(3–7) Answer the following quiz questions and discuss the limitations of human problem solving capabilities.

   (i) Count the number of occurrences of the letter 'f' in the following sentence.

      'The final version of the software is the result of years of scientific study'

   Now, count the number of occurrences of the letter 'f' again, but this time start counting backwards from the last character of the line. Is the result the same as the result you got at the first time?

   (ii) Cover up the list of numbers with your hand or a piece of paper, then reveal one number at a time as you add up the numbers in your head.

$$
\begin{array}{c}
1000 \\
50 \\
1000 \\
20 \\
1000 \\
40 \\
1000 \\
30 \\
1000 \\
10
\end{array}
$$

   The answer should be 5150. Is your answer correct?

(3–8) An important part of design activity is problem solving. Use various problem solving strategies to solve the following puzzle problems.

(i) *Chessboard.* How many squares are there on a chessboard?

(ii) *Coffee can.* A coffee can contains some black beans and some white beans. The following process is to be repeated as long as possible:

- Randomly select two beans from the can.
- If they have the same colour, throw them out, but put another black bean in. (Assume that there are enough extra black beans are available to do this.)
- If they have different colours, place the white one back into the can and throw the black one away.

What can be said about the colour of the final bean based on the number of white beans and the number of black beans initially in the can?

(iii) *Neighbours.* There are five houses in a row, all of different colours. In each house lives a person of different nationality. These five people each take different drinks, smoke different brands and keep different pets. Use the following knowledge to find out who keeps fish as his pet.

- The Englishman lives in a red house.
- The Swede keeps a dog.
- The Dane drinks tea.
- The green house is just to the left of the white house.
- The green house occupant drinks coffee.
- The person who smokes Pall Mall keeps birds.
- The occupant of the yellow house smokes Dunhill.
- The person in the house right in the centre drinks milk.
- The Norwegian lives in the leftmost house.
- The person who smokes Blend lives next to the person who keeps cats.
- The person who keeps horses lives next to the person who smokes Dunhill.
- The person who smokes Blue Master drinks beer.
- The German smokes Prince.
- The Norwegian lives next to the blue house.
- The person who smokes Blend lives next to the one who drinks water.

(3–9) Consider software design methods SSADM. Answer the following questions:

(i) What is the representation part of the method?

(ii) What is the process part of the method?

(iii) Give some examples of the heuristics rules of the method.

(3–10) Consider the design that you made in exercise (1–10). Answer the following questions.

(i) What strategy you used in the design?

(ii) What is your design procedure?

(iii) How do you represent the design? (*Hint: you may need different notations to represent the design of the product and the design of the process for making the product.*)

(iv) What are the alternatives of the design?

(v) Are Witt, Baker and Merritt's axioms and principles applicable to your design?

REFERENCES

1   Brooks, F. P. Jr, No silver bullet: essence and accidents of software engineering, *IEEE Computer*, 1987, pp10–19.

2   Parnas, D. L. and Weiss, D. M., Active design reviews: principles and practices, *Journal of Systems and Software*, Vol. 7, p259, 1987.

3   Bernard Witt, Terry Baker and Everett Merritt, *Software Architecture and Design*, Van Nostrand Reinhold, New York, 1994

4   Budgen, D., *Software Design*, 2nd Edition, Addison Wesley, 2003.

5   Cross, N., *Engineering Design Methods: Strategies for Product Design*, 3rd Edition, Wiley, 2000.

6   Zhu, H., How powerful are folding/unfolding transformations? *Journal of Functional Programming*, UK, January 1994.

7   Jackson, M. A., *Principles of Program Design*, Academic Press, 1975.

8   Jackson, M. A., *System Development*, Prentice-Hall, 1983.

9   Yourdon, E. and Constantine, L. L., *Structured Design*, Prentice-Hall, 1979.

10 Yourdon, E., *Modern Structured Analysis*, Yourdon Press, 1989.

11 Robinson, P. J., *Hierarchical Object-Oriented Design*, Prentice-Hall, 1992.

12 OMG, *UML Specification*, Version 1.5, March, 2003. Available online at URL: http://www.omg.org/technology/documents/formal/uml.htm.

13 Jacobson, I., Booch, G. and Rumbaugh, J., *The United Software Development Process*, Addison Wesley, 1999.

14 Jones, C. B., *Software Development: A Rigorous Approach*, Prentice-Hall, 1980.

15 Jones, C. B., *Systematic Software Development using VDM*, Prentice-Hall, 1986.

16 Sannella, D. and Tarlecki, A., Algebraic methods for specification and formal development of programs, *ACM Comput. Surv.* Vol. 31, No. 3es, Article 10, Sept. 1999.

17 Lehman, M. M. and Ramil, J. F., Rules and Tools for Software Evolution Planning and Management, in *Annals of Software Eng.*, special issue on software management, vol. 11, issue 1, 2001, pp15–44.

4 Software Architecture

This chapter introduces the notion of software architecture and architectural styles and discusses its role in software design. The objectives of the chapter are:

- To understand the general concept of architecture;

- To understand different views to the concept of software architecture;

- To understand the notion of software architectural styles;

- To understand the roles of software architecture and architectural styles in software design.

This chapter is organised as follows. Section 4.1 examines the general notion of architecture in other disciplines, which include buildings and computer hardware. Section 4.2 presents the most influential models of software architecture in the literature and discusses the roles of software architecture in software design. Section 4.3 introduces the notion of software architectural styles.

4.1   THE NOTION OF ARCHITECTURE

The original meaning of the word architecture, as defined in the *Oxford English Dictionary*, is *the art or science of building, especially the art or practice of designing edifices for human use taking both aesthetic and practical factors into account*. It also means *a style of building, a mode, manner, or style of construction or organisations, and structure*. Therefore, let's start the examination of the notion with buildings.

4.1.1   Architecture in the discipline of buildings

Buildings can be classified according to their main function, or purpose. For example, houses are for residential accommodation; dovecotes are for housing doves; lighthouses are coastal towers with lights to warn approaching ships of dangers, etc. The basic lesson that we can learn from buildings' architecture is that the main function of the system is the most important and basic factor and determines its structure. While the main function of a building largely determines its structure, other constraints also affect the structural and other features of the building. For example, each type of building can be further classified by the structure and its specific usage. Bastel houses are homes in which the residential quarters are above livestock shelters and storage space. Bungalows are one-storey houses. Semi-detached houses are two houses joined to form one building. Terraced houses are a row of connected houses, etc.

While structure in the above sense plays an important role in building, at the heart of the science and art of architecture are the so-called architectural styles. The house that my family lives in is not a Georgian house or Victorian house not only because it is not old enough, but more importantly, because its style is not Georgian or Victorian. Features of Georgian design include symmetry, simplicity and classical details such as columns in the classical orders of Doric, Ionic and Corinthian. The panelled front doors are large, with columns or decorations both sides and a semi-circular window, known as a fanlight, above. Sash windows, introduced in the early 18th century, are tall and well proportioned. They have delicate wooden glazing bars and the panes of glass are all the same size. A typical example of Georgian houses is the 18th century building the Royal Crescent in Bath; see Figure 4.1. Victorian houses are those built during the reign of Queen Victoria from 1837 to 1901. Much of the domestic Victorian housing was modest and terraced or semi-detached.

Figure 4.1 The 18th century crescent of terraced Georgian houses in Bath

The change of architectural styles in history clearly demonstrates the impact of development of building techniques. When the Normans invaded and conquered Britain in 1066, they brought the Romanesque style with them. Their skills as masons and engineers were demonstrated in their massive, solid-constructed churches and cathedrals. They had perfected the roof-covering technique of vaulting developed 1000 years earlier by the Romans. This involved the use of semicircular stone arches extending the length of the roof space to form a barrel vault. The Norman style has the features that walls are thick, with large smooth-faced, rectangular dressed stones and an infilling of small stones. Broad buttresses support the walls. Windows are narrow and semicircular. Doors are surrounded by semicircular arches, often colourfully decorated with a zigzag and dog-tooth pattern. Columns are massive circular structures, sometimes covered with ascending spirals or diamonds and with circular bases sitting on square footings. Capitals are either square with cushion-type decoration or circular. Norman architects had encountered difficulties when creating intersections between aisles of different widths. Their early English successors solved these problems either by constructing pointed arches because the height of a pointed arch is not determined by its width, or by raising the level of the springers (the bottom stones) on the narrower semicircular arch. Churches after the 12th century had lighter, thinner structures with aisles and naves of varying width. To support the increasingly high and thin walls, the flying buttress was introduced, which transferred the downward thrusts to supports away from the main inner wall. This allowed structures to have larger windows because the walls took less of the overall weight. Because of the use of pointed arches, the width of doors no longer needed to relate to the height of the arch. Entrances acquired a more graceful appearance. These are the basic characteristics of Gothic church architecture. During the 14th century, architects felt free to add decoration to all surfaces of their buildings. Advanced engineering skills were matched by ever greater sculptural quality. Tracery within windows developed elaborate curves and great delicacy, and the art of stained glass was taken to great heights. Fonts, gargoyles, eagle lecterns, choir stalls and pulpits were also added to enrich interiors. By the time of the 16th century, repetitious vertical mouldings and fluting gave interiors an illusion of heightened space, which gave rise to the term 'perpendicular architecture'. This style marked the culmination of British Gothic.

It is worth noting that the design knowledge associated to an architectural style is often codified in the form of a vocabulary that defines the types of components in the architecture and their roles and interrelationships. For example, Figure 4.2 illustrates the vocabulary associated to the components of Gothic churches.

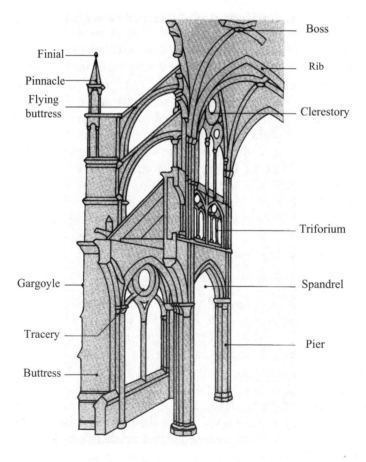

Figure 4.2 Structural characteristics of Gothic churches

As pointed out by Perry and Wolf [2], although the subject matter for building and software is quite different, there are a number of interesting points in building architecture that are also applicable for the study of software architecture.

(1) *Multiple views*. A building architect works with the customer by means of a number of different views in which some particular aspect of the building is emphasised. For example, there are elevations and floor plans that give the exterior and interior views, respectively. The elevation views may be supplemented by contextual drawings or even scale models to provide the customer with the look of the building in its context.

(2) *Architectural styles*. As we have seen from the above discussion, architectural style plays a central role in art and the science of building. Style is particularly useful from both descriptive and prescriptive points of view. Descriptively, architectural style defines a particular codification of design elements and formal arrangements. Prescriptively, style limits the kind of design elements and their formal arrangements. In other words, an architectural style constrains both the design elements and the formal relationships among the design elements.

(3) *The impact of implementation technique on design*. The development of architectural styles clearly demonstrated the impact of implementation techniques on the style of architecture. For example, the airy feel of the perpendicular style of King's College, Cambridge, cannot be built by using Romanesque engineering skills. There are two key factors of building techniques: the tools and the materials. Today's skyscraper cannot be built only using wooden posts and beams or steel without modern building tools.

4.1.2 Architecture in the discipline of computer hardware

In the study of computer hardware, computer scientists have developed a number of computer architectures as successful designs of computer systems. For example, almost all the computers in daily use today are of a von Neumann architecture. Figure 4.3 depicts the overall structure of the von Neumann computer architecture. It contains two main parts: the Central Processing Unit (CPU) and the main memory. The basic ideas of the design are:

(1) *Stored program*. The data and instructions are both stored in the main memory. The content of the memory is addressable by location without regard to what is stored in the location.

(2) *Sequential execution*. Instructions are executed sequentially from one instruction to the next in the order of their location in the memory unless the order is explicitly modified.

The primary function of the CPU is to execute the instructions fetched from the main memory. The instruction tells the CPU to perform one of its basic operations including arithmetic or logic operation, transference of data from/to main memory, etc. Typically, it consists of three components. The control unit (CU) interprets (decodes) the instruction to be executed and tells the other component what to do. A set of registers is the temporary data storage used to hold intensively used data and intermediate results. The arithmetic/logic unit (ALU) performs arithmetic and logic operations.

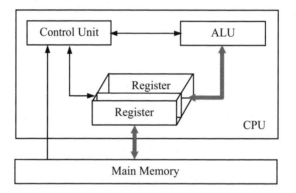

Figure 4.3 The von Neumann architecture

In the von Neumann architecture, a small set of circuits can be driven to perform very different tasks depending on the program which is stored in the memory and executed at run time. It successfully achieves the design target of *general purpose computer* within the boundary of physical implementation capability.

In the past five decades, modern technology has significantly improved the performance of von Neumann computers through fast integrated circuit technology and new architectural features such as large caches, multiple fast buses, pipeline, etc. However, there are a number of fundamental shortcomings of the architecture. For example, von Neumann computers execute instructions sequentially. Computers running with a single CPU are often unable to meet the performance requirements in certain application areas such as in fluid flow analysis and aerodynamics. Applications in such domains are characterised by very large amounts of numerical computation and a large quantity of input data. A solution to the need for high performance is architectures that contain several processing units executing in parallel. Hence, parallel computer architectures have been designed. Figure 4.4 shows a single instruction flow multiple data flows (SIMD) architecture with shared memory.

The SIMD architecture contains one control unit and a number n (n>1) of processing units connected through an interconnection network to a shared memory. The control unit sequentially decodes and interprets the instructions fetched from a shared memory and tells the processing units to perform arithmetic and logic operations on the data also fetched from the shared memory. Although the processing units are executing the same instructions all the times, the data they operate on may be different. It is in this sense, the architecture has a single instruction flow and multiple data flows.

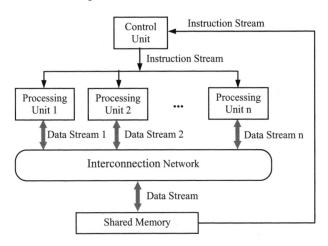

Figure 4.4 Architecture of SIMD with shared memory

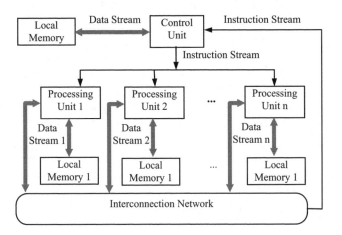

Figure 4.5 Architecture of SIMD without shared memory

As the number of processing units increases, the traffic on the interconnection network increases rapidly. To avoid traffic jam on the interconnection network, local memories can be introduced. Since each processing unit has a local memory, the accesses to the shared memory through interconnections can be reduced. The complexity of the architecture can be reduced by excluding the shared memory. Information exchanges between the processing units are obtained through an interconnection network. The SIMD architecture without shared memory is depicted in Figure 4.5.

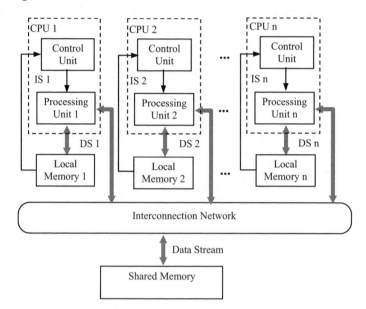

Figure 4.6 The architecture of MIMD with shared memory

While SIMD computers can achieve a very high performance, they have a fundamental limitation. That is, only certain applications can benefit from the parallelism implemented by the hardware and specially programmed by the software. MIMD architectures can achieve high performance by utilisation of a wider range of parallelism contained in programs. Figure 4.6 and Figure 4.7 depict the architecture of MIMD with and without shared memory, respectively.

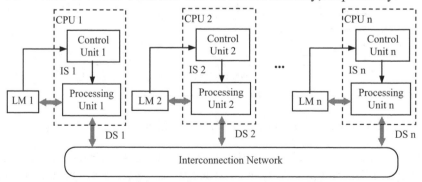

Figure 4.7 The architecture of MIMD without shared memory

From the discussion made above, we can see how computer scientists in the hardware area use the notion of computer architecture to design and realise computer systems.

(1) *The concepts of components*. A number of basic elements that occur frequently in various structural designs of computers at highest level are recognised. Their functionality and basic features are understood and explicitly defined. These elements become the components of the system and the basic elements to define the overall structure of the system, i.e. the architecture.

(2) *The inference of system property*. The system level properties of a computer system can be inferred from the collection of elements contained in an architectural design and the ways these elements interconnect. Such inferences are less dependent on the details of the component's implementation. Instead, they rely on the abstract properties of the components. Similar inferences are also embodied in building architectures.

(3) *The design space*. The architecture serves as a means of classification of computer systems. Various specific computer systems can be classified according to their highest level structures. In the discussion above, we have seen that computer architectures can be classified into three types; that is, von Neumann architecture (i.e. SISD), SIMD and MIMD architectures.[1] The elements in the architecture can also be further classified in the same architectural way. For example, the control unit can be classified into hardwired or microprogrammed according to the way it is realised. Interconnection network can also be classified according to its structure or the way it is realised, such as using buses or switches. Such classifications provide guidelines for the design of computer architecture when a specific set of design constraints and requirements become clear. It explicitly defines the design space and associates each possible design decision with its consequences and impact on system properties, such as performance and cost. Such association of design decisions with the consequences is represented in the form of the rationale of the design decision and usually backed up by a great amount of scientific research and experiment data. One of the most important advantages of such an understanding of computer architecture and their classifications is that the components can be standardised. Hence, they can be designed and manufactured independent of other components and used in various different computer systems.

---

[1] For those who are familiar with computer organisation and architecture, this classification is the Flynn's classification.

4.1.3   The general notion of architecture

From the examination of the notion of architecture in building and computer hardware, we observe the following common features of the notion.

(1) *Architecture is an abstract model.* Architecture is an abstract representation of a complicated system. Details below a certain level are hidden. For example, in the description of hardware architectures, the implementation of the components is ignored, which is not the concern at architectural level.

(2) *Architecture is a structural model.* Architecture is a model of a complicated system in terms of a collection of components and the relationships between the components. In fact, structure is a fundamental part of the meaning of the word 'architecture'. The abstraction from a complex system to an architectural model is reflected in the way that components and the relationships among them are represented. A component is either represented as an abstract entity characterised by a collection of properties, or represented in turn as a composition of such components. Another means of abstraction from a system to its architectural model is to select a subset of the elements of the system as components and/or to group certain subsets of elements into one component. Some elements may be simply ignored in the abstract model.

(3) *Architecture is a model with a certain engineering purpose.* Architecture is a model with a specific engineering purpose or a number of interrelated purposes. A descriptive purpose is usually to demonstrate or analyse the properties of interest of the system. A prescriptive purpose may be to provide guidelines for further design and implementation of the system in addition to demonstration and analysis of the properties of interest. An architectural model must enable the users (e.g. the engineer or customer) of the model to achieve the purpose. The purpose or the property of interest determines what details of the system can be ignored and what should be presented and how details are represented, e.g. as the properties of the components and/or their interrelationships. The existence of multiple views in building architecture shows that different purposes and properties of interest may result in different types of models, i.e. different models of architecture.

Based on the above observation, we give a discipline independent definition of the notion of architecture as follows.

Architecture is an abstract representation, or model, of a complicated system in terms of its structure that consists of a collection of components together with some relations among them to achieve certain engineering purposes and to manifest a certain set of properties of interest on the system. The details of the components and their relationships are hidden and replaced with abstract entities and relations. These abstract entities are either represented by a number of characteristic properties that affect the properties of interest on the system or a composition of such abstract entities of lower level.

4.2   THE NOTION OF SOFTWARE ARCHITECTURE

When describing the top-level design of a software system, people often draw diagrams to show its components and the links between the components. For example, the following diagram depicts the software structure of WWW client-server pair.

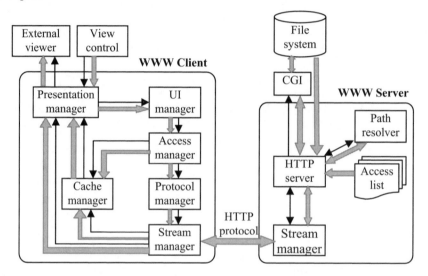

Figure 4.8 The structure of WWW client-server pair

Such a diagram abstracts from a complicated system and provides a comprehensible representation of the system to facilitate reasoning about the system, such as to show how it works to fulfil the required tasks and to analysis its quality. The gross organisation of a software system as a collection of interacting components is the intuition of the notion of software architecture [1]. It is analogous to the notion of computer architecture in computer hardware, network architecture in computer networks, and building architecture in buildings. The past decade has seen rapid growth of research in software architecture. Considerable progress has been made in developing the technological and methodological base for treating architectural design as an engineering discipline.

One of the main aims of the study of software architecture is to achieve an understanding of how software structure at the highest level affects a software system's property and its development process. It has evolved by observations of the design principles that designers follow and actions that they take when working on real systems. It is a young discipline; hence there is no single accepted definition of the term. On the other hand, there is no shortage of definitions, either.[2] Most of the commonly circulated definitions are consistent in their themes – structure, components, and connections among them – but they vary widely in the details and are not interchangeable.

4.2.1 Prescriptive models

Perry and Wolf made one of the most influential definitions in 1992 [2]. After examining the notions of architecture in other disciplines including computer hardware, computer network and building, Perry and Wolf defined software architecture by the following formula.

Software Architecture = {Elements, Form, Rationale}

In this definition, a software architecture is a set of architectural *elements* (or design elements) that have a particular form. Three different classes of architectural elements were distinguished. They are:

- *Data elements.* The data elements are those that contain the information that is used and transformed;

- *Processing elements.* They are those components that supply the transformation on the data elements;

- *Connecting elements.* They are the *'glue'* that holds the different pieces of the architecture together. For example, procedure calls, accesses to shared data, and messages are examples of connecting elements that serve to 'glue' architectural elements together.

The architectural *form* consists of weighted properties and relationships.

- *Relationships.* Relationships are used to constrain the 'placement' of architectural elements – that is, they constrain how the different elements may interact and how they are organised with respect to each other in the architecture.

---

[2] For a list of various definitions of the notion of software architecture, readers are referred to the website on software architecture at the Software Engineering Institute of Carnegie Mellon University. The URL is:

http://www.sei.cmu.edu/architecture/definitions.html

- *Properties*. Properties are used to constrain the choice of architectural elements – that is, the properties are used to define constraints on the elements to the degree desired by the architecture.

- *Weight*. Properties and relationships together define the minimum desired constraints on the software architecture. A *weight* can be associated to a property or relationship to indicate the importance of the property or relationship, or to express the preference among a number of choices among alternatives.

In Perry and Wolf's definition, the *rationale* for the various choices made in defining an architecture is an integral part of software architecture. The rationale captures the motivation for the choice of architectural style, the choice of elements, and the form. It explicates the satisfaction of system constraints determined by users' requirements both functional and non-functional.

Perry and Wolf's definition considers software architecture from a prescriptive point of view. From this viewpoint, software architecture is a design document that prescribes how the system is to be built. In Perry and Wolf's own words, '*architecture is concerned with the selection of architectural elements, their interactions, and the constraints on those elements and their interactions necessary to provide a framework in which to satisfy the requirements and serve as a basis for the (detail) design*'. Therefore, the rationale is an integral part of software architecture and treated as first-class citizen. Barry Boehm and his students at USC Center for Software Engineering [3] further require that an architecture contains a statement of stakeholders' requirements of the system. From this point of view, not every complex of diagrams and symbols is an architecture if there is no sufficient rationale to ensure the components, connections and constraints will define a system that satisfies the set of stakeholders' requirements of the system. The existence of a software architecture becomes a key milestone in software development life cycle. Similarly, Hofmeister, Nord and Soni [4] regard software architecture as '*purposeful design plan of a system*', although they agree with the philosophical statement that every implemented software system has an architecture regardless whether there is an explicit documentation describing it, and/or whether it is good or bad.

4.2.2 Descriptive models

An alternative approach is the descriptive point of view, which considers architecture as a description of the high level structure in terms of architectural elements and the interactions between them. For example, Shaw and Garlan [5] wrote '*abstractly, software architecture involves the description of elements from which systems are built, interactions among those elements, patterns that guide their composition, and constraints on these patterns'*. Although Shaw and Garlan agree that architecture provides some rationale for the design decisions by showing the correspondence between the system requirements and elements of the constructed system, their model of software architecture only consists of two parts:

- *Components*. A component is a unit of software that performs some function at run-time. Examples of components include programs, objects, processes, clients and servers, databases, etc.

- *Connectors*. A connector is a mechanism that mediates communication, coordination, or cooperation among components. Connectors describe the interactions among these components. Implementations of connectors are usually distributed over many system components; often they do not correspond to discrete elements of the running systems. Examples of connectors include shared variable access, procedure calls, remote procedure calls, message-passing protocols, data streams, and transaction streams.

Shaw and Garlan emphasise the abstract nature of software architecture that specifies the structure and topology of the system. Details of the implementation of the components and connectors are hidden at architectural level. However, architectural models can be composed to define larger systems. A component can be specified by an architectural model of the sub-system.

4.2.3   Multiple view models

In contrast to Shaw and Garlan's view of components as units that have some function at run-time, Bass, Clements and Kazman [6] look at software architecture from multiple views. Hence, the structure of a software system is not unique. It can be viewed from different perspectives and results in a number of different structural models of the same system. For example, a software system can be analysed according to the modules and their interrelationships. It can also be analysed according to the processes at the run-time and their interrelationships. These two structures are usually different. Bass, Clements and Kazman believe that although each of them contains certain architectural information of the system, none of them gives a complete picture of the architecture. Therefore, they define software architecture as follows.

'The software architecture of a program or computing system is the structure or structures of the system, which comprise software components, the externally visible properties of those components, and the relationships among them' [6].

The following are the key concepts used in the definition.

- *Components*. Because architecture can comprise more than one kind of structure, there is more than one kind of component, more than one kind of interaction among components. By intention, the definition does not specify what architectural components and relationships are. What Bass, Clements and Kazman's emphasise is that '*an architecture is foremost an abstraction of a system that suppresses details of components that do not affect how they use, are used by, relate to, or interact with each other*'.

- *Externally visible properties*. Externally visible properties refer to those assumptions other components can make of a component, such as its provided services, performance characteristics, fault handling, shared resource usage, and so on. The intention of this definition is that a software architecture must abstract away some information from the system and yet provide enough information to be a basis for analysis, decision making, and hence risk reduction.

- *Structures*. Software systems exhibit many structures. Each structure is an abstraction with respect to different criteria. Each abstraction 'boils away' details of the software that are independent of the concern reflected by the abstraction. Consequently, each structure can use its own notation, reflect its own choice of architectural style, and define independently what is meant by component, interrelationship, rationale, principles and guidelines. The definition itself does not restrict what is an architectural structure. However, they listed a number of structures that were considered as the most common and useful software structures [6].

The following brief descriptions of the software structures come from Bass, Clements and Kazman's book [6]. Each description characterises the structure by what are the components, which are called the *units*, and what are the relationships between the units, which are called the *links*. Each structure is also associated with its uses in software development.

(1) *Module structure*. The units are *work assignments* in the development of a software system and have products associated with them, such as interface specification, code, test plan, etc. They are linked by the *is-a-sub-module-of* relation. Module structure is useful to allocate a project's labour and other resources during the development and maintenance of the system.

(2) *Conceptual*, or *logical*, *structure*. The units are abstractions of the *system's functional requirements*. These abstractions are related by the *shares-data-with*

relation. This view is useful for understanding the interactions between entities in the problem space and their variation.

(3) *Process structure*, or *coordination structure*. The units are *processes or threads*. The links include the relations of *synchronises-with, cannot-run-without, cannot-run-with, pre-empts*, or any relations dealing with process synchronisation and concurrency. This view deals with the dynamic aspects of a system. It is useful to analyse run-time properties of the system.

(4) *Physical structure*. The units are *hardware entities* (such as processors) and the links are the *communication pathways*. Links between the units are the *communicates-with* relation. This view shows the mapping of software onto hardware. It is particularly of interest in distributed or parallel systems. It allows an engineer to reason about performance, availability, and security.

(5) *Uses structure*. The units are *procedures* or *modules*. They are linked by the *assumes-the-correct-presence-of* relation. It is useful to engineer systems that can be easily subset or extended such as using an incremental approach to integration.

(6) *Calls structure*. The units are usually (*sub*)*procedures*. They are linked by the *calls* or *invokes* relation. The calls structure is used to trace flow of execution in a program.

(7) *Data flow structure*. The units are *programs* or *modules*. The links are *may-send-data-to* relation. The links are labelled with names of the data transmitted. The data flow view is most useful for requirements traceability.

(8) *Control flow structure*. The units are *programs, modules* or *system states*. The relation is *becomes-active-after*. This view is useful for verifying the functional behaviour of the system as well as timing properties. If the only mechanism for transferring control is the program call, this is identical to the calls structure.

(9) *Class structure*. The units are *classes* and *objects*. The relation is *inherits-from* or *is-an-instance-of*. This view supports reasoning about collections of similar behaviour and parameterised differences from the core, which are captured by sub-classing.

Based on observations and examinations of industrial practices, Hofmeister, Nord and Soni [4] identified four loosely coupled views of software architecture that are present in every system and provide a relative complete picture of the software architecture. These views are code view, module view, execution view and conceptual view[3].

(1) *Code view*. A software system's source code is usually split into many files, and many kinds of files, e.g. for the interface specification, for the module body, and so forth. To enable sophisticated building of software systems, the object code and binary code generated from source code have their own right and are mapped into libraries and/or files. These software artefacts also have multiple versions, so configuration management is an important task. The code view is concerned with the organisation of source code into object code, binary code, and libraries, and further into versions, files, and directories etc. Such organisation strongly affects the reusability of the code and the build time of the system. Important engineering concerns for this view are the following.

- *How can time and effort for product upgrades be reduced?*

- *How should product versions and releases be managed?*

- *How can build time be reduced?*

- *What tools are needed to support the development environment?*

- *How are integration and testing supported?*

(2) *Module view*. Software systems are implemented in programming languages using a number of modules or classes. The module view is concerned with the following questions.

- *How the product mapped to the software platform?*

- *What system support/services does it use?*

- *How can testing be supported?*

- *How can dependencies between modules be minimised?*

- *How can the reuses of modules and sub-systems be maximised? etc.*

---

[3] These views should not be confused with Bass, Clements and Kazman's structures. They are different.

(3) *Execution view*. Systems have always had a dynamic aspect. Execution view is concerned with how functional components are allocated to run-time entities, how to handle communication, co-ordination, and synchronisation among them, and how to map them to the hardware. This view should enable software engineers to answer questions like the following.

- *How does the system meet its performance, recovery and reconfiguration requirements?*

- *How can one balance resource usage, such as load balance?*

- *How can one achieve the necessary concurrency, replication, and distribution without adding too much complexity to the control algorithms?*

- *How can the impact of changes in the run-time platform be minimised? etc.*

(4) *Conceptual view*. The conceptual view of a software system's architecture describes the system in terms of its major design elements and the relationships among them. This is the view of software architecture that most authors in software architecture mean by software architecture. It plays a primary role in the four views. The engineering concerns addressed by the conceptual view include the following.

- *How does the system fulfil the requirements?*

- *How can the impact of changes in requirements or the domain be minimised?*

- *How are the commercial off-the-shelf (COTS) components integrated and how do they interact at the functional level with the rest of the system?*

- *How is functionality partitioned into product releases? etc.*

In the remainder of this book, we will mostly take the conceptual models of software system as the architectural model. The following is our working definition of the notion software architecture.

Software architecture is an abstract representation, or model, of a software system in terms of a structure that consists of a collection of elements together with the relationships among them to achieve software design purposes and to manifest a certain set of design properties of the system. The details of the elements and relationships are hidden and replaced with abstract computational entities called components and connectors, respectively. These abstract entities are either represented by a number of characteristic properties that affect the properties of the system or an architectural model of the lower level.

4.2.4 The roles of architecture in software design

As discussed in section 4.1, an architectural model of a system is determined by the purpose of the model. In this book, our main purpose of architectural models is for software design. In particular, as Kazman pointed out [7], there are three fundamental reasons why software architecture is important.

(1) Communication among stakeholders

As Mayall pointed out in his *Principle of Relationships*, establishing a work relationship between the stakeholders is very important in design process. Software architecture represents a common high-level abstraction of a system that most, if not all, of the system's stakeholders can use as a basis for creating mutual understanding, forming consensus, and communicating with each other.

(2) Manifestation of early design decisions

As discussed in Chapter 1, design process is a decision-making process. Software architecture is the manifestation of the earliest design decisions about a system, and these early bindings carry weight far out of proportion to their individual gravity with respect to the system's remaining development, its deployment, and its maintenance life. Architecture defines constraints on its implementation, dictates organisational structure, and inhibits or enables a system's quality attributes. It is also the earliest point at which the system to be built can be analysed. A system's quality can be predicted by studying its architecture. It makes reasoning about and managing changes easier. It helps in evolutionary prototyping.

(3) Representation of transferable abstraction of a system

Software architecture constitutes a relatively small, intellectually comprehensible model for how a system is structured and how its components work together. The design knowledge represented in this model is transferable across systems. In particular, it can be applied to other systems exhibiting similar requirements and can promote large-scale reuse.

For the software design methodology perspective, the systematic study of software architectural styles enables us to draw a relatively complete picture of the design space of software systems, to associate properties of software systems with architectural design decisions and styles, and hence to facilitate the interferences at software design stage. It is a significant milestone in the progress in the development of software design methodology.

4.3   SOFTWARE ARCHITECTURAL STYLE

As pointed out by Shaw and Garlan [5], one of the hallmarks of software architectural design is the use of idiomatic patterns of system organisation. Many of these patterns have been developed over the years as designers recognised the values of specific organisational principles and structures for certain classes of software systems. These patterns of organisational principles and structures play a role in software design similar to the notion of architectural styles in other disciplines such as in building architecture and computer architecture. This section studies the notion of software architectural style.

4.3.1   Introductory examples

Let's first examine some examples of software architectures in detail.

Example 1: Audio transcription system

Consider the audio transcription software [8] depicted in Figure 4.9.

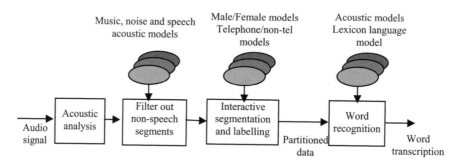

Figure 4.9 Overview of transcription system for audio stream

    The system automatically generates text transcriptions from audio data streams of English speech in radio broadcast. As shown in the diagram, it consists of four parts. The input to the system is a continuous stream of audio signals. The *acoustic analysis* partitions the stream of audio signals into a sequence of homogeneous acoustic segments. Non-speech segments are identified and removed by the *filter*. The speech segments are clustered and labelled according to bandwidth and gender by the *segmentation and labelling* component. The result of this partitioning process is a sequence of speech segments with speaker, gender and telephone/wideband labels. Finally, *word recognition* component recognises the words using a language model, and a transcription is generated as a sequence of words. Figure 4.10 shows the input and output of the system and the intermediate data streams passing through the components of the system.

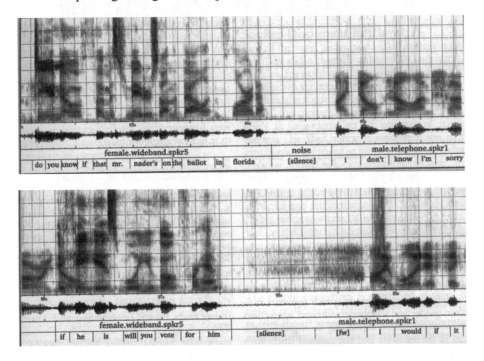

Figure 4.10 Spectrograms illustrate the input, output and intermediate data streams passing through the components

Example 2: Projection keyboard

The second example is the software that realises the projection keyboard for handheld devices shown in Figure 4.11.

A prototype full-size projection keyboard like the one shown in Figure 4.11 is made entirely of light projected onto desktops, airplane tray tablet, even kitchen counters. It functions, feels and sounds like its mechanical counterpart. The keyboard uses a single tiny sensor to observe the user's fingers and transform motions into keystrokes. Typing can be as fast as their fingers allowed on a full-size keyboard. There is no need to carry around a physical keyboard, neither to be stowed, nor folded away, but merely switched off. According to Tomasi, Rafii and Torunoglu [9], the projection keyboard developed at Canesta Inc., San Jose, CA, will soon be available to be integrated into users' devices of choice such as in cell phones and PDAs with a few extra grams and a few more cubic millimetres.

Figure 4.11 Projection keyboard for handheld devices

The projection keyboard consists of three main physical parts, as outlined in Figure 4.11. The optical system (component A in Figure 4.12) projects the keyboard onto the typing surface. The infrared light source (component B) generates an invisible fan shaped beam grazing the surface. The sensor (component C) is a camera that looks down at the typing surface at a shallow angle through a wide lens sensitive only to infrared light. A finger striking the typing surface breaks the infrared beam, thereby becoming visible to the camera; triangulation then determines the position of the finger on the typing surface.

Figure 4.12 The components of the projection keyboard

Figure 4.13 below shows the structure of the software that transforms the images caught by the camera into keystrokes. From the continuous stream of images that are caught by the camera, the candidate fingers are identified and segmented from other possible background objects by the *Segmentation* component. It generates a stream of identified segments of candidate fingers and outputs to the Localisation component. The *Localisation* component takes the stream of images from the camera and the original stream of segments as input and determines the position and time of a keystroke for each segment of image. It generates a stream of finger positions in the sensor's coordinates. This stream of coordinates is fed into the *Event Classification* component to determine the type of action: *landing*, *hold*, *move*, and *takeoff*. The stream of finger positions is also fed into the *Triangulation* component, which transforms image points into keyboard positions. It uses a table to map each sensor coordinate position to the identity of the key associated to the position. The output of the Triangulation component is a stream of key identities, which together with the stream of event types determines the appropriate stream of keystroke events by the *Event Generation* component.

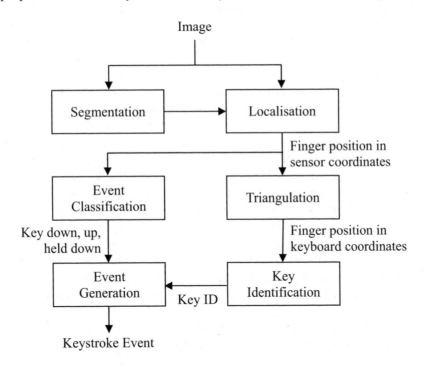

Figure 4.13 The structure of keystroke interpretation algorithm

Although the projection keyboard interpretation software and the audio transcription software are from different application domains, their overall structures have a few common features.

First, for both software systems, the components are all taking continuous streams of input data although the specific formats and semantics of the input data may be significantly different.

Second, the connections between the components serve as the pipes through which data flows from one component to another.

Finally, all components process data incrementally. They do not rely on global information of the whole stream of the input. There is no system-wide global state variables shared between the components. They are independent with each other.

These common features determine that the systems have a number of common features about their run-time behaviours as well as development and maintenance related properties. For example, both of the systems can handle continuous streams of input data of unlimited length and can generate a stream of corresponding output data in the same order of the sequence of input data. As an example of development and maintenance related properties, we can see that certain functions of the system can be easily changed by simply replacing certain components. For the audio transcription system, by changing the word recognition component, the system can be easily modified to recognise speeches in French, German and other languages. For the projection keyboard interpretation software, the table used to map sensor positions to key identities in the Key Identification component can be easily replaced by other tables for different keyboard layouts. In fact, the software enables dynamic changes of keyboard layout through reconfigurable tables. This is a feature that is hard to achieve on a conventional keyboard. Such common development and maintenance related properties and the common characteristics of run-time behaviours are logical consequences of their common features at architectural level. Therefore, we can infer that any system that has the above architectural features will also have these derived development and run-time properties. Because of the common features of the architectural structures of the above systems, we can say that they are of the same architectural style. In fact, they are in the *pipe-and-filter* architecture style, which is one of the most well studied software architectural styles; see Chapter 6 for more detail. In other words, a software architectural style is a set of consistent architectural features that characterise a collection of software systems that satisfy the features.

Example 3: DVD rental management system

To further explain the concept of architectural style, let's examine one more example of software system that is not in the same style as the above two.

The third example software system that we are examining is an information management system for a DVD rental shop. The system is required to help the management of the stock of a collection of DVD discs held by the shop for customers to rent. The shop has a number of customers registered as its members who can rent the DVD discs. The software is also required to manage the information about the customers such as their names, addresses, contact telephone numbers, and payment details (e.g. credit card numbers), etc. In particular, the system needs to fulfil the following functions.

(a) *A user interface.* It should allow the users (i.e. the staffs of the DVD rental shop) to log on into the system with a user name and a password, to receive and execute users' commands from a graphical user interface, and to display information on the screen.

(b) *DVD management.* It should manage the collection of DVDs. In particular, it should have the following functions.

- Add a new DVD title into the stock and assign each copy of the DVD disc with a shelf number;
- Remove an existing DVD disc or title from the collection;
- Search for a DVD by its title, or shelf number, or other information;
- Display and print out detailed information of a DVD title/disc;
- Check out a DVD disc when it is rented to a customer;
- Check in a DVD disc when it is returned by a customer;
- Display and print out the rental history of a DVD title or disc;
- List all DVD discs that are rented out;
- List all DVD discs that are in the stock.

(c) *Customer management.* It should manage the list of customers and fulfil the following functions.

- Add a new member;
- Delete an existing member;
- Search for detailed information about a member;
- Check if a member satisfies the condition for renting a disc, for example, no overdue discs and that the number of rented discs is not over the limit;
- Display and print out a member's rental history, etc.

(d) *User management.* It should keep a list of users and their log in passwords. In particular, it has the following functions.

- Add a new user;
- Change an existing user's password;
- Change an existing user's type, e.g. from shop assistant to manager;
- Delete an existing user;
- Display and print out the transactions issued by a user within a specific period of time and date.

The system implements each of the main functions by a component in the form of a module with a set of procedures or functions. The details of the data structures managed by the component, which is implemented by using a relational database, are encapsulated inside the module and hidden from other components. Components interact with each other through procedure and function calls. For example, in the implementation of checking out a DVD disc to a customer, the DVD Manager component calls the Customer Manager to check if the customer is a valid customer to rent the DVD. The DVD Manager also calls the User Manager to check if the user has the access permission to delete a DVD disc or title, because only managers can delete a DVD from the collection. The architecture of the system is represented as follows in Figure 4.14.

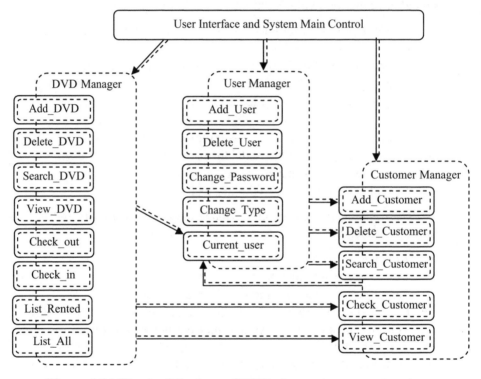

Figure 4.14 The Architecture of DVD shop management system

This overall structure does not have the features of the audio transcription and projection keyboard interpretation systems. It differs from the other systems in a number of architectural aspects as follows.

Firstly, components in the DVD shop management system are not filters. They do not take streams of data as input and they are not transformations on input data. Instead, each component has a number of different functions which are called by other components. Some procedures do not even generate an output as the result of a call. Instead, components in the system encapsulate data and their operation into one unit so that the integrity of the data can be preserved and their implementation details are hidden from the components that use the data. Such components are often called *managers*.

Second, the connections between the components are not data pipes. Instead, they are procedure and function calls, which transmit not only data, but also the control.

Finally, the computational model of the system is different from the pipe-and-filter systems. Components do not execute concurrently. A component is executed only if one of its procedures and functions is called. Moreover, if one component calls another component's function or procedure, the control will be passed to the other component and resumes its execution when the called procedure terminates and returns the control.

Therefore, the DVD shop management system is not in the pipe-and-filter style. Consequently, we cannot expect that the DVD system has the same run-time behaviour features and development and maintenance related properties associated to the pipe-and-filter style. In fact, it is in another well studied architectural style called *data abstraction*, which will be also discussed in more detail in Chapter 6.

4.3.2 The notion of software architectural style

From the examples given above, we can see that a software architectural style is in some ways analogous to an architectural style in buildings such as Gothic or Greek Revival. It consists of a few key architectural features and rules for combining features so that architectural integrity is preserved. A software architectural style is determined by the following types of features.

- *A set of component types.* Not all types of components can appear in a software architecture. Instead, a software architecture often limits the types of components that can be included in the system. For example, a pipe-and-filter system consists of a number of filters. Other types of component cannot be included in the system. A data abstraction architecture consists of a number of instances of abstract data types and/or objects. Such specific types of components are often given specific names, such as *filter* in the pipe-and-filter architectural style and *manager* in the data abstraction architectural style.

- *A set of connectors.* Connectors are the mechanisms that mediate communication, coordination or cooperation among components. A software architecture limits the uses of connectors in the system. For example, in a pipe-and-filter system, only pipes can be used as connections between filters. The specific types of connectors that can be used in an architectural style are often given certain specific names, for example, *pipes* in the pipe-and-filter style.

- *A topological structure.* A software architecture also limits the choices of the topological structure that components are interconnected through connectors. For example, we will see in section 6.3 that a layered system must have a hierarchical organisation.

- *A set of semantic constraints.* In addition to the limitations imposed on components, connectors and topological structures, software architecture may also impose semantic constraints at system level. For example, the state of an object in a data abstraction architecture can only be changed through calls to its methods. The filters in a pipe-and-filter architecture do not share states with each other.

Therefore, a style is not the architecture of a particular system. Instead, it is an abstraction for a set of architectures that have a set of common architectural features. Similar to the term Gothic determines what a building looks like, software architectural style determines a class of architectures that meet the style's constraints. Therefore, styles are usually ambiguous about some detailed issues, which is intentionally so. In particular, a style ignores details about the following aspects of a system.

- *The function of the system and components.* For example, one of the components in an architectural style may be a database, but the kind of data may vary.

- *The number of components involved.* For example, a pipe-and-filter architecture may have 2 filters connected together by 1 pipe, or 20 filters connected by 19 pipes. How many filters or pipes in the system is not the concern of architectural style.

- *The mechanism of interaction.* For example, in a layered system, the call to the lower layer can be local procedure calls, or remote procedure calls, or other process communication mechanisms. All of these mechanisms are acceptable for the architectural style of layered systems.

Software architectural styles are abstractions of good architectural designs of software systems that developed over the past decades. The principles and structures represented in a style often appear in the same application domain repetitively and many are applicable to a number of application domains.

To summarise the discussion on the notion of software architectural style, we quote Shaw and Garlan's definition [5] of the notion below.

An architectural style defines a family of systems in terms of a pattern of structural organisations. More specifically, an architectural style defines a vocabulary of components and connector types, and a set of constraints on how they can be combined. For many styles, there may also exist one or more semantic models that specify how to determine a system's overall properties from the properties of its parts.

SUMMARY

The notion of architecture has been developed in a number of engineering disciplines, which include building and computer hardware. Generally speaking, architecture is an abstract representation, or model, of a complicated system in terms of a structure that consists of a collection of components together with some relations among them. An architectural model can be used to achieve certain engineering purposes and to manifest a certain set of properties of interest on the system. For different engineering purposes, different architectural models can be built for the same system. The details of the components and their relationships are hidden in the architectural model. They are replaced with abstract entities and relations. These abstract entities are either represented by a number of characteristic properties that affect the properties of interest on the system or a composition of such abstract entities of lower level. From the studies of architectures of complicated systems in other engineering disciplines, we can learn the following lessons. First, certain system properties can be inferred from appropriate architectural models. Second, an architectural style represents a consistent set of design decisions, which has been proven to be well-established and can be applied to solve a certain type of similar problem.

In the literature, a large number of software architectural models have been proposed. A *prescriptive* model use software architecture as a blueprint of the system to be developed and guidelines for further design and implementation of the system. A *descriptive* model describes the system as an existence no matter whether it already exists or to be developed. Multiple view models emphasise the need to present a complicated system using a number of different models for different purposes. Among the most influential models of software architecture are:

(1) Perry and Wolf's definition of software architecture as a triple of elements, forms and rationale;

(2) Shaw and Garlan's definition of software architecture as structures consisting of components and connectors;

(3) Bass, Clements and Kazman's definition as a collection of structures comprising software components characterised by externally visible properties and the relationships among them;

(4) Boehm *et al.*'s definition as a triple of structure, requirements, and rationale, and the use of software architecture as a software development milestone of the complete documentation of architectural design;

(5) Hofmeister, Nord and Soni's definition from four views: the code view, the module view, the execution view and the conceptual view.

Software architecture plays three fundamental roles in software design. It is a language that facilitates the communications among stakeholders. It is a model of the system that manifests early design decisions. It is a notation that represents transferable knowledge of a system at an abstract level. In the context of software design, in the remainder of this book, we use the following working definition of software architecture.

Software architecture is an abstract representation, or model, of a software system in terms of a structure that consists of a collection of elements together with the relationships among them to achieve software design purposes and to manifest a certain set of design properties of the system. The details of the elements and relationships are hidden and replaced with abstract computational entities, called components and connectors, respectively. These abstract entities are either represented by a number of characteristic properties that affect the properties of the system or a composition of such abstract entities of lower level in the form of an architectural model.

An architectural style defines a family of systems in terms of a pattern of structural organisations. More specifically, an architectural style defines a vocabulary of components and connector types, and a set of constraints on how they can be combined. For many styles, there may also be one or more semantic models that specify how to determine a system's overall properties from the properties of its parts.

FURTHER READING

Software architecture became a subfield of software engineering in the late 1980s and early 1990s. Prior to that, many computer scientists contributed to the formation of the notion of software architecture. Among the most important are Parnas' recognition of the importance of system families [10], and architectural decomposition principles based on information hiding [11], and Dijkstra's exposing certain system structuring principles [12]. Professor Mary Shaw and David Garlan's book on *Software Architecture: Perspectives on An Emerging Discipline* [5] published in 1996 is perhaps the first textbook on software architecture. It contains a modern treatment of the concept of software architecture and architectural styles, and a large number of examples and case studies on the applications of the concept. Bass, Clements and Kazman's book *Software Architecture in Practice* [6] is more targeted at an audience who have more experiences in software development than undergraduate or postgraduate students. However, I found that most parts of the book, including its discussion on the concept of software architecture should still be a good supplementary reading for students. The papers [1] by David Garlan and [7] by Rick Kazman are introductory overviews of the current state and recent development in the research on software architecture. The *IEEE Transactions on Software Engineering, ACM Transactions on Software Engineering and Methodology*, the annual *International Conferences on Software Engineering* organised by IEEE are where top research papers on software architectures are often published. The annual *Working IFIP Conferences on Software Architecture (WICSA)* are devoted to the topic. The first WICSA conference was held at San Antonio, USA, in Feb. 22–24, 1999. The website on software architecture hosted by the Software Engineering Institute at Carnegie Mellon University contains a comprehensive list of literatures on the topic and a list of various definitions on the concept of software architecture. The URL of the website is http://www.sei.cmu.edu/architecture/.

EXERCISES

(4-1) What are the main factors that an architect may take into consideration in the design of the structure of a building? Should software engineers consider the similar factors in the design of a computer software system?

(4-2) As demonstrated in the study of computer architectures, an architectural design can be used to infer a computer system's important properties without detailed information of the components. Similar inferences can be made on architectural designs of buildings. For example, a bungalow is suitable for those who have difficulties to move up and down stairs because it is a one-storey house. Will software engineers also benefit in such inferences? What are the main properties that software engineers would want to infer from software architectural designs?

(4–3) In the study of computer networks, the notion of network architecture has been developed. Discuss the following in the context of computer networks.

(i) What is architecture? Does the notion conform to our discipline independent definition of the notion?

(ii) How are computer network systems classified according to their architectures?

(iii) Why is architecture important in the design and implementation of computer networks?

(4–4) According to Perry and Wolf's definition [2], software architecture is a triple consisting of architectural elements, form, and rationale. Architectural elements can be classified into data elements, processing elements and connection elements. Analyse the www client-server architecture depicted in Figure 4.8. Identify its architectural elements and classify them into the above three kinds.

(4–5) Apply Shaw and Garlan's definition of software architecture to analyse the structure of the WWW client/server structure depicted in Figure 4.8. Compare the result of the analysis with the result of exercise (4–4).

(i) Identify the components and the connector between the components.

(ii) Discuss what feature you can infer from the description of the structure.

(4–6) The following diagram depicts the structure of rule-based systems. Identify the components and connectors of the system.

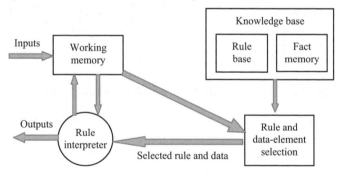

Figure 4.15 Basic rule-based system

(4–7) The following diagram depicts the structure for usage-based web personalisation software [13]. From a descriptive point of view, discuss what are the components and connectors (or connections) of the system.

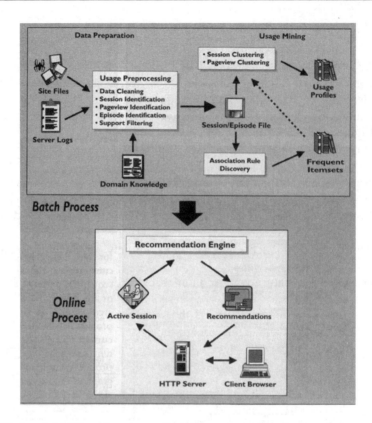

Figure 4.16 The structure of a web personalisation system

(4–8) Consider the transcription system discussed in section 4.3.1.

(i) Identify the components and connectors in the software;

(ii) Discuss the architectural features of each component and connector;

(iii) Use software architecture visual notation to describe the architecture of the system;

(vi) Discuss the main features of the topological structure of the architecture of the system.

(4–9) Consider the projection keyboard software discussed in section 4.3.1.

(i) Identify the components and connectors in software;

(ii) Discuss the architectural features of each component and connector;

(iii) Use software architecture visual notation to describe the architecture of the system;

(vi) Discuss the main features of the topological structure of the architecture of the system.

(4–10) Compare the audio transcription system and the projection keyboard software discussed in section 4.3.1.

(i) Identify the common features as well as the differences in the architectural features of the components and connectors, and the topological structures;

(ii) Discuss the significance of the identified similarity and differences to answer why they should be considered as in the same style;

(iii) Analyse the structures of the input/output data of the applications of the systems and identify their common properties. Then, discuss if these common properties in the structures of input and output should be considered as a condition to apply the architectural style.

(4–11) Consider the DVD rental shop management software system discussed in section 4.3.1.

(i) Identify the components and connectors of the system;

(ii) Discuss the architectural features of the components and connectors of the system;

(iii) Compare the system with the audio transcription software and projection keyboard software.

(a) Identify differences in architectural features of the components and connectors of the systems;

(b) Discuss the significances of the identified differences in architectural features to answer why they should be considered as in different styles.

REFERENCES

1   Garlan, D., Software Architecture: A Roadmap, Proc. of The ACM Workshop on Future of Software Engineering, Limerick, Ireland, 2000, pp91–101.

2   Perry, D. E. and Wolf, A. L., Foundations for the study of software architecture, *Software Engineering Notes*, Vol. 17, No. 4, pp40–52, Oct. 1992.

3   Gacek, C., Abd-Allah, A., Clark, B. and Boehm, B., On the definition of software system architecture, In Proc. of 1st International Workshop on Architectures for Software Systems – In Cooperation with the 17th International Conference on Software Engineering, 1995. (*Also available as Technical Report USC/CSE-95-TR500, Center for Software Engineering, University of Southern California, April. 1995*).

4   Hofmeister, C., Nord, R. and Soni, D., *Applied Software Architecture*, Addison Wesley, 2000.

5   Shaw, M. and Garlan, D., *Software Architecture: Perspectives on an Emerging Discipline*, Prentice Hall, 1996.

6   Bass, L., Clements P. and Kazman, R., *Software Architecture in Practice*, Addison Wesley, 1998.

7   Kazman, R., Software Architecture, in *Handbook of Software Engineering and Knowledge Engineering, Vol.1 Fundamentals,* World Scientific Publishing, 2002.

8   Gauvain, J. L., Lamel, L. and Adda, G., Transcribing broadcast news for audio and video indexing, *Communications of ACM*, Vol. 43, No. 2, Feb. 2002, pp64–70.

9   Tomasi, C., Rafii, A. and Torunoglu, I., Full-size projection keyboard for handheld devices, *Communications of ACM*, Vol. 46, No. 7, July 2003, pp71–75.

10   Parnas, D. L., Designing software for ease of extension and contraction, *IEEE Transactions on Software Engineering*, Vol. 5, Mar 1979, pp128–138.

11   Parnas, D. L., Clements, P. C. and Weiss, D. M., The modular structure of complex systems, *IEEE Transactions on Software Engineering*, Vol. 11, No. 3, March 1985, pp259-266.

12   Dijkstra, E. W., The structure of 'THE' multiprogramming system, *Communications of the ACM*, Vol. 11, No. 5, 1968, pp341–346.

13   Mobasher, B., Cooley, R. and Srivastava, J., Automatic personalisation based on web usage mining, *Communications of the ACM*, Vol. 43, No. 8, August 2000, pp142–151.

5 Description of Software Architectures

As discussed in the previous chapter, software architecture plays a significant role in the communication between stakeholders of software development. Therefore, how to describe software architecture is of particular importance. This chapter presents a visual language for the description of software architectures. This chapter's objectives are:

- To understand the basic requirements of a visual notation for the representation of software architecture;

- To learn a specific visual notation.

The chapter is organised as follows. Section 5.1 introduces the visual notation in detail. Section 5.2 to section 5.4 present some examples of the uses of the notation.

5.1   THE VISUAL NOTATION

A description of software architecture must enable us to answer questions such as:

- What are the components in the architecture? What are the main features of a component? In particular, is it a process, or a file, a database or just a variable whose value is stored in the memory? What does a component do? How does it behave? What other components does it rely on?

- What are the relationships between the components? Do they mean 'send data to', 'sends control to', 'calls', 'is a part of', some combination of these, or something else? What are the mechanisms used to fulfil these relations?

Although a number of software architecture description languages have been proposed in the literature, to date, architectures have largely been represented by box-and-line drawings in which the nature of the components, their properties, and the semantics of the connections and the behaviour of the system are represented by visual notations. Such visual notations improve the visibility of software design, but the use of such notations suffers from informal definition of their semantics.

The notation used in this book is based on *Software Architecture Visual Notation*, which comes from a recent book on software architecture by Bass, Clements and Kazman [1]. The visual notation not only supports the description of software architecture, but also other aspects related to software architectural design such as system architecture, reference models and development processes. In this book, we only use the software architectural part of the visual language.

5.1.1   Active and passive elements

In the visual notation, architectural elements (i.e. components) are represented as nodes and relationships (i.e. connectors) between the architectural elements are represented as arrows between the nodes. Architectural elements of different natures are depicted using different kinds of nodes in the visual notation. There are three kinds of node:

- *square corner rectangles*: they represents hardware components;

- *round corner rectangles*: they represent software components that are not active;

- *rectangles with corners cut off*: they represent active software components, i.e. run-time processes, i.e.

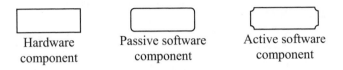

Hardware component   Passive software component   Active software component

Figure 5.1 Visual notation for representation of components

For example, a procedure is a software component. It is passive because it only executes when it is called. Therefore, in the visual notation a procedure is represented by a round corner rectangle. A process is a run-time entity. It is active and can execute concurrently with other processes. Therefore, in the visual notation, it is presented by a rectangle with corners cut off.

5.1.2 Data and control

The visual notation distinguishes control and data features of all architectural elements and indicates *data* via dotted lines and *control* via solid lines to depict both architectural elements and their relationships.

A component that has a control feature means that it is executable. A component that has a 'data' feature means that the component stores data as its internal state. If it is also executable, the component retains the states between executions of the component. A typical example of such computation component is object.

For example, if a computation component is depicted as a rounded rectangle with a pair of lines, one solid and one dotted, the component must have both data and control features. That is, it must be executable and it also contains storage of data to store its state. By contrast, a passive data component that is not executable, such as a text file, is described by a single dotted line indicating that a file only contains data. Figure 5.2 below gives a number of examples of commonly used software architectural elements.

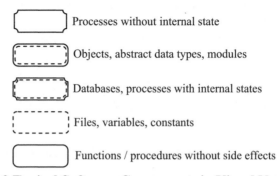

Processes without internal state

Objects, abstract data types, modules

Databases, processes with internal states

Files, variables, constants

Functions / procedures without side effects

Figure 5.2 Typical Software Components in Visual Notation

5.1.3 Relationships

Relationships between architectural elements are represented as arrows between the nodes. A connection has a control feature, if the connection can pass the control from one component to another and causes its execution. A connection has a data feature, if data is passed from one component to another.

For example, data connections, such as socket connections, are shown as dotted lines, whereas control connections, such as process spawning, are shown as solid lines. A procedure call that passes data from the caller to a procedure is depicted as an arrow consisting of two lines, one solid line and one dashed line. The solid line indicates that the procedure call causes the control transmitted to the procedure. The dashed line indicates that data are also passed from the caller through parameters to the procedure.

⟶ Uni-Directional Control Flow

⟷ Bi-Directional Control Flow

- - -▶ Uni-Directional Data Flow

◀- -▶ Bi-Directional Data Flow

===▶ Uni-Directional Data and Control Flow

◀==▶ Bi-Directional Data and Control Flow

Figure 5.3 Visual notation for connections

In addition to such arrows, there are also arrows for relationships between architectural elements of different views. For example, there are arrows for one element which implements another, arrows for one element which is an aggregate of a number of others, and an element that inherits the features of another; see Figure 5.4 for details.

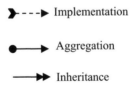

Figure 5.4 Visual notation for representation of relationships between architectural elements

Notice that, having a data and control flow between two components (shown in Figure 5.5(a)) is different from having a data flow and a control flow between them (as shown in Figure 5.5 (b)). The former shows one connector between two components that data and control are passed from component A to B at the same time. In contrast, the latter shows two connectors between the components, which means that control and data can be passed separately, e.g. at different times.

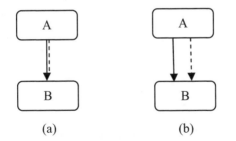

Figure 5.5 Data flow and control flow between components

5.1.4 Decomposition/composition of architectural elements

When an architectural element is a composition of a number of lower level elements, the node can be extended into a box so that the lower level elements and their interrelationships can be drawn inside the box. In such cases, the node looks more like a box which binds the elements together.

For example, the following diagram in the visual notation shows a procedure that has three procedure and one local passive data elements (i.e. a local variable) as its components and the relationships between these elements. As shown in the diagram, Proc1 calls procedures Proc2 and Proc3, and passes data through parameters to the procedures. Procedure Proc1 also writes data into and reads data from the local variable Data1. Procedure Proc2 only writes into Data1. Procedure Proc3 only reads from Data1.

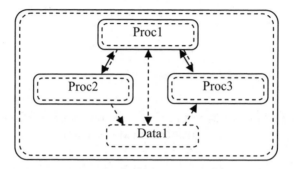

Figure 5.6 Example of compositional element represented in the visual notation

In particular, a class (or an object) may have a number of methods that can be called by other components. These methods are drawn on the boarder of the class to indicate that they are visible from the outside of the element; see Figure 5.7 below.

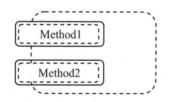

Figure 5.7 Representation of classes

Now, let's see some examples of representation of software architecture in the visual notation.

5.2 EXAMPLE 1: WWW CLIENT-SERVER PAIR

Consider the WWW client-server structure given in Figure 5.8.

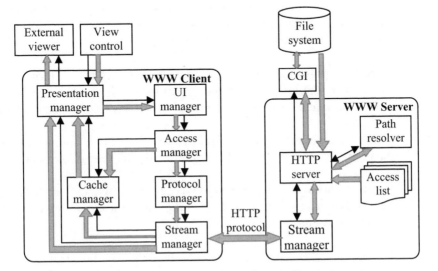

Figure 5.8 Illustration of WWW client-server structure

At the top level, there are 6 components in this architecture: the external viewer, the view control, the Client side (WWW browser), the web server, the common gateway interface (CGI), and a file system.

- An external viewer is a program that is used to view certain types of contents of a web page, such as a postscript viewer, QuickTime for playing video and audio streams, etc. They are active run-time processes.

- The view control component maintains a configuration file and aids the mapping of document types to external viewers when consulted by the presentation manager of the browser.

- On the server side, the file system maintains a collection of files in HTML format and other data as well. These files are retrieved by the WWW server when requested by the browser.

- CGI executes the scripts embedded in HTML files and provides extended functionality of the system for implementation of web-based applications.

- The WWW browser executes on the client side. It can be decomposed into a number of components, which include:

  ✧ User interface (UI) manager handles the look and feel of client's user interface.

  ✧ Presentation manager delegates information display to UI manager or external programs (external viewers) to view resources that are not directly supported by the user interface manager.

  ✧ Access manager accepts the information requests in the form of URLs captured by the UI manager and determines if the requested URL exists in the Cache and also interprets history based navigation, such as 'back'.

  ✧ Cache manager manages a collection of retrieved files and passes a file to the presentation manager if it is requested by the access manager.

  ✧ Protocol manager determines the types of a request for information captured by access manager and invokes the appropriate protocol suite to service the request.

  ✧ Stream manager uses the protocol invoked by protocol manager to communicate with the server in order to obtain the requested information.

- On the WWW server side, there are also a number of components, which include:

  ✧ Stream manager communicates with the stream manager on the client side to receive information requests and send back the requested information.

  ✧ Access list stored a list of clients that are authorised for the documents.

  ✧ Path resolver resolves the location of the requested documents in the files system.

  ✧ The HTTP server ensures transparent access to the file system where the source documents are stored. It also consults an access list to determine if the requesting client is authorised to access the data pointed to by the URL. CGI scripts are passed to CGI to execute.

This architecture can be represented in the visual notation as follows.

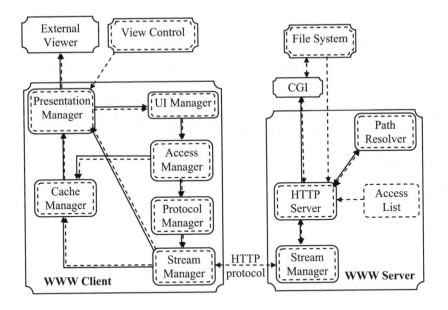

Figure 5.9 Description of WWW client-server structure in the visual notation

5.3   EXAMPLE 2: ROBOT SOCCER UNSW

Since 1997, the American Association for Artificial Intelligence organises and sponsors Robotic Soccer World Championship, called RoboCup, annually. In 2000, the champion of the fourth RoboCup in the Sony Legged Robot League is UNSW which is developed by the School of Computer Science and Engineering at the University of New South Wales, Australia [2]. Each participant team consists of three players, one of which was the goalie. The field is 1.8 metres by 2.8 metres. The robots are the quadruped robot platform, which is similar to the commercial entertainment robot AIBO ERS-110; see Figure 5.10.

UNSW's software consists of the following four components to implement the basic skills such as dribbling, head butting and kicking, as well as game strategies.

- *Vision*: The images captured by the robot's camera are processed to recognise blobs, converting them into objects such as beacons, goals, or the ball. Metrics such as direction and distance are generated at the same time.

- *Localisation*: It maintains three variables: the x and y coordinates and the heading of the robots. It updates the position and direction of the robot each time field objects are recognised and each time the robot moves.

- *Locomotion*: It drives the legs and head effectors based on directions from the strategy module.

- *Strategy module*: It combines various skills and behaviours to achieve the goal of winning the matches.

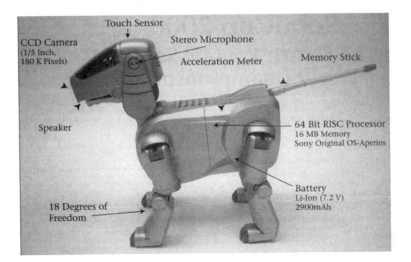

Figure 5.10 The legged robot platform

Weight: 1.59 kg, Size: 2.75 x 156 x 266 mm (without tail)

The information flow between the components is shown in Figure 5.11.

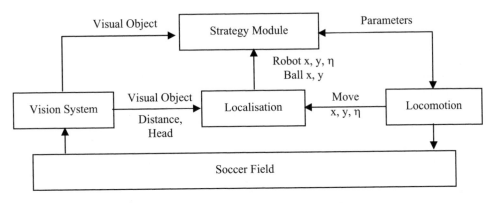

Figure 5.11 The software structure of UNSW

It is clear that the software system consists of 4 components. These components are all active processes. The connections between the components only pass data between them. Therefore, the architecture of the software system can be described as follows.

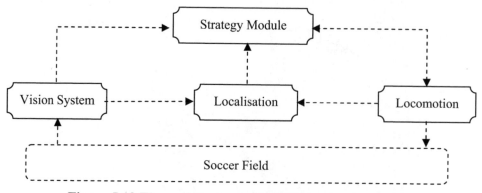

Figure 5.12 The architecture of UNSW in visual notation

5.4   EXAMPLE 3: TRAINING CENTRES' MANAGEMENT INFORMATION SYSTEM

The example to be discussed in this sub-section is a large administrative system developed by the Dept of Defence Telematics Agency for the Dutch Dept of Defence (DoD). The system is described in Lassing, Rijsenbrij and van Vliet's case studies of software architectures [3]. It was developed for use by 15 Dutch army training centres that provide the various services to the Dutch army for the registration of data concerning their courses and students. These training centres are located throughout the Netherlands and part of Germany. Each training centre is a separate organisational unit responsible for their own operating results and belongs to exactly one branch of military service.

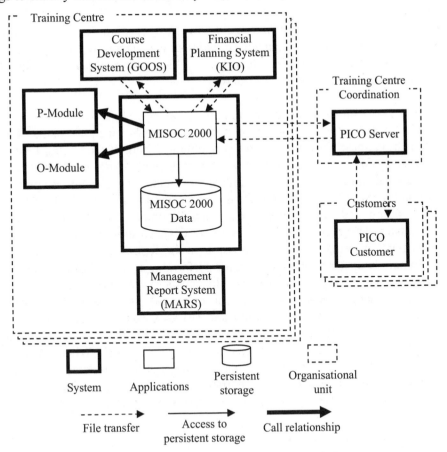

Figure 5.13 Computer systems in Dutch army training centres

As shown in Figure 5.13, each training centre has a number of computer systems interconnected together. Their functions and interrelationships are described below[1].

- The *course development system* (*GOOS*) is used for developing new courses. It uses information from MISOC 2000, such as the number of registrations for a course and the availability of locations. After new courses have been developed with GOOS, they are imported into MISOC 2000. From then on it is possible to register students for these courses. The data exchanges between MISOC 2000 and GOOS consist of files being imported and exported.

- The *financial planning system* (*KIO*) is used for calculation of the costs. KIO feeds MISOC 2000 with information concerning cost centres and retrieves information from MISOC 2000 concerning the organisation, instructors, locations, and resources. These data exchanges take the form of file transfers.

- The *management reporting system* (*MARS*) is a management information system that is used for generating various management reports. This system is implemented using a COTS report tool. This tool directly accesses the MISOC 2000 database to retrieve information.

- The *P-module* is a part of the *human resource* (*HR*) information system. The HR system stores information about employees, such as name, rank and qualifications. This information is maintained both at the central level for the whole DoD, and at the local level for each unit. At the local level, each unit uses an instance of the P-module for managing the information of the employees of that unit. Periodically, the central system feeds the P-module of each unit with information concerning the employees of that unit using file transfer. These downloads are one way only, so global updates to the human resource information are only possible at the central HR system. However, the P-module does provide facilities for performing updates, but these changes are not carried through to other units. This enables units to register temporary staff. The P-module plays two different roles: (a) as a stand-alone system for managing personnel information and (b) as a 'service' for other systems to access personnel information. MISOC 2000 uses the P-module in the latter role, mostly to retrieve information about instructors. When MISOC 2000 invokes the P-module, one of the applications of the P-module is started on the user's workstation and control is transferred to that application. After the user has performed the necessary actions, the application is closed and control is

---

[1] Notice that, Lassing, Rijsenbrij and van Vliet's case study was focused on one particular sub-system MISOC 2000. Hence, the description of the whole system is incomplete.

returned to MISOC 2000. Other systems use the P-module in similar ways.

- The function of the *O-module* is to provide access to information concerning the organisation and its resources. Just like the human resource information, this information is stored at both the central and the local level and the central mainframe performs periodical downloads to local instances of the O-module.

- *MISOC 2000* is also related to the *PICO* (*Planning and Development System for Courses and Training*) system outside the training centres. PICO gathers the course information of all training centres and enables their customers, i.e. all organisational units, to enrol employees for these courses. The information concerning the courses is transferred from the training centres to a central server, the PICO server. The customers of the training centres use a local system, 'PICO customer', to retrieve this information and enrol their employees for these courses. Finally, these enrolments are transferred from the PICO server to MISOC 2000 at the appropriate training centre. All of these flows of information are file transfers.

Based on the above description of the system, we can represent the system in visual notation in Figure 5.14.

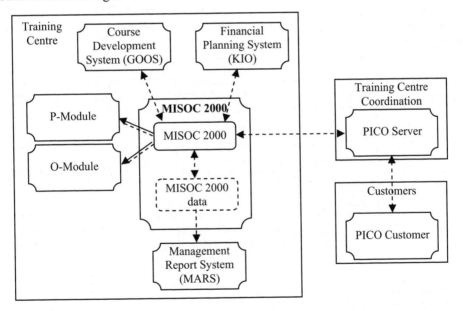

Figure 5.14 Representation of the information systems in visual notation

As shown in Figure 5.15, MISOC 2000 consists of a number of sub-systems. The choice of sub-systems in the design of MISOC 2000 was driven by the processes of the training centres: each sub-system supports a specific group of users. The following sub-systems were recognised.

- *Product*: formulating course catalogues and production plans for a training center

- *Sales*: distribution of course catalogues and recording agreements with customers

- *Student*: registration of student information

- *Programming*: creating short-term schedules

- *Logistics*: management of the availability of locations and items

- *Economics*: exporting cost information to KIO and importing information about cost centres from KIO

- *Personnel*: an extension of the P-module to record personnel information specific for training centres

These sub-systems communicate through a shared database. Figure 5.15 shows the sub-systems, the information they share and their communication with the systems in the environment.

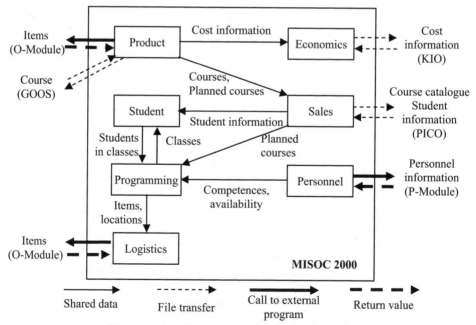

Figure 5.15 The structure of MISOC 2000

There is also another sub-system of MISOC 2000, called 'General'. This sub-system is not aimed at supporting a specific group of users. Instead, it is used for administrative purposes, like maintenance of authorisation and configuration data. Information recorded by this sub-system is used by all other sub-systems. It was not shown in Figure 5.15 to enhance readability.

Therefore, we have the following architectural description of the system MISOC 2000 in visual notation as follows in Figure 5.16. Notice that, although data flows between various components are identified and depicted in the original diagram given in [3], the actual connections between these components are indirectly through the database. Moreover, the component 'General' is also explicitly represented in Figure 5.16.

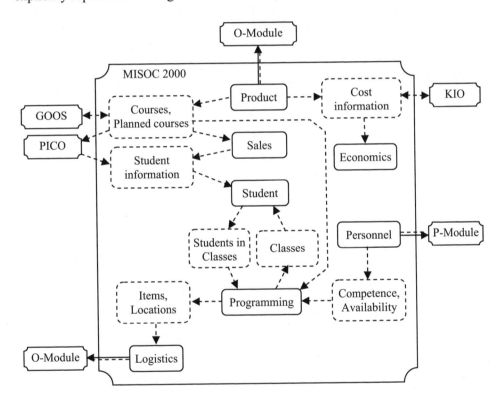

Figure 5.16 Representation of MISOC 2000's architecture in visual notation

Orthogonal to this division in sub-systems, MISOC 2000 is also divided into three layers. The first layer consists of a number of client executables, which are installed on the users' workstations. The second layer consists of a number of server executables, which are installed on an application server. The third layer consists of the database tables that are placed on the database management server. This layering spreads the required processing over a number of machines.

MISOC 2000 is protected from unauthorised use by an authorisation mechanism. The authorisation strategy is function-oriented, i.e. groups of users are authorised to perform certain sets of functions. The authorisation mechanism consists of a number of elements. The first element is the maintenance of the authorisation data. As mentioned before, this function is performed by the sub-system 'General'. The second element is the storage of authorisation data. This function is performed by the MISOC 2000 database server, which has a separate database for authorisation data. The next element is the authentication client that logs users in to and out of MISOC 2000. It is installed on each user's workstation that registers a user with the database. This authentication client is also used for other systems. The final element of the authorisation mechanism is the authorisation functions. To do so, each function checks the authorisation database to see whether the current user is authorised to perform that function. This structured was represented in Figure 5.17.

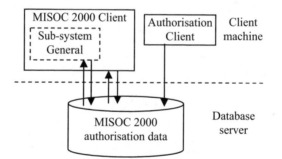

Figure 5.17 The elements of authorisation

According to the above description, we can have an alternative view to the architecture of the MISOC 2000 system represented below in Figure 5.18.

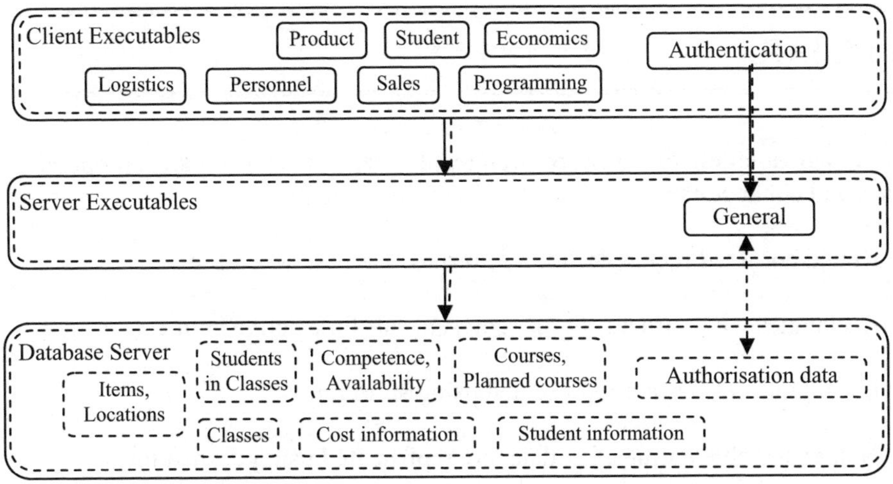

Figure 5.18 An alternative view of the architecture of MISOC 2000

SUMMARY

The visual notation of software architecture represents software components as nodes and connectors as arcs between them. In particular,

- Round cornered rectangles represent run-time passive entities;

- Rectangles with corners cut off represent run-time active entities;

- Executable entities are represented using solid lines;

- Non-executable entities, i.e. data, are represented using dashed lines;

- Data flows between components are represented as dashed line arcs;

- Control flows between components are represented as solid line arcs.

FURTHER READING

The visual notation of software architecture presented in this chapter is devised by Bass, Clements and Kazman, who are among the forefront of researchers on software architecture. The notation was used in their book *Software Architecture in Practice* [1] published in 1998. The visual notation used in this book is only a part of their notation. The original notation also contains symbols and diagrams to describe other aspects of systems related to software architecture such as the business models in which the software is used. In the literature, a number of languages have also been proposed to describe software architectures. Such languages are called software architecture description languages (ADLs). A brief introduction to ADLs can be found in Mary Shaw and David Garlan's textbook on *Software Architecture: Perspective on An Emerging Discipline*. Among the best known examples of architecture description languages are Rapide [4], SADL [5], UniCon [6], and Wright [7]. These languages provide formal notations for representing and analysing software architectural designs with the intention to solve the problems caused by the informality of most box-and-line depictions of architectural designs. Examples of these are the possible ambiguity and inaccuracy in the meanings of a design, and the lack of support to reasoning about the design to uncover the inconsistency and incompleteness of a design.

EXERCISES

(5–1) Use the visual notation to represent the following software components:

(a) A file that can be read and written;

(b) A function that has no side-effect;

(c) A procedure that assigns a value of an output parameter (i.e. a call-by-reference parameter) according to the value of a global variable and has the side-effect of modifying the global variable according to its parameters;

(d) A filter that receives a value from its input port and outputs a value calculated only from the input value;

(e) A process that receives requests of database queries and updates and responds with corresponding actions on database queries and database updates;

(f) Data stored in a ROM (read only memory);

(g) An object O that contains two methods A and B;

(i) A module M that contains two procedures A and B and a global variable C, where procedure A may read and write values to variable C while procedure B may only read values of variable C;

(j) A library $LFPA$ of long float-point arithmetic operators that contains the following functions and constants:

- *Functions*: Addition, Subtraction, Multiplication, Division, greater_than, long-equal;

- *Constants*: Zero, Overflow, Underflow.

(k) A server process S that receives messages from the internet and takes one of a set of pre-defined actions $A_1, A_2, ..., A_n$ on its maintained database DB according to the content of the message, where each action is defined as an internal procedure.

(5–2) Use the visual notation to represent the following links between software components.

(a) Procedure A calls procedure B, which has no parameters;

(b) Procedure A calls procedure B, which has at least one parameter;

(c) Procedure A uses the value of a global variable B to fulfil its functionality;

(d) Procedure A modifies the value of a global variable B, but does not use its value in its computation;

(e) Procedure A uses the value of a global variable B in its computation and also modifies its value;

(f) Process A sends messages to process B, but does not receive any messages from B;

(g) Process A communicates with process B by sending and receiving messages;

(h) Process A running on machine C communicates with process B on machine D via a communication network by sending and receiving messages;

(i) Process A and B communicate with each other through accessing a global variable V stored in shared memory.

(5–3) Fill the blank cells of the following table, which defines the properties of software components represented in the visual notation.

Table 5.1 Properties of components represented in the visual notation

Node	Properties				Example
	Executable	Has state	Passive	Active	
	Yes	No	Yes	No	Function
	Yes		No	Yes	Filter
	No	Yes			
	Yes				
				No	

(5–4) Identify the properties of the components and connectors of the software systems in exercise (4–6). The structure of the system depicted in Figure 4.15 is reproduced below as Figure 5.19. Use the software architecture visual notation to describe the architecture of the software system.

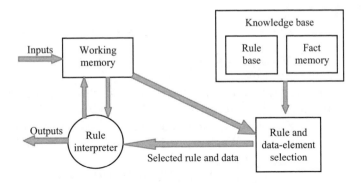

Figure 5.19 Basic rule-based system

(5–5) Identify the properties of the components and connectors of the software system studied in exercise (4–7). Its structure depicted in Figure 4.16 is reproduced below as Figure 5.20. Use the software architecture visual notation to describe the architecture of the software system.

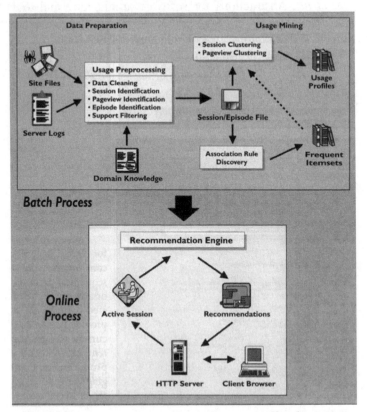

Figure 5.20 The structure of a web personalisation system

REFERENCES

1   Bass, L., Clements P. and Kazman, R., *Software Architecture in Practice*, Addison Wesley, 1998.

2   Stone, P. (ed.), RoboCup-2000: The fourth Robotic Soccer World Championships, *AI Magazine*, Vol. 22, No. 1, Spring 2001, pp11–38.

3   Lassing, N., Rijsenbrij, D. and van Vliet, H. Towards a Broader View on Software Architecture Analysis of Flexibility, *Proc. Asian-Pacific Software Eng. Conf. (APSEC'99)*, 1999.

4   Luckham, D. C., Augustin, L. M., Kenny, J. J., Veer, J., Bryan, D. and Mann, W., Specification and analysis of system architecture using Rapide, *IEEE Transactions on Software Engineering*, Special issue on Software Architecture, Vol. 21, No. 4, pp336–355, April 1995.

5   Moriconi, M., Qian, X. and Riemenschneider, R., Correct architecture refinement, *IEEE Transactions on Software Engineering*, Special issue on Software Architecture, Vol. 21, No. 4, pp356–372, April 1995.

6   Shaw, M, *et al.*, Abstractions for software architecture and tools to support them, *IEEE Transactions on Software Engineering*, Special issue on Software Architecture, Vol. 21, No. 4, pp314–335, April 1995.

7   Allen, R. and Garlan, D., A formal basis for architectural connection, *ACM Transactions on Software Engineering and Methodology*, July 1997.

6 Typical Architectural Styles

As discussed in the previous chapters, an architectural style is an abstraction of the structural designs of a family of software systems. These styles serve as idiomatic patterns of system organisation. They have been developed over the years as designers recognised the values of specific organisational principles and structures for certain classes of software systems. These patterns of organisational principles and structures play a role in software design similar to the notion of architectural styles in other disciplines such as in building architecture and computer architecture. In this chapter, we examine a number of well understood software architectural styles in detail. The objectives of the chapter are:

- To learn various software architectural styles;

- To learn how different software architectural styles are interrelated.

As Shaw and Garlan pointed out [1], based on the notion of software architectural styles defined in the previous chapter, a particular style can be characterised by answers to the following questions.

- *What is the design vocabulary?* An answer to this question clarifies the types of components and connectors that can be used in the systems of a specific style. It represents a part of the design knowledge associated with the architectural style in the form of a vocabulary that software engineers denote these types of components and connectors, and the ways they are combined. However, design vocabulary may go beyond these nicknames of components and connectors of a specific architectural style to include design activities and run-time phenomena etc.

- *What are the allowable structural patterns?* An answer to this question clarifies the features and properties of the topological structure of the system in the form of constraints on how components and connectors can be combined and interconnected in a system in the style.

- *What is the underlying computational model?* An answer to this question usually describes how the system is executed, i.e. the mechanisms that enable the system to operate. It clarifies the features about the run-time behaviours of the systems in the style.

- *What are the essential invariants of the style?* An answer to this question provides additional characteristic features of the architectural style not covered by the above questions, such as semantic constraints. These features form an important part of the characteristics of the architectural style. It often enables us to infer other properties about run-time behaviours and development and maintenance processes.

- *What are the most important properties of software systems that can be derived from the style?* Especially, *what are the advantages and disadvantages of using the style?* An answer to this question provides a guideline for the uses of the style, which forms an important design knowledge that links from architectural features to design considerations such as quality.

- *What are the common specialisations of the style?* An answer to this question provides information about the variable aspects of the architectural style. It clarifies the choices that designers can have and represents a design space within the architectural style. A specialisation often forms a sub-type of the style. Such relationships can form a systematic knowledge of software architectural styles and provide further guidelines for the effective uses of architectural styles in software design.

- *What are the typical examples of its uses?* Concrete examples of software systems in the style illustrate the uses of the architectural style and demonstrate its usefulness as well as possible problems associated with the style. It helps software designers to learn from existing experiences and good practices. Examples also indicate the application domains that can often benefit from the architectural style. However, it is worth noting that an architectural style is usually not bound to such application domains.

Therefore, in the following we will organise the discussions of each architectural style by addressing its computational model, design vocabulary, structural pattern, essential invariants, properties derived from the style such as the advantages and disadvantages, and sub-types of the styles. We will also illustrate the styles by examples and discuss their typical applications.

The chapter is organised as follows. Section 1 introduces the data flow architectural style and its sub-styles. Section 2 discusses the architectural style of independent components and its main sub-styles. Section 3 is devoted to the call and return style and its main sub-styles. Section 4 and 5 are about data centred and virtual machine architectural styles, respectively.

6.1 DATA FLOW

Data flow is a software architectural style that is widely used in various application domains where data processing plays a significant role. The pipe-and-filter architectural style discussed in Chapter 4 is a special case of data flow style. Here, we start with the data flow architectural style to illustrate how design knowledge can be associated to an architectural style. More software architectural styles will be presented in the chapter.

6.1.1 The general data flow style

A. Computational model

The computational model of an architectural style is the overall mechanism that a system in the style works.

The data flow style is characterised by viewing the system as a series of transformations on successive pieces of input data. Data enter the system and then flow through the components one at a time until they are assigned to some final destination (output or data store). The structure of the design is dominated by orderly motion of data from component to component. The availability of data controls computation.

B. Design vocabulary

Associated to each architectural style is a set of design vocabulary about the specific types of components and connectors that can be used in the systems of the style, the particular design considerations often concerned the designers of such a system, and so on.

For example, a system in the data flow style consists of a collection of components which are called *processing elements* or *units*. A *processing element* starts its computation when its inputs are available. It then processes the data and produces outputs, which are fed into other processing elements as input. The connections and interactions between these processing elements are called *data flows*, or simply *flows*.

C. Structural pattern

Systems of a particular style often have a specific topologic structure in which components are connected together. A data flow system can be viewed as a directed graph, where nodes are processing elements and arcs are data flows between the elements. Figure 6.1 illustrates the data flow style.

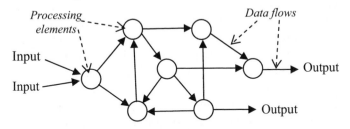

Figure 6.1 Illustration of data flow style

In the software architectural visual notation, the structure of a data flow system can be illustrated by the following diagram.

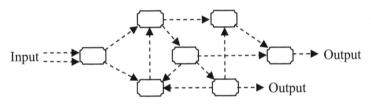

Figure 6.2 Representation of data flow style in visual notation

D. Essential invariants

Systems of a style may be different from each other on a number of features. It is important to understand what features are variable so that different systems can be different but still regarded as in the same style, as well as what are the essential features that all systems of the style must have. One of the essential invariants for data flow systems is that there is no interaction between processing elements other than data flows. Moreover, each processing element must be on a path from the input to an output.

E. Sub-types of the style

A way of understanding what can be different for systems in a style is to recognise its sub-styles. They form the most important variants of the style; hence the design choices within the style. There are two main subtypes of data flow style, *batch sequential processing* and *pipe-and-filter*. We have seen 2 examples of pipe-and-filter systems in the previous section.

F. Properties derived from the architecture

As we have seen in Chapter 4, systems of the same style tend to have a set of common features. Such common features of each architectural style provide transferable design knowledge and can be used as guidelines of software design.

In the data flow architecture, components are highly independent. There is no global control of the components' behaviour. The processing elements can be executed concurrently, even on different computers. They are capable of processing continuous streams of data, which may be theoretically without a limit on the length of input data, and provide continuous control and monitoring functions of real-time process control systems. The components are reusable and can be relatively easily integrated into other systems of the same architectural style. The modification of the system can be easily performed at two levels. At the component level, the processing elements can be modified without requiring modifications of other processing elements provided that formats and types of the data flows into and out of the element are compatible with the original ones. At the system's structural level, new processing elements and data flows can be relatively easily added into the system to extend the system's functionality. Data flow architecture can be analysed for its performance by applying well-established methods, such as queue theory.

A possible difficulty in the design and implementation of a data flow architecture is the synchronisation of the computations of more than one processing element, if such synchronisations are necessary.

G. Examples

Typical examples of software systems in the style help us to understand how such a system works as well as the advantages and disadvantages of design systems in the style. We can learn from such examples when the style is useful when given a design problem.

Many web-based applications can be regarded as in the data flow architectural style. For example, an e-business system depicted in the following diagram (Figure 6.3) consists of four components. The *client side* executes on the user's computer and is connected to the *web-server* through the internet. The web server processes sequences of user's requests, which is in the form of messages, and passes the requests to a *database server* for processing database queries. The results of database queries are processed by the html *page generator* to produce an html file, which is sent back to the client side to display on the user's computer screen.

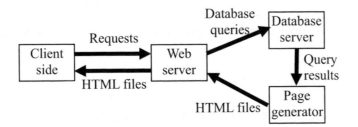

Figure 6.3 The structure of a typical web-based application

6.1.2 The pipe-and-filter sub-style

A. Computational model

The pipe-and-filter architectural style is a sub-type of data flow style. Therefore, the computational model of data flow is also the model for pipes-and-filters style. In particular, as discussed in section 4.3, each component in a software system of pipe-and-filter style incrementally reads in streams of data on its inputs and incrementally produces streams of data on its outputs. This is usually accomplished by applying a local transformation to each individual datum of the input streams and computing incrementally, so that output begins when an element of the input stream arrives and before the whole input stream is consumed. The outputs from one component are directly fed to another component as its inputs. The connectors of this style serve as conduits for the streams, transmitting outputs of one filter to another filter's input.

B. Design vocabulary

The components in a pipes-and-filters architecture are called *filters*. The connectors in pipe-and-filter systems are called *pipes*. As already discussed in section 4.3, there are three important constraints on the components and the connectors of pipe-and-filter architecture.

(1) *Independence*. Filters must be independent entities. In particular, they should not share state with each other. There should be no global state variables as well.

(2) *Anonymity*. Filters do not know the identity of their upstream and downstream filters. Their specifications might restrict what appears on the input pipes or make guarantees about what appears on the output pipes, but they may not identify the components at the ends of those pipes.

(3) *Concurrency*. The correctness of the output of a pipe-and-filter network should not depend on the order in which the filters perform their incremental processing – although fair scheduling can be assumed. The dynamic execution can be best understood by considering all the filters are executing in parallel or concurrently.

Therefore, a filter differs from a processing element of the general data flow architectural style in two ways. First, a processing element is not required to be anonymous to its upstream or downstream processing elements, but anonymity is a key feature of filters. Second, generally speaking, in a data flow architecture, processing elements are not required to execute concurrently, although they can in some systems. However, in a pipe-and-filter system, filters must execute concurrently.

C. Structural pattern

There is no structure restriction in addition to that of the restrictions of data flow architectural style. Figure 6.4 illustrates in the visual notation the structure of a pipe-and-filter system.

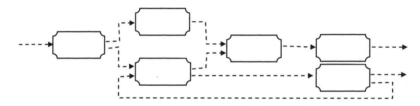

Figure 6.4 Illustration of pipe-and-filter architecture in the visual notation

D. Properties derived from the architecture

Pipe-and-filter systems have a number of nice properties. First, they allow the designer to understand the overall input/output behaviour of a system as a simple composition of the behaviours of the individual filters. Second, they support reuse. Any two filters can be hooked together, provided they agree on the data that are being transmitted between them. Third, systems are easy to maintain and enhance. New filters can be added to existing systems, and old filters can be replaced by improved ones. For example, for the transcription system depicted in Figure 4.9, the word recognition component can be replaced by components to recognise new broadcasts in French and German with an error rate acceptable for information retrieval. Fourth, data are incrementally processed. This enables the system to process long streams of input data. For example, the audio transcription system can process hours of unrestricted radio and video news broadcasts. Moreover, they permit certain kinds of specialised analysis, such as throughput and deadlock analysis. Finally, they naturally support concurrent execution. Each filter can be implemented as a separate task and potentially executed in parallel with other filters.

However, these systems also have their disadvantages. First, pipe-and-filter systems often lead to a batch organisation of processing. Although filters can process data incrementally, they are inherently independent, so the designer must think of each filter as providing a complete transformation of input data to output data. In particular, because of their transformational character, pipe-and-filter systems are typically not good at handling interactive applications. Second, they may be hampered by having to maintain correspondence between two separate but related streams. Third, depending on the implementation, they may force a lowest common denominator on data transmission, resulting in added work for each filter to parse and unparse its data. This, in turn, can lead to loss of performance and to increased complexity in writing the filters themselves.

E. Sub-types of the style

The main sub-type of this style is pipeline. Pipeline architectures are pipes-and-filters systems in which there is no cycle of data flows. Figure 6.5 below illustrates the pipeline architectural style. In fact, the examples given in section 4.3 are pipelines.

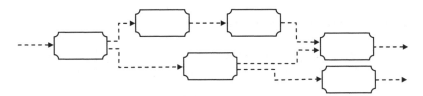

Figure 6.5 Illustration of pipeline architectural style

F. Examples

We have seen two examples of software systems audio transcription and projection keyboard interpretation in the pipe-and-filter architectural style in Chapter 4. The best-known examples of pipe-and-filter architectures are programs written in the Unix shell. Unix supports this style by providing run-time mechanisms for implementing pipes. For example, typing in the following into the command line of a Unix system 'ls –l | more' is actually building a program by using the pipe-and-filter architecture. It combines two programs 'ls' and 'more' through the pipe connector '|'.

6.1.3   The batch sequential processing sub-style

A. Computational model

Batch sequential processing is also a sub-type of data flow architectural style. In addition to the common features of the data flow architectural style's computational model, in the batch sequential style, components are independent programs. They are executed sequentially, i.e. one component runs to completion before the next starts. The data is transmitted between components as a whole batch rather than a stream of data elements.

B. Design vocabulary

The computational components in a batch sequential processing architecture are often called *processing steps* or *phases*.

C. Structural pattern

Batch sequential processing architectures usually consist of a finite number of steps linearly connected. However, some batch sequential processing systems contain loops that repeat some processing steps for a finite number of times.

E. Properties derived from the architecture

Batch sequential processing architectures inherit almost all advantages of the data flow architectural style, especially the reusability and modifiability. In addition, it avoids complicated issues related to the synchronisation between components by executing them one after another. On the other hand, because the components do not execute concurrently, the performance of the system may be less satisfactory than other data flow systems. In particular, it usually cannot deal with continuous streams of inputs with unbounded lengths.

D. Examples

Figure 6.6 depicts an example of a transaction processing system that illustrates batch sequential processing style, where data passed from one step to another is stored on tapes.

Figure 6.6 An example that illustrates batch sequential processing style

The system contains four components. The *Validate* component validates the validity of each transaction stored on a tape. It removes invalid transactions and stores all valid transactions on another tape. The *Sort* component executes when validation is completed. It reads in all transactions stored on the tape that the previous step generated and sorts the transactions according to the time that transactions are issued. The result is then stored in another tape. Since this step is after the completion of validation, all transactions stored on the tape must be valid and they must also be listed in the order that earlier transactions are listed first. After sorting the transactions, the *Update* component updates the contents of a business database by processing the transactions one by one according to their order stored on the tape generated by the Sort component. The results of the update are recorded on another tape, which was input to the final step of processing to generate a summary report by the *Report* component.

Compilers are essentially in batch sequential processing styles. A simplified view of the architecture of compilers is depicted in Figure 6.7 below.

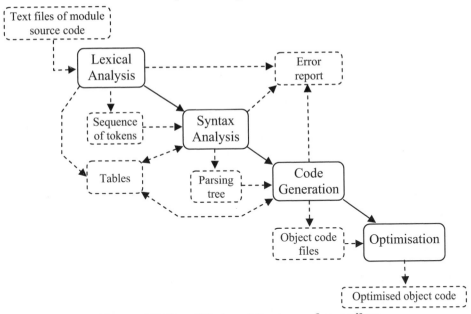

Figure 6.7 Simplified architecture of compilers

The *lexical analysis* reads in the source code of the modules to be compiled, which are in the form of a sequence of characters stored in a text file. It generates a table of identifiers and a sequence of tokens that each token represents a lexical element in the source code. The outputs are stored in a number of files. These files together with files previously generated in the compilation of the imported modules are passed to the *syntax analysis* phase, which then parse the sequence of tokens into a parsing tree and generates some more tables, for example, those associate variables to their types, etc. These outputs are also stored in files for consumption by the code generation phase. The *code generation* phase reads in these files and produces object codes and more tables, such as tables providing information about the exported procedures, variables and types for the linker program. These outputs are also stored into files. The *optimisation* phase is optional, which improves the efficiency of the object code. Of course, in each phase, errors in the source code of the program may be discovered. In such cases, an error report may be generated and either displayed on the screen or written into an error report file. The compilation will terminate after an error is discovered.

6.2 INDEPENDENT COMPONENTS

The architectural style of independent components has attracted increasing interest recently for its strong support to software reuse and evolution due to its ease of integration of components into a system. It has a number of sub-types of style including *communicating processes*, *event-based implicit invocation* and *multi-agent systems*.

6.2.1 The general independent components style

A. Computational model

Independent component architecture consists of a number of components that communicate through messages. They send data to each other but typically do not directly control each other. The message may be passed to named participants or passed among unnamed participants in case of using the publish/subscribe paradigm.

B. Design vocabulary

All components of a system in the independent component style must be executable. They are often called *processes* if the component is active. Otherwise, they are often just called *modules*. However, each specific sub-type of the architectural style, which will be discussed later, has its own vocabulary.

C. Structural pattern

There is no general pattern of system structure for the whole class of independent component architectural style with regard to the topological structures of the systems.

D. Essential invariants

The essential invariant of all sub-types of the independent component style is that the only means of information exchange among the components is message passing. There is no shared state variable or data between the components. Components are autonomous in the sense that they are not controlling each other in the sense that one component cannot decide whether the receiver of a message will take an action accordingly or which action is to be taken if any. In case of more than one component receiving a message, the sender cannot even decide which of the receivers will react on the message first.

E. Properties derived from the architecture

Independent component architectures achieve modifiability by decoupling various portions of the computation. It enables concurrent executions of the components, even parallel executions of components on various computers over a network. Scalability of the system can be achieved through balancing the load of clients and the servers, which is usually running on more powerful hardware systems. Figure 6.8 illustrates various possible partitions of software functional components to be distributed on computers in a two tier client-server system in order to achieve load balance.

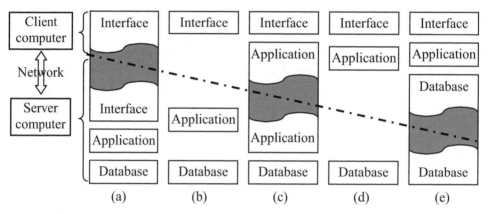

Figure 6.8 Possible partitions of software functional components to be distributed to client and server computers

Another advantage of decoupling computation into independent components is that it eases component integration. It strongly supports system evolution at two levels. At the component level, a component can be replaced by a revised one without affecting the interfaces of other components in the system. At the systems level, new components can be easily integrated into the system, say, simply by registering it for the events of the system.

The main disadvantage of independent component architectures is also due to the independency between the components. When a component announces an event or send a message to another component, it cannot assume the receiver(s) will respond to it. To overcome this problem, interaction protocols must be designed and implemented for all components to follow. This may result in heavy overhead of the system. Moreover, reasoning about correctness can also be problematic due to components' autonomous behaviour.

F. Sub-types of the style

There are a number of sub-types of independent component architectural styles including the communicating process systems and the event-based implicit invocation systems, which will be discussed in detail in sections 6.2.3 and 6.2.2, respectively. In addition to these sub-types, there are also interrupt-driven process systems and multicast message with dynamic binding systems. Multi-agent systems are also a sub-type of the independent component style. They emerged from artificial intelligence research and attracted considerable attention recently.

G. Examples

A typical example of independent component architecture is the client-server architecture, which, in fact, can be considered as a sub-type of the architectural style. A client-server system usually consists of a number of clients and one or more servers; as shown in Figure 6.9.

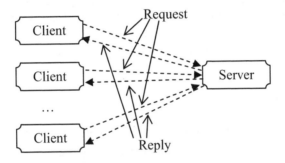

Figure 6.9 Client-server structure

A client component sends messages to a server to request the execution of a certain computational task to be performed by the server. Upon receiving such a request, the server decides whether to perform the requested task, and if it decides to do so, the outcome or the result of the task is fed back to the client by sending a message. There are numerous concrete examples of such client-server systems in web-based applications. In fact, the www client-server system described in Chapter 4 and studied in Chapter 5 is a typical example of this architectural style.

6.2.2   The event based implicit invocation systems sub-style

Event-based systems are a sub-type of independent component architectures in which control is part of the model.

A. Computational model

Individual components in an event-based implicit invocation system announce data that they wish to share with their environment – a set of unnamed components. These other components may register an interest in this class of data. If they do so, when the data appears, they are invoked and receive the data. Typically, event systems make use of a message manager that manages communication among the components, invoking a component (thus controlling it) when a message arrives for it. This paradigm is important because it decouples component implementation from knowing each other's names and locations. This decoupling eases component integration.

B. Design vocabulary

A component's announcement of data is usually called *publishing* the data. Such an announcement is also called an *event*. A component's registration of its interests in certain data is called *subscription*. A message manager in an event-based implicit invocation system is also often called *event handler*. It is responsible for keeping a record on all components that registered their interests in certain events. When an event takes place, the event handler distributes the data to those registered components.

C. Structural pattern

The general structural pattern of event-based implicit invocation systems is shown in Figure 6.10. The interface of a component in event-based implicit invocation systems usually contains a collection of events that it can raise and a collection of procedures or functions that other components can call directly. Therefore, in addition to message passing through the event handler, components may communicate with each other directly through procedure/function calls.

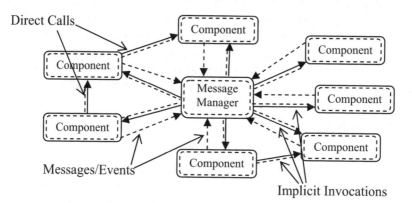

Figure 6.10 Structure of event-based implicit invocation systems

D. Properties derived from the architecture

As a sub-type of independent components architectural style, event-based implicit invocation style inherits all the advantages and disadvantages of independent components architectures. The implicit invocation architecture strongly supports reuse and software evolution. A new component can be integrated into the system while the system is executing simply by registering it for the events of that system. One component can be replaced by another component or components without affecting the interfaces of other components of the system. Such replacement can be done without stopping the execution of the system. This property is of particular importance for systems that must run uninterrupted continuously for a long period of time such as continuous process control systems.

E. Examples

Typical examples of software systems in the event-based implicit invocation style can be found in programming environments to integrate various tools, in database management systems to ensure various consistency constraints, in graphical user interface systems to separate presentations of data from applications that manage the data, etc.

The following example is an integrated programming environment called Field that integrates a number of tools with an event-based implicit invocation architecture [2]. The structure of the system is described in Figure 6.11 below.

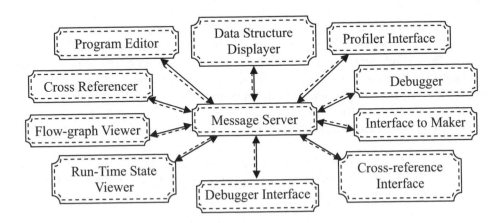

Figure 6.11 The architecture of Field programming environment

As shown in Figure 6.11, the Field system consists of a set of programming tools, which include the following.

Program Editor: a full functioned extensible editor for C and Pascal programs. It allows association of annotations with each line of code. Annotations can be created, removed and queried. Multiple windows of the editor can be active simultaneously.

Cross Referencer: it collects a relational database about a software system. The database is generated the first time when cross-referencing is done. It is then incrementally rescanning only those source files that have changed.

Cross Reference Interface: a menu-oriented interface that enables simple database queries to be made by filling a dialogue box. It is used by other tools, such as the Program Editor to implement commands like 'find and display the declaration of this procedure', and the Debugger to implement high level commands such as 'set breakpoints at all assignments to this variable', etc.

Data Structure Displayer: it is adapted from another programming environment and incorporated as a pair of tools, which graphically displays a data structure and describes how the data structure should be displayed, respectively.

Flow Graph Viewer: it displays a hierarchical flow graph of an area of the program interactively selected by the user.

Run-Time State Viewer: it displays various types of run-time state of the program when executed for debugging, such as the run-time stack, values of variables and expressions, and debugger events such as breakpoints.

There are also other tools in the system. The readers are referred to [2] for more details. These tools are integrated through the component called *Message Server*. Each tool registers a set of message patterns with the server. Tools communicate by sending messages to the server and receiving those messages that match their registered patterns. The message server in the Field system serves as the message manager. The messages are in text format of variable lengths. They are sent by the tools and then the Message Server rebroadcasts to other tools.

This system has a typical event-based implicit invocation system. The Field system achieved high flexibility by letting independent tools cooperate through such a simple convention of implicit invocation.

6.2.3   The communicating processes sub-style

Another sub-type of independent component architectures is the architectural style of communicating processes. These are the classic multi-process systems.

A. Computational model

The components of a system in the communicating processes style are active processes. They communicate with each other through fixed channels of communications. They pass messages to each other to synchronise their executions and to achieve mutual exclusion in accessing shared resources.

B. Design vocabulary

The components in a communicating processes system are called *processes* and they communicate with each other through *communication channels* and *ports*, where messages are sent and received.

There are a number of different communication mechanisms that are provided by various operating systems and can be used by the system. Communications between processes can be *synchronous*, which means two processes must engage in the communication at the same time in order for one message to be passed from one to another. Alternatively, the communication can be *asynchronous*, when one message can be delivered without the receiver's engagement in the communication. Communications among processes can also be *point to point*, or *one-to-one*, if a message is only received by one specific process. Alternatively, it can be *broadcasted* to all processes in the system, or *group broadcasted* to a sub-group of the processes.

C. Structural pattern

The general structure of communicating processes systems is a network of processes connected by communication channels. It differs from event-based implicit invocation in that there is no event handler that is responsible for redistribution of the messages among the processes. Although communicating processes systems with fixed communication channels can be regarded as a sub-style of data flow architectural style, they usually have a more complicated flow of information between processes rather than only having more or less simpler patterns of data flow. The messages passed between processes usually contain requests of performing certain tasks rather than just the data to be processed.

D. Sub-types of the style

Client-server architecture is a well-known sub-type of communicating processes. A server exists to serve data to one or more clients, which are typically located across a network. The client originates a call to the server, which works, synchronously or asynchronously, to service the client's request.

6.3 CALL AND RETURN

Call-and-return architecture has been the dominant architectural style in large systems for the past 30 years. This is directly supported by the classical and current programming paradigms. A number of sub-types of the style have emerged including main-program-and-subroutine with shared data, layered systems, abstract data types and object-oriented systems, etc. Each of these has its own interesting features.

6.3.1 The general call and return style

A. Computational model

A software system in call and return style is essentially decomposed into smaller pieces to deal with complexity and to help achieve modifiability. There is typically a single thread of control. Each component executes only when it gets this control from another component and returns the control to that component when it terminates execution. During its execution, it may pass the control along to other components. Each component usually has a fixed *entry* where the executions of the components start. A component also has some fixed locations called *exits* where executions terminate. Such components are called *subroutines*. The passes of control from one component to another are called subroutine *calls* or *invocations*, which are often combined with passing data as the parameters. The component that has the entrance to the whole program is usually called the *main program*. It controls the executions of subroutines. In a system of the style, there may also be some passive data components, which store shared data for accesses by the subroutines. Shared data that all components can access are usually called *global variables* or *global state* of the system.

The structural organisation and dynamic control of execution in the call and return style are directly supported by almost all high-level programming languages with the *procedure/function* facility. Therefore, subroutines are also called *procedures*, and subroutine invocations are called *procedure/function calls*.

B. Structural pattern

As illustrated in Figure 6.12, a system in the call and return style can have any topological structure that links subroutines by subroutine calls. However, a common practice is to organise the connections between subroutines in certain patterns and to pack a number of interrelated subroutines into program units. This results in a number of sub-types of the style.

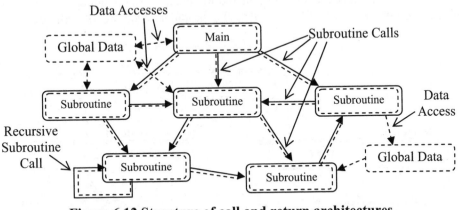

Figure 6.12 Structure of call and return architectures

C. Design vocabulary

A common practice in the design of a call and return system is to organise subroutines into a hierarchy as shown in Figure 6.13. A call and return architecture with a hierarchical structure is often called the *main-program-and-subroutine with shared data*. In fact, this can be considered as a sub-type of the call and return style. Figure 6.13 illustrates the structure of systems in this style.

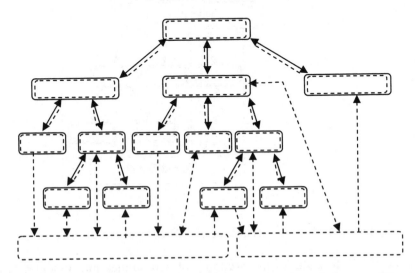

Figure 6.13 The main-program-subroutine with shared data architecture

In a call and return system, a group of subroutines that share a common data store can be grouped together to form a *module*. The module facility in almost all high level programming languages supports flexible control over the visibility of variables and procedures and functions defined in a module so that accesses to these entities are restricted and implementation details can be hidden from the users of the module. Figure 6.14 illustrates the modular structure of call and return architectures.

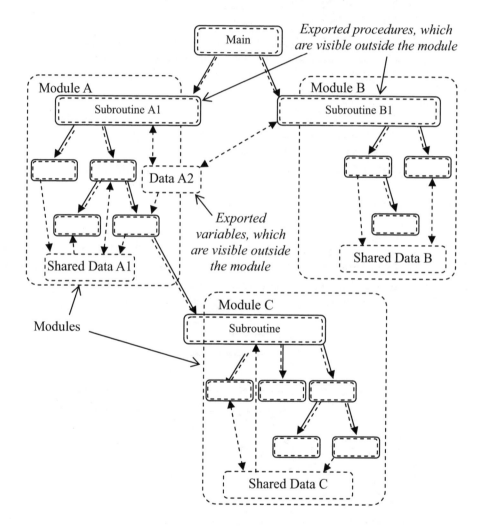

Figure 6.14 Modular structure of call and return architecture

A basic rule that guides the grouping of subroutines into modules is *loose coupling* and *high cohesion*. *High cohesion* means that the subroutines within one module should have intensive interconnection in terms of the number of calls between the subroutines and, perhaps more importantly, the frequency that one subroutine calls another at run-time. *Loose coupling* means that there are few interconnections across the boundary of modules in terms of both statically the links between the subroutines of different modules and dynamically the frequency of subroutine calls across module boundary at run-time. The basic idea underlying this rule is also applicable to the decomposition of a program into subroutines. We would like a subroutine to have intensive interaction within its body, i.e. high cohesion, and few interactions between subroutines, i.e. loose coupling.

Another concept related to the modular design of a software system through decomposition of a program into subroutines and grouping subroutines into modules is *granularity*. A module (as well as a subroutine) should not be too small because that will result in a large number of inter-module (or inter-subroutine) interactions. It should also not be too large, which diminishes the benefit of modularity.

D. Properties derived from the architecture

As discussed in section 3.1, one of the basic causes of the difficulty in software development is the complexity. A basic vehicle to deal with complexity is separation of concerns. The decomposition of a complex program into subroutines enables programmers to separate the concerns in programming a large system into a number of less complex programming problems. Therefore, larger scale software systems can be developed through the collaboration among a team of software developers, each of whom deals with a smaller and less complicated sub-problem. The concept of information hiding and the modular programming facility further enables software developers to decompose an even larger scale of systems into manageable sized units and provides a more flexible means of integrating them into a system. This also achieved a good modifiability of the system. A modification of the internal body of a procedure without affecting the interface will not affect the whole system. Similarly, a modification of the body of a module without affecting the interface will also not affect the whole system.

However, loose coupling and high cohesion alone are not enough to deal with the complexity in large scale software development, which often contain hundreds even thousands of modules. More disciplined organisation of system's structure leads to two interesting sub-types of the call and return architectural style.

E. Sub-types of the style

There are two interesting sub-types of the style that worth discussing in detail. One is layered systems, which is discussed in section 6.3.2; the other is data abstraction including abstract data types and its advanced form object-oriented systems, which is discussed in section 6.3.3.

F. Example

The MISOC 2000 system discussed in section 5.4 and the DVD shop management system discussed in section 4.3 are examples of systems in the call and return style. This is a style that should be familiar to students who have learned structured programming.

6.3.2 The layered systems sub-style

Layered systems form a sub-type of the call and return style. They are commonly seen in system software as well as application systems.

A. Computational model

The computational model of layered systems is the same as that of call and return systems. The main characteristic of the style is its way of organising subroutines into a simple topological structure.

B. Structural pattern and design vocabulary

As illustrated in Figure 6.15, in a layered system, subroutines are organised into a number of groups, which are called *layers*. Each layer contains a collection of subroutines that provide services at a certain abstract level to the layer or layers above it. At the same time, the implementation of the subroutines of the layer depends on calls to the subroutines in the lower layers. In some layered systems, an inner layer is hidden from all outer layers except the adjacent one, while in other systems certain functions are carefully selected for export to all outer layers.

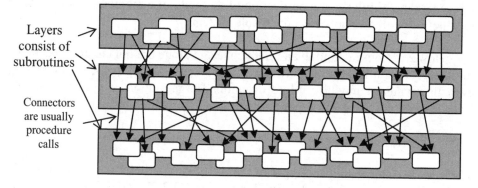

Figure 6.15 Structure of layered systems

C. Properties derived from the architecture

Layered systems have several desirable properties. First, they support designs based on increasing levels of abstraction. This allows implementers to partition a complex problem into a sequence of incremental steps. Second, they support enhancement. Changes to the function of one layer only affect those layers above. Third, they support reuse. Like abstract data types, they allow different implementations of the same layer to be used interchangeably, provided they support the same interfaces to their adjacent layers. This leads to the possibility of defining standard layer interfaces upon which different implementers can build.

However, layered systems also have disadvantages. Not all systems are easily structured in a layered fashion. Even if a system can logically be structured in layers, considerations of performance may require closer coupling between logically high-level functions and their lower level implementations. Additionally, it may be quite difficult to find the right levels of abstraction. This is particularly true for standardised layered models.

D. Typical examples

The best known examples of this kind of architectural style are layered communication protocols. Other application areas for this style include database systems and operating systems.

6.3.3 Data abstraction: the abstract data type and object-oriented sub-styles

Data abstraction, including the basic abstract data type style and its advanced form object-oriented style, is the current mainstream of software development paradigm.

A. Computation model

The computational model of the data abstraction style is the same as the call and return style. However, in the advanced form, i.e. in the object-oriented style, dynamic binding enables a variable to refer to objects of different classes. Consequently, a call statement may actually invoke different procedures at different times during one execution of the program. This is achieved through the introduction of inheritance relation between program unit classes, which will be discussed below.

B. Structural pattern and design vocabulary

In the basic data abstraction style, a particular type of data's representation and all its associated operations are encapsulated into one unit, which enables the data to be used and operated the same way as data of preliminary data types like integers and real numbers directly defined by programming languages. Therefore, such a unit is called an *abstract data type*. The components of this style are instances of the abstract data types. Such components are often called *managers* because they are responsible for preserving the integrity of a resource, here the representation of various types of entities. They interact through function and/or procedure invocations as operations on the data. There are two important aspects of this style. First, a component is responsible for preserving the integrity of its representations. Second, the representation is hidden from other components. All access to the data must be through operations defined by the abstract data type. Figure 6.16 illustrates the structure of abstract data type systems in software architectural visual notation.

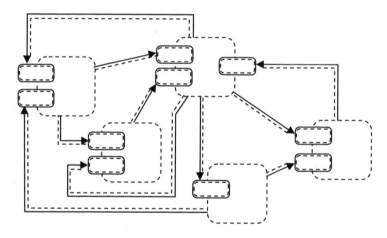

Figure 6.16 Description of an OO architecture in visual notation

Object-oriented style further extends the idea that abstract data types are representations of real world entities and lays its foundation on the philosophy that everything in the world is an object. Therefore, in a pure object-oriented system there is only one type of run-time component, which is object. Moreover, objects can be classified into *classes*. Each class represents a set of *objects*, which are the instances of the class, by a collection of *attributes* for instances' states and a collection of *methods* for the operations on the objects to change their states. Therefore, in the same way as abstract data types, classes are encapsulations of data and operations. However, the metaphor of objects and their classifications into classes in object orientation enables us to talk about one class being a *generalisation* or *specialisation* of another. A class *A* is a *specialisation* of class *B* means that all objects in class *A* are also members of class *B*. Therefore, an object in class A automatically has all the attributes and methods defined in class B; but in addition, it can also have some additional attributes and methods. For objects in class A, those attributes and methods defined in class B are called *inherited* from class B. Moreover, a specialisation of a class can also redefine the type of an attribute and/or the body of a method. Such redefinition is called *overriding*.

Suppose that class A inherits class B, a variable x declared to be of class B can also hold a value of class A because instances of class A are also members of class B. Calling a method m of the object held by variable x, write $x.m$ in object-oriented notation, may result in actually invoking different operations because a specialisation of the class may override the original definition of the method. Determining which semantics are to be associated to an expression or a statement at run-time is called *dynamic binding*. It is one of the basic features of object orientation. A consequence of dynamic binding is that the same method name may refer to a number of different operations, which is called *polymorphism*. These features of object orientation are all based on the inheritance relation on classes. Therefore, inheritance relation plays a significant role in the design of object-oriented systems.

C. Properties derived from the architecture

Data abstraction based, including abstract data types and object-oriented systems have many nice properties, most of which are well known. Because an object hides its representation from its clients, it is possible to change its implementation without affecting its clients. Additionally, the building of a set of accessing routines with the data that they manipulate allows designers to decompose problems into collections of interacting agents.

However, object-oriented systems also have disadvantages. The most significant is that in order for one object to interact with another (via procedure call) it must know the identity of that other object. This is in contrast, for example, to pipe-and-filter systems, where filters do not need to know what other filters are in the system in order to interact with them. In object-oriented systems, then, whenever the identity of an object changes, it is necessary to modify all other objects that explicitly invoke it. In a module-oriented language this manifests itself as the need to change the 'import' list of every module that uses the changed module. There can also be side-effect problems: if object A uses object B and object C also uses B, then C's effects on B look like unexpected side effects to A, and vice versa.

6.4   DATA-CENTRED

A. Computational model and design vocabulary

The term data-centred architecture refers to systems in which the access and update of a widely accessed data-store is an apt description.

There are two types of components in a data centred system. One is a data store, which stores the data that other components can access. It is called shared data. The other components are active and run on independent threads of control. They access the shared data to fulfil their functionality and to collaborate with each other. These components are usually called clients. The shared data is the central means of communications among the clients.

B. Structural pattern

A sketch of this style is shown in Figure 6.17.

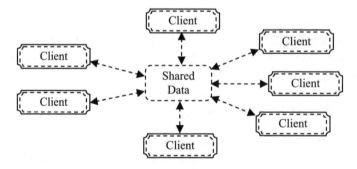

Figure 6.17 Data-centred style

C. Sub-types of the style

The shared data that all clients access and update may be a *passive repository* such as a file or an *active repository* such as a blackboard. The means of communication (sometimes called the coordination model) distinguishes two sub-types: *repository* (which is shown in the figure above) and *blackboard*. A blackboard sends notification to subscribers when data of interest changes, and thus is active.

D. Properties derived from the architecture

The data-centred style offers a structural solution to integrability especially when building from existing systems. They have the advantages that the clients are relatively independent of each other, and the data store is independent of the clients. Thus the system is scalable because new clients can be easily added. It is also modifiable with respect to changing the functionality of any client because other clients will not be affected. Coupling among clients will lessen this benefit but may occur to enhance performance. However, modifiability of the representation of the data stored in the shared data component could be problematic because it may affect all clients in the system.

6.5   VIRTUAL MACHINE

A. Structural pattern

A software system of virtual machine architecture usually consists of 4 components interconnected as follows (Figure 6.18).

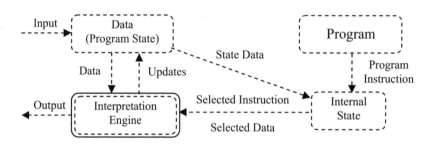

Figure 6.18 Virtual machine architecture

B. Computational model and design vocabulary

Virtual machines are software systems that simulate a computer system, but with some functionality that is not native to the hardware and/or software on which it is implemented.

Similar to the hardware architecture of a computer, the structure of a virtual machine consists of three passive data components and one active component as shown in Figure 6.18. Their functions are as follows.

(a) The *program* component stores the 'program' being interpreted, which is an abstract representation of the process of data. It is usually in the form of a sequence of structured data elements. Each element represents an '*instruction*' or '*statement*' for how to process the data. It is analogous to the program instructions run on the hardware computer system, hence called '*program*'.

(b) The *data* component stores the information to be processed. Such information is analogous to the values assigned to variables in the execution of a program. The data component is analogou to the memory of computer hardware.

(c) The *interpretation engine* is the active component in the system. It selects an instruction from the '*program*' being interpreted, updates the program's data according to the instruction, and updates its internal state. It is analogous to the CPU in computer hardware.

(d) The *internal state* stores the current state of the interpretation engine. It is analogous to the registers or the instruction count in computer hardware.

C. Properties derived from the architecture

Virtual machine architectures have the goal of achieving the quality of portability. Executing a program via an interpreter also adds flexibility through the ability to interrupt and query the program and introduce modifications at run-time, but there is a performance cost.

This can be useful in a number of ways. It can allow one to simulate and test platforms that have not yet been built such as new hardware, and it can simulate 'disaster' mode that would be too complex, costly or dangerous to test with the real system.

D. Examples

Common examples of virtual machines are *interpreters*, *rule-based systems*, *syntactic shells*, and *command language processors*. For example, the Java language is built to run on top of the *Java virtual machine*, which allows the Java programs to be platform independent. A Java program can therefore be executed on all computer platforms that have an implementation of Java virtual machine.

A Java virtual machine is a software system that enables compiled Java programs to be executed. However, the term Java virtual machine also refers to the abstract specification of any specific implementation of such a system. This specification defines the architecture of the software, its dynamic behaviour, format of the object code generated from a compilation of Java programs, as well as various issues that may affect the portability of the Java programs. There are a number of implementations of the abstract specifications on various hardware and software platforms. The term Java virtual machine may also refer to any run-time instances of the software. The following gives a very brief introduction to the architecture of Java virtual machine as specified in the abstract specification in [3]. Figure 6.19 shows the components and their connections in a Java virtual machine.

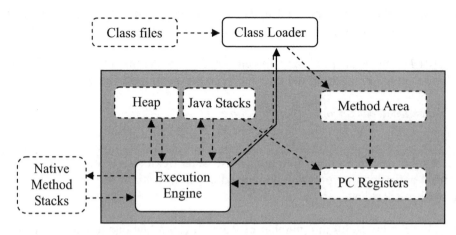

Figure 6.19 Architecture of Java virtual machine

Compiled code of Java programs to be executed by a Java virtual machine is represented using a hardware and operating system-independent binary format called *class file* format. The *Class Loader* finds the correct class files and loads them to the data areas of the virtue machine, links the codes on files together, initialises variables and then invokes the compiled Java code. The data areas in a Java virtual machine consist of the following parts.

Method Area. The method area is analogous to the storage area for compiled code of a conventional language. In other words, method area is the '*Program*' component of the virtue machine architectural style. It stores data related to class structures, such as the run-time constant pool, field and method data, and the code for methods and constructors, including the special methods used in class and instance initialisation and interface type initialisation.

PC Register. A Java virtual machine can support many threads of execution at once. At any point, each thread is executing the code of a single method, the current method for that thread. Each thread has its own program counter pointing to an instruction of the method that the thread is currently executing, which is called PC register.

Java Stack. Each Java virtual machine thread has a private data area, called Java Stack, created at the same time as the thread. It holds local variables and partial results of the method that the thread is currently executing, and hence, it plays a part in method invocation and return. The data related to one method invocation is packed into one frame. When a thread invokes a method, the Java virtual machine pushes a new frame onto that thread's Java stack. When the method completes, the virtual machine pops and discards the frame for that method. A Java virtual machine stack is analogous to the stack of a conventional language such as C directly running on computer hardware.

Heap. The heap is the run-time data area from which memory for all class instances (i.e. objects) and arrays is allocated. A Java virtual machine has one *heap* that is shared among all Java virtual machine threads. The heap is created on virtual machine start-up. Heap storage for objects is reclaimed by an automatic storage management system known as a *garbage collector.*

Native Method Stacks. The Java virtual machine also allows a Java program to call libraries written in other programming languages and to execute them in hardware machine code. Native Method Stacks serves this purpose.

Execution Engine. At the core of any Java virtual machine implementation is its execution engine, which performs the computation of the instructions. In the Java virtual machine specification, the behaviour of the execution engine is defined in terms of an instruction set. For each instruction, the specification describes in detail *what* an implementation should do when it encounters the instruction, but says very little about *how.* The implementations of the execution engine can be interpretation, just-in-time compilation, executing natively in silicon, use a combination of these, or dream up some brand new technique.

The Java virtual machine has a typical example of virtual machine architecture though it has a few additional components such as the Native Method Stacks and a Class Loader.

SUMMARY

In this chapter, we examined a number of software architectural styles. The following summarises the interrelationships between the software architectural styles discussed in this chapter.

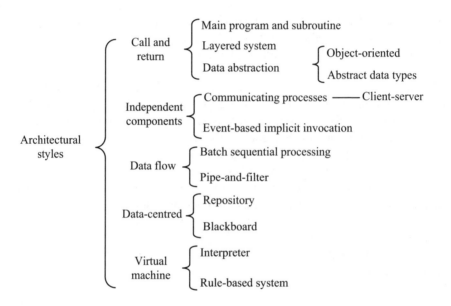

Figure 6.20 A catalogue of software architectural styles

FURTHER READING

Architectural styles and the interrelationships between them can help us recognise when two styles are similar. It also tells us the circumstances in which it is appropriate to apply a style. The definitions of styles and discussions about their interrelationships given in this chapter are mostly from Mary Shaw and David Garlan's work [1]. A large number of case studies can also be found in the book.

EXERCISES

(6–1) Discuss the following questions

(i) What is software architectural style?

(ii) What design knowledge can be included in software architectural styles?

(6–2) Discuss what the components, connectors and constraints are for the pipe-and-filter architectural style.

(6–3) Give a brief description to each of the following terms in the design vocabulary associated to data flow architecture style:

(a) Processing unit (or processing elements);

(b) Data flow (or simply flow).

(6–4) Consider a typical e-business system depicted in Figure 6.3.

(i) Identify the components and connectors of the system and discuss their architectural features.

(ii) Use software architectural visual notation to describe the architecture.

(iii) Discuss how the architectural features of the components and connectors and the topological structure of the system match the data flow style.

(6–4) Give a brief description to each of the following terms in the design vocabulary associated to pipe-and-filter architecture style.

(a) filter, (b) pipe.

(6–5) (i) Discuss if a filter can also be considered as a processing element in the data flow style;

(ii) Discuss if a pipe can also be considered as a data flow in the data flow style.

(6–6) Discuss the advantages and disadvantages of using the pipe-and-filter architectural style.

(6–7) In the Unix command shell environment, a set of small specialised programs can be connected together by the pipeline operator '|' so that they interact with each other by feeding the output of one into the input of the next. By stringing simple programs together in this way, rich behaviour can emerge. The following are some of the Unix commands.

- **ls**: produces a list of files in the current directory.

- **wc**: counts the number of words, lines, and characters in its input. In particular, the –l option counts the number of lines in its input.

- **grep**: reports those lines in its input that match a pattern. For example, grep '[zhu]' can find out all lines in the input that either contains the character 'z', or 'h', or 'u'.

- **cat**: it concatenates a list of text files and produces lines of texts as output.

(i) Use these command to complete the following functionalities.

(a) To count how many files in a directory;

(b) To list all files whose name contains the letter 'z';

(c) To count how many files in a directory whose name contains the letter 'z';

(d) To count the total number of lines in the text files in a directory whose names contain the letter 'z'.

(ii) Two words are an anagram if they use exactly the same characters but in different orders. For example, 'lived' and 'devil' are anagrams, so are 'emit' and 'mite'. The anagram analysis problem is to get a list of words (assume they are stored in a text file) and bring all the anagrams in the list together. Design a set of small programs and use the Unix pipeline operator to combine them together to solve the anagram analysis problem.

(6–8) Give a brief description of the terms *phase* in the context of design vocabulary associated to batch sequential processing architecture style.

(6–9) What is the constraint imposed on the topological structure of the batch sequential processing architectures?

(6–10) Discuss the advantages and disadvantages of using the batch sequential processing architectural style.

(6–11) Discuss the advantages and disadvantages of using the independent components architectural style.

(6–12) Give a brief description to each of the following design vocabulary in the context of event-based implicit invocation architecture style:

(a) publish, (b) subscribe, (c) event handler.

(6–13) Analyse the architectural features of components and connectors and the topological structure of the Field system described in section 6.2.2. Discuss how the architecture of the system matches the description of event-based implicit invocation style.

(6–14) Give a brief description to each of the following design vocabulary in the context of communicating processes architecture style.

(a) process, (b) communication channel, (c) synchronous communication, (d) asynchronous communication, (e) broadcast, (f) one-to-one communications.

(6–15) (i) Discuss what types of component a data-centred architecture can have and how are they connected.

(ii) Discuss the advantages and disadvantages of data-centred architectures.

(6–16) Consider the architecture of a rule-based system as depicted in Figure 4–15 of Chapter 4. Discuss which architectural style it belongs to.

(6–17) Give a brief definition for each of the following design vocabulary associated to the call and return architectures.

(a) subroutine; (b) subroutine call; (c) module; (d) visible variables; (e) visible procedures/functions; (f) exported variables, procedures/functions and data type definitions; (g) loose coupling; (h) high cohesion; (i) granularity.

(6–18) Give a brief definition of the term layer in the context of layered systems architectural style.

(6–19) Discuss the similarities and differences between the main-program-and-subroutine with shared data architectural style and the layered systems architectural style.

(6–20) In the context of the abstract data types and object-oriented systems architectural style, give a brief definition to each of the following design vocabulary:

(a) inheritance; (b) instance; (c) overriding; (d) dynamic binding; (e) polymorphism; (f) encapsulation.

(6–21) Discuss the similarities and differences between modules, abstract data types, and classes.

REFERENCES

1   Shaw, M. and Garlan, D., *Software Architecture: Perspectives on an Emerging Discipline*, Prentice Hall, 1996.
2   Reiss, S. P., Connecting Tools Using Message Passing in the Field Environment, *IEEE Software*, July, 1990, Vol. 7, No. 4, pp57–66.
3   Lindholm, T. and Yellin, F., *The Java Virtual Machine Specification*, 2nd Edition, Addison-Wesley, 1999.

7 Using Styles in Design

In this chapter, we study how to use architectural styles in software design. We will first give a number of design rules for choosing an architectural style when a design problem is given. We then discuss how architectural styles can be combined to solve a design problem. Finally, we illustrate how to apply various architectural styles to one design problem to obtain diversity in designs with different features. We will also compare the design informally to demonstrate the differences between the architectural styles. The objectives of the chapter are:

- To learn how to design software systems in various architectural styles;

- To understand how architectural styles affect the quality of the software.

The chapter is organised as follows. Section 7.1 presents a set of design rules for the proper uses of architectural styles. Section 7.2 discusses different ways that architectural styles can be combined together to solve design problems. Section 7.3 is a case study with a specific design problem. Four designs in different styles of a design problem will be provided and compared, which include designs in main program/subroutines with shared data style, abstract data type style, implicit invocation style, and pipe-and-filter style.

7.1 CHOICES OF STYLES

Given a design problem, which software architectural style should you choose to use? The answer is, of course, that it depends on the nature of the computation underlying the problem to be solved and, equally important, the quality or qualities that most concern you. In many cases, there are a number of architectural styles that are suitable to the nature of the computation involved in solving the problem. In that case, the quality attributes that are most concerned play the central role in the choice of architectural style. As discussed in Chapter 2, for many quality attributes, system structure provides the most leverage on the quality. Therefore, a style appropriate to the quality concern should be considered. The following table summarises the design knowledge embodied in the architectural styles we have discussed in the previous chapters in the form of rule of thumb for choosing an architectural style.

Table 7.1 Rules for appropriate uses of architectural styles

Style	Nature of Computation	Quality Concerns
Data flow	The input and output data of the problem to be solved are both well defined and easily identified. The computation is to produce output from the input as the direct result of sequentially transforming an input in a time-independent fashion.	Integratability from relatively simple interface between components. Reusability by interchanges of components to change functionality.
Batch sequential	There is a single output operation that is the result of reading and processing a single collection of input. The processing of the input consists of a number of sequentially connected intermediate transformations.	Reusability and modifiability, especially when performance is not a major concern and synchronisation related complexity can be reduced.

Pipe-and-filter	The computation involves transformations on continuous streams of data. The transformations are incremental, i.e. applied on the elements of the stream of data. One transformation can begin before the previous step has completed.	Scalability, especially to process the input data of unbounded length of data stream. Performance, to respond to the input as soon as an element of the input data is fed into the system before the whole stream of data is obtained.
Call and Return	The order of computation is fixed. Components cannot make useful progress while waiting for the results of requests to other components.	Modifiability, integratability, reusability.
Layered systems	The computational tasks can be divided between those specific to the application and those generic to many applications but specific to the underlying computing platform.	Portability across computing platforms. Reuse of an already developed computing infrastructure layer, such as operating system, network packages, etc.
Main-program-and-subroutine with shared data	The problem to be solved at a higher level of abstraction can be decomposed into a number of smaller problems at a lower level of abstraction that can be solved and their results can be put together to solve the higher level problem.	Performance, especially the space of memory used to store intermediate results can be significantly reduced without duplication when shared with components, and time to access the intermediate results can be reduced through direct access rather than other means of communication. Reusability, especially when a subroutine solves a problem that reoccurs in the application domain frequently.

Data abstraction	Computation is based on a relatively fixed variety of entities and each of these entities has a fixed number of operations.	Reusability, especially the reuse of the components that represent those computational entities that reoccur frequently in the application domain. Modifiability, especially when the representations of the computational entities are likely to change.
Abstract data type		Integratability, especially through careful attentions to the design of the interfaces between the components.
Object-oriented	In addition to the common features of the computation in all data abstraction sub-styles, the entities in the system have commonalities and fall into a nature hierarchy of inheritance.	Reusability and modifiability as in all data abstraction sub-styles. Moreover, it also aims at reusability and modifiability when the types of entities are relatively stable in the application domain while the system's functionality is likely to be changed, especially enhanced, in the future.
Independent components	One component can continue to make progress some what independent of the states of other components. The system is to be run on a network of computer systems.	Modifiability, especially when performance tuning via reallocating work among processes and reallocating processes to computers is necessary. Performance, especially to achieve maximal utilisation of the computational resource is important.
Communicating processes	Message passing is sufficient as an interaction mechanism.	

Event-based implicit invocation	Computations are triggered by a collection of events. Event originators and event processors can be decoupled.	Flexibility for the modification system's functionality especially enhancement of functionality. Scalability in the sense of adding processes that are triggered by the events already detected/ signalled in the system. Modifiability for change the way that events are processed.
Client-server	Computation can be reviewed as providing services to a number of users who share the access to the information and/or computation resources. Computation tasks can be divided between instigators of service requests and executors of those requests or between producers and consumers of data.	Scalability in terms of the number of users who can have access to the system simultaneously as well as from a wide geographic area. Modifiability, especially when users' interface may change and/or new functionality is likely to be added into the system as new services.
Data-centred	The central issue in the computation is the storage, representation, management and retrieval of a large amount of interrelated long-lived data. The data are usually highly structured. The order that components are executed in is determined by a stream of incoming requests to access/update the data.	Scalability in terms of the amount of data to be stored and processed by the system. Modifiability to change the producing and processing the data while the structure of the data remains relatively stable.
Virtual machine	Data consists of two parts; one is the information to be processed and the other controls how the first part is to be processed.	Portability of the processing of the data in different hardware and software platforms.

It is worth noting that, while the rules given above provide a set of guidelines for the uses of architectural styles in the architectural designs of systems, it is a good idea to make several architectural designs of the same problem and to evaluate and compare these designs so that their quality attributes can be fully understood in the specific context of the design problem. A consequence of making such a number of design and evaluation/comparisons usually results in better understanding of the design problem and subsequently modifications to the designs with better solutions. This design, evaluation and modification process may repeat for several cycles before a final design decision can be made to settle on a specific architectural design. In this context, the design rules discussed above can be used as a quick guide to rule out certain choices of styles which are obviously inappropriate to the problem at hand and to make a quick selection of possible candidate styles as the first step.

7.2 COMBINATIONS OF STYLES

Most software systems are not built from a single style. Instead, the design of a software system at architectural level often needs to combine different styles to solve the design problem. Software systems that are not in a single style are called heterogeneous styles. In [1], Shaw pointed out that there are three kinds of ways architectural styles can be combined together.

7.2.1 Hierarchical heterogeneous styles

The hierarchical combination of different styles in the design of a software system is to use one architectural style at one level of abstraction while using a different style in the design of a component of the higher level.

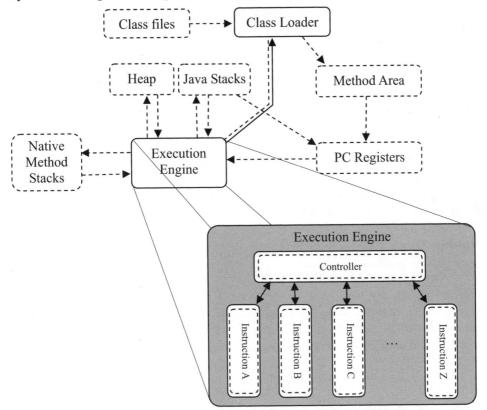

Figure 7.1 Java virtual machine in hierarchical heterogeneous styles

For example, at the top level of abstraction we can use virtual machine style to design the Java virtual machine as given in Chapter 6. The key component of the architecture is the execution engine. We can use the main-program-and-subroutine style to implement this component. As illustrated in Figure 7.1, the component consists of a controller that decides which instruction to be executed while each instruction is implemented by a procedure.

7.2.2   Simultaneously heterogeneous styles

Software architectural styles discussed in the previous chapter do not form a disjoint classification of software architectures. In many cases, the architecture of a software system can be aptly described as in a number of different architectural styles.

For example, an architecture in the data centred style consists of a number of clients that access and update the data in the shared data component. In many cases, the system can also be viewed as in the independent component style, especially when the shared data is an active repository and the clients have their own thread of controls.

Another example of the overlaps between two types of architectural styles is the pipe-and-filter system. A pipe-and-filter system can be implemented as a number of processes that operate independents, waiting until input is at their ports. Such a system can also be viewed as in the independent component style.

A concrete example of system in simultaneously heterogeneous style is the MISOC 2000 system described in Chapter 5. It can be viewed as in the client-server style as shown in Figure 5.17. It can also be viewed as a layered system as shown in Figure 5.18, where the clients call the server via remote procedural calls. Moreover, since the system is implemented in an object-oriented programming language. We can also view the system from an object-oriented style point of view.

When a system like MISOC 2000 can be aptly described as in a number of different styles, we may analyse the system as described in different styles to understand its features and problems. Each of the styles may shed a light on its behaviour and structural features from a different angle. Therefore, it is important to understand the system from all views.

In the design of a software system, due to the overlapping between different architectural styles, several designs in different styles can be merged into one design that shares all the advantages of different styles and avoids the disadvantages. Therefore, understanding simultaneous heterogeneous styles is of particular importance in the application of architectural styles. Of course, things could go wrong when combining a number of architectural styles into one design to form a simultaneous heterogeneous architecture which inherits all the disadvantages of the styles without any benefit of their advantages.

7.2.3 Locationally heterogeneous styles

A software system seldom appears in the exact form of an architectural style as theoretically defined in the previous chapter. For example, the Java virtual machine described in Chapter 6 can be regarded as in the virtual machine architecture if we focus on the subset of components and connectors within the boxed area in Figure 7.2, which is reproduced below.

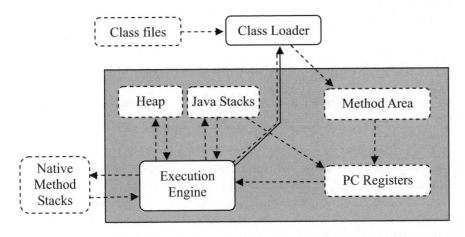

Figure 7.2 Example of locationally heterogeneous style: JVM

A software system's architecture is in a locationally heterogeneous style if it can be considered as in one style when taking a subset of its components and connectors, meanwhile it can also be viewed as in another style when taking a different subset of the components and connectors.

For example, if we redraw the architecture diagram of the Java virtual machine as in Figure 7.3 below, we can find that it is in the main-program-and-subroutine with shared data style.

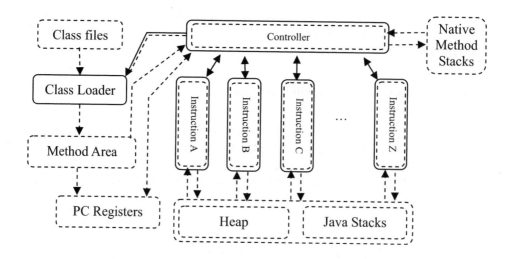

Figure 7.3 Alternative view to the architecture of JVM

Software systems' architectures in locationally heterogeneous styles exist for the following reasons.

First, the theoretical definitions of architectural styles are abstractions of collections of software systems that have common features in their architecture structures and behaviours. Those components and connectors have no significant impact on the systems' most important features hence do not necessarily appear in all of the systems and are therefore hidden from the theoretical definition. This enables the most important and dominating features and dynamic behaviours of the systems to be clearly demonstrated and inferred from the definition without interference of unnecessary and less important components. However, in practical uses of a style, it is inevitable to add and/or modify some of the structural or behavioural features into the architectural design of the systems. For example, the theoretical definition of the virtual machine architectural style has ignored the issue how programs and initial data are loaded on to the virtual machine. This issue cannot be ignored in the design of Java virtual machine because it must allow the program code for classes to be dynamically loaded to the system. It is, therefore, no surprise to see a class loader component in the architecture of JVM in addition to those relatively standard components of a virtual machine.

Second, the architectural styles that we have recognised are still far away from a complete catalogue. In fact, it is doubtful if such a complete catalogue could even be developed. Therefore, it is inevitable that sometimes we can only partially recognise the architectural style of a system and have several different such partial understandings of a software system's architectural style. When there are several different views of a system's architectural style, a question remains for which style should be used in the analysis of the system. This is an open problem that has no ready made answer in the literature so far.

Third, locationally heterogeneous styles also often occur as a result of software evolution process. When components and connectors are added into an existing system and existing ones are modified or deleted to enhance its functionality or fix bugs, the style of the system's architecture may change as well. For example, new components and connectors added into the system may not fit into the style but solve the problem. After a long period of evolution, the original style of the system becomes less recognisable and no longer plays a dominant role. Alternative understanding of the system's style may well appear. The worst case is that the evolution process results in a system that is hard to understand and impossible to further modify. In such cases, the system comes to the state of *dead* according to Peter Naur [2] although it may still be in operation. A question is how to modify an existing system while keeping the system in a good style. This may involve restructuring the system's architecture and changing its style. In the context of object-oriented design, this is called refactoring; see for example [3, 4]. It is one of the current active research topics.

Finally, systems in locationally heterogeneous styles can be the result of bad designs where conceptual integrity is poor. As discussed in Chapter 2, *conceptual integrity* refers to the property of a design that exhibit harmony, symmetry and predictability. A well-designed system with conceptual integrity should faithfully adhere to a single concept. If a system's architecture has to be understood partially as in one style for one part and as in another completely different, even conflicting style, for another part, it is hard to say that the system has a good conceptual integrity. Therefore, such situations should be avoided as much as possible.

7.3 CASE STUDY: KEYWORD FREQUENCY VECTOR

In this section, we demonstrate how to make designs in a given architectural style. We apply four different architectural styles to one design problem to show the differences in the quality attributes of the designs of different styles.

7.3.1 Specification of the problem

The keyword frequency vector (KFV) of a text file is a sequence of pairs of keywords and their frequency of appearance in the text. It is a good representation of the contents of the text. Keyword frequency vectors are widely used in information retrieval. For example the following is the keyword frequency vector of this paragraph.

Word	Frequency
keyword	5
frequency	4
text	4
vector	4
appearance	1
content	1
example	1
file	1
follow	1
good	1
information	1
pair	1
paragraph	1
representation	1
retrieval	1
sequence	1
use	1
widely	1

The vector clearly indicates that the paragraph is about keyword, frequency, text, and vector. When a user searches for information about 'keyword frequency vector', this paragraph matches the query because the searched words have a high frequency of occurrences in the text. Another advantage of keyword frequency vector is that it is usually more compressive than the original text. This technique works better when small words (such as 'a', 'the', 'is', 'it') are removed from the vector as we did in the example above. Moreover, the same word of different forms should be treated as one. For example, 'keywords' and 'keyword' are treated as one word rather than two words in the above example. Most importantly, keyword frequency vectors can be extracted from texts automatically. Our design problem is to design the architecture of such a system.

7.3.2 Designs in various styles

We now make some architectural level designs of a software system that extracts a keyword vector from an input text. We will apply the following architectural styles: (a) main program/subroutines with shared data, (b) abstract data type, (c) pipe-and-filter, and (d) event driven.

A. Design 1: Main program/subroutine with shared data

We start with a design in the style of main program/subroutine architecture, which is perhaps what we are most familiar with.

In this architectural style, data are stored in memory and/or file system that are accessible by all components of the system. The functionality is decomposed into a number of subroutines, which are usually procedures or functions in a programming language. These functions and procedures are invoked by a main program, which plays the role of system controller.

For this particular design problem, we decompose the computation into a number of tasks as follows. Each task is a subroutine, i.e. procedure or function. A main program controls the execution order of the tasks.

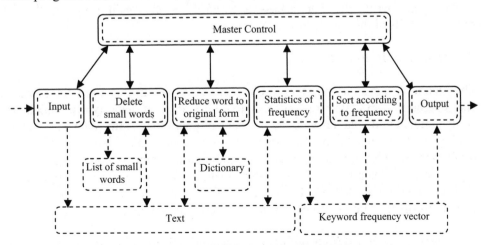

Figure 7.4 KFV in shared data storage architecture

(1) *Input*: The first step is to get the input text from the input device or any other source of information and to store the text into internal memory in an appropriate format. The design of internal format will be determined by detailed design.

(2) *Delete small words*: At this step, the small words contained in the text are deleted from the text as it is stored in the internal memory. It will use a list of small words to check on each word in the text.

(3) *Reduce word to its original form*: Each word left in the text is then reduced to its original form, e.g. 'architectures' is reduced to 'architecture'; 'calculi' is reduced to 'calculus'; and 'followed' is reduced to 'follow'. A dictionary will be used to reduce each word into its original form.

(4) *Statistics of frequency*: The frequency of the occurrences of a word in the text is counted to generate a sequence of pairs comprising the word and its frequency. This sequence of pairs is not necessarily ordered according to the frequency, but may be in the alphabetic order of keywords. The result will be stored in another memory storage.

(5) *Sort according to the frequency*: Now the sequence of pairs of keywords and their frequencies are put into an order according to the frequency.

(6) *Output*: Finally, the keyword frequency vector is translated into required output format and output to the device.

The information exchanges between the subroutines are through the uses of two shared data structures *Text* and *Keyword frequency vector*; see Figure 7.4. The data storages in the architecture are shared with all the components as both readable and writeable. The access is control by the main program through sequential calls of the subroutines.

B.   *Design 2: Abstract data type*

The second design is in the style of abstract data types. In this style, the accesses and operations on data are encapsulated into abstract data types, which are computational units that provide the interface of operations on the data and hide the implementation details of the operations. Computations can, therefore, be performed by invoking the operations on the data in a similar way as using basic data types. To design a software system in this style, we need to recognise the abstract data type, that is, to recognise the data structure and the required operations on the data to implement the required functionality.

For the specific design problem, we recognised the following three abstract data types.

(1) *Word ADT*: It provides the following two operations on words.

(a) *Is-small-word*: This is a Boolean function that checks if the parameter is a small word. It returns TRUE if the word is listed in a list of small words, otherwise it returns FALSE.

(b) *Reduce*: This is a function on words that changes a word to its original form according to a dictionary of words and returns it back.

(2) *Text ADT*: It provides the following operations on texts.

(a) *Setup*: It gets the text from the input component and translates it into an internal format and stores it in its internal data storage.

(b) *Take-word*: It is a function that returns one word in the text and deletes it from its internal data storage.

(c) *Is-text-empty*: It is a Boolean function that returns TRUE if the internal storage is empty, otherwise returns FALSE when it contains at least one word.

(3) *Keyword Frequency Vector ADT*: It is an abstract data type on keyword frequency vectors. It provides the following operations.

(a) *Add-word*: It adds a word to the keyword frequency vector. It calls is-small-word function of the word ADT. If the function returns TRUE, it does nothing. Otherwise, it further calls the reduce function of the word ADT, and then searches for the word in the keyword frequency vector. If the vector already contains the word, its frequency is increased by 1, otherwise the keyword is added into the vector with frequency 1.

(b) *Is-KFV-empty*: It is a Boolean function that returns TRUE if the keyword frequency is empty, otherwise, it returns FALSE.

(c) *Take-KWF*: It is a function that returns the keyword that is of highest frequency and its frequency. It then deletes the keyword from the vector.

(d) *Initialise*: It initialises the internal representation of keyword frequency vector.

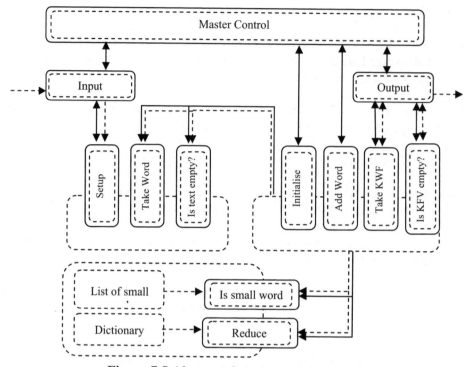

Figure 7.5 Abstract data type architecture

In addition to these abstract data types, the system also contains input, output components, whose functions are very similar to the shared data storage design, but they call the operations provided by the abstract data type to access the data. Figure 7.5 gives the architecture of the design.

C.   Design 3: Implicit invocation

The implicit invocation architecture also uses three abstract data types to access the data abstractly. However, the computations are invoked implicitly when data is modified. That is, each time when the data is modified an event is generated and the event drives a corresponding event handling function to execute. Thus, interactions are based on an active data model. For example, the act of inserting or deleting a word from the text will cause the extract component to call the add-word or delete-word operation on the keyword frequency vector, which consequently changes the vector's value. This allows the system to produce keyword frequency vector interactively and keep the stored vector consistent with the text while the user is editing the text. Figure 7.6 gives the architecture of the design.

The abstract data types are slightly different from those in the abstract data type architecture. The representation of text in the text ADT will also be different to make the architecture work. The detail of their functionality is omitted here, but included as an exercise for the readers to work out the detailed description of the components.

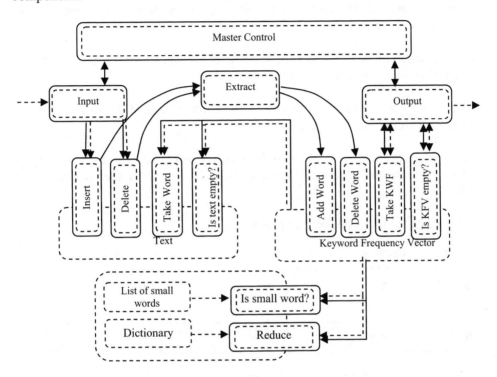

Figure 7.6 Implicit invocation architecture

D. Design 4: Pipe-and-filter

The pipe-and-filter architectural style is also applicable to this problem. In this style, the computation is decomposed into a number of filters and data are passed between the filters in the form of streams of elements. To design a software system in this style, we must decompose the computation into such filters and to decide the structures of the data elements passed between the filters.

For this particular design problem, we can recognise the following filters:

(1) *Input*: Takes the stream of characters in the text and breaks it down to a stream of words.

(2) *Delete small words*: Removes the small words in the input stream of words.

(3) *Reduce words to original forms*: Changes each word in the stream of words into its original form.

(4) *Sort words alphabetically*: Takes the stream of words and sorts it into alphabetical order.

(5) *Count the frequency*: Counts the occurrences of each word in the stream and generates a stream of keyword-frequency pairs.

(6) *Sort vector according to frequency*: Sorts the stream of keyword-frequency pairs according to frequency.

(7) *Output*: Takes a stream of keyword-frequency pairs that is sorted according to the frequency and generates a keyword frequency vector in the required output format.

The architecture is depicted in Figure 7.7.

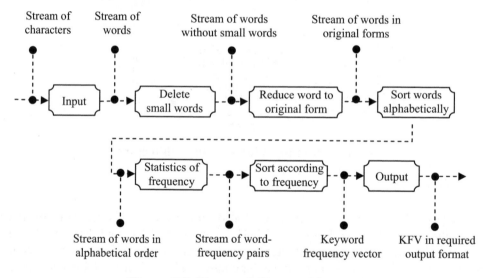

Figure 7.7. Pipe-and-filter architecture

7.3.3 Analysis and comparison

To compare the advantages and disadvantages of the designs, we consider the following quality attributes.

1. *Modifiability*: How difficult it is to modify the system after its implementation to meet new requirements. The following possible types of changes should be considered.

   - *Use of the system*: For example, extracting keyword frequency vector can be performed incrementally paragraph by paragraph as it is read from the input device, or on the whole text file after they are read, or on demand when the keyword frequency vector is required.

   - *Input/output data representation*: For example, text, words, and characters can be stored in various ways. Similarly, the keyword frequency vector can be stored explicitly or implicitly, e.g. as pairs of index and frequency.

   - *System function*: For example, modify the system to treat synonyms as the same word, change the systems to be interactive, and allow the user to delete and insert words from the original text.

2. *Performance*: The performance of the system in terms of the space used and the time needed to execute the program.

3. *Reusability*: To what extent can the components serve as reusable entities?

A system of shared data architecture will be difficult to modify the data representation. A change on the representation of text in the system will force you to modify the code in at least four components including the input, delete small words, reduce word to original form, and statistics of frequency. A change in the representation of the keyword frequency vector will force you to modify at least three components including statistics of frequency, sort according to frequency and output. It is also very difficult to make changes to meet the requirements of changing usage. For example, if the system is developed to process a text after it reads in all the text, it will need additional components and change of the master control component to be able to process the text paragraph by paragraph. To enhance system functionality to be able to treat synonyms as the same word, only the dictionary and the reduce component need to be changed. However, if we want to treat phrases as a synonym of a single word, the change will involve deleting small words and the control component. Things become much more complicated. It is also difficult to change the system into interactive mode if the user is allowed to insert and delete words in the text. The system is good at performance with respect to both space and time. The reusability of components is poor, because they have a great number of assumptions on the environment of the components.

A system in abstract data type architecture will be relatively easier to change the representation of data because the access of the data is limited by using the operations defined by the abstract data type. Changes will be local to the abstract data type. A change of the usage will force the system to modify the master control component, and probably the text and vector abstract data types. The enhancement of functionality to treat synonyms as the same word will need to modify the word abstract data type. It is very difficult to deal with phrases in this architecture. Changing the system into an interactive system will involve modifications of two main abstract data types. The performance of the system will be good at space, but less efficient on time because a lot more procedure calls are needed in comparison with shared data architecture. The components are more reusable than components in shared data architecture because abstract data types are more independent.

A system using implicit invocation architecture is easy to modify if the usage needs change. Since the data is also accessed through abstract data types, changes to data representation are local and relatively easier than shared data store architecture. Enhancement of functionality is the same as abstract data type, but it is much easier to handle interactive insert and delete operations on text. However, the performance of the system is less easy to control because of the implicit invocation of the extraction. Similar to the design in abstract data type style, the components in this system are quite reusable.

The pipe-and-filter architecture is easy to change the processing algorithm, which can be made by replacing the input filter with new ones. A change in the data representation of a stream only involves two adjacent filters. It should not be too difficult. The enhancement of function to treat synonyms as the same word can be achieved by modifications on the reduce word filter. Similar to other architectures, dealing with phrases is more difficult, which may need to swap the order of filters and modifications on the filters. It is also very difficult to modify the system into an interactive one to allow the user to insert and delete words in the text. The performance of the system is less satisfactory on both time and space because each filter needs its own internal space to store the stream. Reusability is an advantage of the architecture because each filter is quite independent.

Table 7.2 summarises the above discussion. There are two points that are worth noting. Firstly, there is no architectural design that is satisfactory over all design considerations. Therefore, a trade-off must be made in the decision on selection of the design. Alternatively, a new design should be made to meet all the design requirements. This decision must be based on good understanding of the priority of the requirements. Secondly, a pattern of quality attributes for an architectural style shown in Table 7.2 occurs in various design problems, such as in the designs of keyword in context problem [5]. This pattern is the basis that architectural styles can provide a useful guidance of design to achieve quality attributes. However, some quality attributes are not uniquely determined by the architectural style. Consequently, it is necessary to analyse an architectural design against the details of quality requirements.

Table 7.2 Summary of the comparison of the architectural designs for KFV

Attribute		Shared data	Abstract data type	Implicit invocation	Pipe-and-filter
Modifiability	Usage	−	−	+	+
	Representation	−	+	+	+
	Function	+	−	+	−
Performance		+	+	−	−
Reuse		−	+	+	+

SUMMARY

The use of an architectural style in design must be determined by the nature of the computation within the design problem inherently and the quality concerns. A set of rules for proper uses of architectural styles is presented in this chapter to provide guidelines for the choices of architectural styles. However, making several designs in different styles and then comparing them in depth is a good idea for making a good design.

Architectural styles can be combined together to make an architectural design. There are three different forms of heterogeneous styles. Hierarchical heterogeneity means a component is in an architectural style different from the whole system's style. Simultaneous heterogeneity is when a system can be regarded as two architectural styles at the same time depending on the view to the system. Locational heterogeneity is when a part of the system can be regarded as in one style while another part is in a different style. Combination of architectural styles in one design plays a significant role in software design practices. However, if not used carefully, it may result in poor conceptual integrity, especially when it is in locationally heterogeneity.

FURTHER READING

The design rules for proper uses of architectural styles stem from Mary Shaw's work. More rules of thumb for the uses of architectural styles can be found in Chapter 5 of Len Bass, Paul Clements and Rick Kazman's book [6], where the conditions on the nature of computation and quality concerns are mixed and stated as when to use the style. More examples can be found in [5] for the uses of several architectural styles to make a number of designs for a single problem, which include the famous keywords in context problem (KWIC). There is also an online repository of example architectural designs, which contains a number of model problems and answers that have multiple designs in different styles. Contributors to the websites are leading researchers in the area of software architecture, including Mary Shaw, David Garlan, Robert Allen, Daniel Klein, John Ockerbloom, Curtis Scott and Marco Schumacher. The URL of the website is: http://www-2.cs.cmu.edu/People/ModProb/ .

Heterogeneous styles are briefly discussed in section 2.10 of Mary Shaw and David Garlan's book [5]. Some examples of systems in heterogeneous styles can be found in Chapter 3 of the same book. The terminology of locational, hierarchical and simultaneous heterogeneity also comes from the work of Mary Shaw and her colleagues; see e.g. Chapter 5 of Len Bass, Paul Clements and Rick Kazman's book [6], which also contains a brief discussion on the topic.

Refactoring object-oriented designs has been an active research topic in the past few years. Research papers can be found in various conference proceedings on agile software development methodology or lightweight methodology. For readers who have extensive experiences in object-oriented design, references [3] and [4] are good starting point text books on the subject.

EXERCISES

(7–1) Generally speaking, the *scalability* of a software system refers to the property that the system can be scaled up to a large scale system, for example to handle a large number of users simultaneously or to store and process a large volume of data.

(i) Discuss various kinds of specific scalabilities;

(ii) For each kind of scalability, discuss which architectural style will support it.

(7–2) Modifications to a software system may be requested for a number of different purposes, for example when the representation of an entity must be changed, or a new function must be added into the system.

(i) Classify various types of modification according to the purposes of modifications;

(ii) For each kind of modification in your answer to the above question, discuss which architectural style(s) can support future requests of the modifications of the kind.

(7–3) For each of the following situations, discuss which architectural style(s) should be applicable.

(i) The application problem has a continuous stream of input data and requires a stream of outputs corresponding to the input stream.

(ii) There are a large number of users who will connect to the application system from a network of computer systems.

(iii) The application needs to be executed on a number of different computing platforms.

(iv) The system must have a very good performance in both time and space.

(v) The system must be easily tuned to achieve the best utilisation of hardware and software resources, which may be added into the system in the future if necessary.

(vi) A key component of the system is to solve a particular problem that occurs frequently in the application domain. It is desirable to make the component reusable in similar systems.

(vii) The application domain has been well recognised and its entities are well understood, but application systems are very likely to change its functionality in the near future.

(viii) There is a set of programs/components readily implemented that can be used in the development of a new application system. However, the functionality provided by the set of existing components is not what is required by the users because the functions provided by the existing components seem at a lower level of abstraction.

(7–4) Consider the Java virtual machine JVM.

(i) Redesign the Java virtual machine JVM using the abstract data type style.

(ii) Discuss the advantages and disadvantages of your design.

(iii) Discuss if your design is in a heterogeneous style.

(7–5) Describe the functionality of each component in the architectural designs of KFV problem.

(7–6) Make as many as possible architectural designs of a software system using different architectural styles to solve each of the following problems. Document your designs by describing:

- *components*: the nature and functions of the components of the system,

- *connectors*: the interactions between the components, and

- *structure*: the structure in the form of a diagram

(i) Text-wrapping

A text consists of a sequence of paragraphs separated by the paragraph break symbol 'new line'. Each paragraph consists of a sequence of words separated by spaces, a punctuation symbol such as ',', ';', ':', '.', etc. Each word consists of a number of letters. Thus, a paragraph can contain an arbitrary number of characters and letters. To display the text on screen or to print the text on pages, a paragraph must be decomposed into a number of lines to fit into the width of the screen or page. Such decompositions should not break in the middle of a word. It should also let each line contain as many words as possible.

Hint: The following assumptions can be used to simplify the design problem:

- The characters are of the same size when printed/displayed.

- The length of a line is fixed to contain a given number of characters.

- A paragraph must start at the beginning of a line.

(ii) Mailing list merge

To broadcast a message to a large number of email users, an email application software system needs to generate a mailing list from a number of pre-stored lists of email addresses. A mailing list merger program takes two mailing lists as input and merges the set of email addresses contained in the lists, but deletes duplications.

(iii) Text capitalisation

A text processing program is required to provide the following functions:

(1) To change all the letters in an input text to the corresponding upper case, if the user commanded the program to do so;

(2) To change all the letters in an input text to the corresponding lower case, if the user commanded the program to do so;

(3) To change all the sentences in an input text into the sentence format if commanded by the user, where sentence format is that the first letter of every sentence is in upper case and all other letters are in lower case;

(4) To change all the sentences in an input text into the title format if

commanded by the user, where title format is that the first letter of each word is in upper case and all other letters are in lower case. For example, 'Software Architectural Design And Analysis' is in title format.

(iv) Anagram analysis

Two words are anagrams if they use exactly the same characters but in different orders. For example, 'lived' and 'devil' are anagrams, so are 'emit' and 'mite'. The anagram analysis program takes a list of words as input and produces a list in which all the anagrams in the input list are put together. Moreover, each group of anagram words will be indicated by the letters of the words in alphabetical order. For example, given the following input

lived, emit, same, mite, devil

it will produce the following output:

aems: *same*; *edilv*: *devil, lived*; *eimt*: *emit, mite*;

REFERENCES

1 Shaw, M., Moving from quality to architecture, Chapter 5 in *Software Architecture in Practice*, by Bass, L., Clements P. and Kazman, R., Addison Wesley, 1998.

2 Naur, P., *Programming as theory building, in Computing: A Human Activity.* ACM Press, pp37–48, 1992.

3 Fowler, M., *Refactoring: Improving the Design of Existing Code*, Addison Wesley, 1999.

4 Wake, W. C., *Refactoring Workbook*, Addison Wesley, 2003.

5 Shaw, M. and Garlan, D., *Software Architecture: Perspectives on an Emerging Discipline*, Prentice Hall, 1996.

6 Bass, L., Clements P. and Kazman, R., *Software Architecture in Practice*, Addison Wesley, 1998.

8 Architectural Design Space

Diversity is present in the solutions of most design problems. Design can be viewed as navigation in the solution space in order to reach the optimal solution. The questions are: what are the structures of the design spaces and how can we know that we are moving towards an optimal solution. Unfortunately, it is not conservative to say that we are still far away from any satisfactory answers to such questions. Since the 1980s, design methodologists have been developing a theory of design spaces as a general theory of design methodology and a basis for developing software systems for computer aided designs [1, 2]. In this chapter, we will study this theory and apply it to software development. The objectives of this chapter are:

- To understand the structure of design space and how design spaces can be used to solve design synthesis and analysis problems;

- To understand the differences between various software architectural elements and how the variety of these elements form a design space;

- To deepen our understanding of software architectural styles by organising various styles into a design space.

The chapter is organised as follows. Section 8.1 is a brief introduction to the theory of design spaces. We will discuss the structures of design spaces and how design synthesis problems and analysis problems can be solved by using a design space in sub-sections 8.1.1 and 8.1.2, respectively. Section 8.2 and Section 8.3 look at the design spaces of architectural elements and styles, respectively.

8.1   THEORY OF DESIGN SPACES

8.1.1   Structure of design spaces

Let's start with an example. Assume that our design task is to design a chair. Consider the chairs depicted in Figure 8.1.

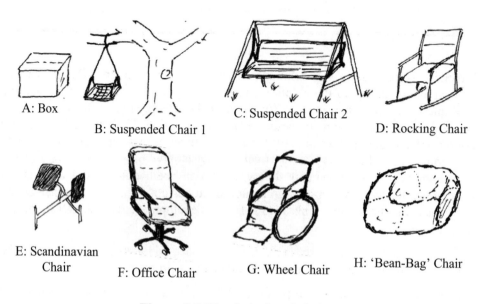

A: Box

B: Suspended Chair 1

C: Suspended Chair 2

D: Rocking Chair

E: Scandinavian Chair

F: Office Chair

G: Wheel Chair

H: 'Bean-Bag' Chair

Figure 8.1 The domain of chairs

Each chair in the figure is an object in the domain that our design task is concerned with. Each real object that existed in the past, exists presently or will exist in the future is called an *entity*. Each entity provides some *functionality* that the design task is concerned with. For example, each chair can provide the functionality of a seat. That is, it prevents a downward movement of the body when a person sits on the object. In addition to this, some of the chairs also provide other functionalities that are also relevant to the design task. For example, some chairs may support the back, i.e. support an upright posture. It may also revolve and constrain the back. These chairs may also have a number of properties. For example, they may be movable, easy to manufacture and aesthetic, etc. These functionalities and properties are called *functional properties* because they display the behaviours of the object when the entity is subjected to a situation. Functional properties play an important role in understanding a design domain. They explicitly describe what the design domain is concerned with in terms of the functional properties that can be realised. Table 8.1 lists a number of functional properties of the chairs given in Figure 8.1.

Table 8.1 Functional properties of chairs

Function	Chair							
	A	B	C	D	E	F	G	H
Seats: prevents a downward movement of the body	+	+	+	+	+	+	+	+
Supports back: supports an upright posture	+	+	+	+	+	+	+	+
Revolves: revolves around a vertical axis	+	+	−	+	+	+	+	+
Movable: can be easily moved	+	−	−	−	+	+	+	+
Constrains back: constrains backward movement of back	−	+	+	−	−	+	+	−
Easy to manufacture: has a simple design with standard components	+	−	−	−	−	+	−	+
Aesthetic	−	+	+	+	+	−	−	−

In addition to these functional properties, there are other types of properties of the entities in the domain. For example, a chair may have a wheel, may have legs, may be lightweight, etc. Such properties can be observed or measured potentially through the use of an instrument no matter whether they are physical, chemical, mechanical, or any other properties. These types of properties are called *observable properties*, or *attributes*, of the entities. The set of attributes and the association of the attributes with the objects in a design domain describe the variety of design choices. Table 8.2 shows a number of attributes that are associated to the entities shown in Figure 8.1.

Table 8.2 Observable properties of chairs

Structure	Chair							
	A	B	C	D	E	F	G	H
Has a seat	+	+	+	+	−	+	+	−
Has a back support	−	+	+	+	−	+	+	−
Has legs	−	−	+	−	−	+	+	−
Has wheels	−	−	−	−	+	+	+	−
Has a vertical rotational degree of freedom	−	+	+	+	−	+	−	−
Is lightweight	+	+	−	−	+	+	+	+
Has a hanger	−	+	+	−	−	−	−	−
Has a brake	−	−	−	−	−	−	+	−

The distinction between functional properties and observable attributes and the use of real objects to link between these two types of property provide a nice approach to codifying design knowledge of specific domains. This representation of design knowledge is empirical. It is worth noting that such empirical knowledge has the following features.

First, some functional properties are directly derivable from the structure or observable properties. For example, a chair that has wheels is movable. A chair that has a vertical rotational degree of freedom can revolve. However, the structure–function relation may be imprecise. For example, a chair with a vertical rotational degree of freedom may not allow 360° of rotation.

Second, not all functional properties are directly derivable from the structure or observable properties. For example, a chair that has no physical back support does not necessarily support the back. For instance, the box chair (A) can support the back if it is located near a wall. Also, Scandinavian chair (E) provides back support although it does not have a physical back support.

Third, functional properties may not be orthogonal or independent. One function may qualify another. For example, the functional property 'constrains back' qualifies the function 'supports back'. Similarly, observable properties may also not be orthogonal or independent.

Finally, the relationships between theses two types of properties are implicitly codified by the entities that serve as sample objects of the domain. The association of objects with certain properties is often based on the empirical knowledge of the domain. Three crucial factors affect the correctness and usefulness of the domain knowledge.

(1) *Entity set*: whether a good sample of real objects was chosen determines whether the knowledge codified in the design space is complete or not.

(2) *Functional properties* and *observable properties*: whether a good set of functional properties and observable properties were chosen determines whether properties of design concerns are included in the design space.

(3) *Association of properties to entities*: the correctness of the domain knowledge represented in a design space is determined by the correctness of the association of properties to the entities.

The general design theory proposed by Yoshikawa [1] provides a set of axioms in terms of topology so that a mathematical analysis of the domain knowledge can be carried out. A full discussion of the mathematical theory is beyond the scope of this book. However, readers are encouraged to refer to the references [1, 2] for further reading.

8.1.2 Solving design synthesis and analysis problems

An important merit of the representation of design knowledge in the above way is that it offers an effective process to solve both synthesis and analysis design problems.

A design *synthesis* problem can be defined as finding an artefact structure that satisfies a number of functionalities. For example, suppose that the specification of our design task is to generate a chair that is movable and constrains the back. Using the knowledge of chairs depicted in Figure 8.1, we can find that the office chair (F) and the wheelchair (G) satisfy our functional requirements. The common observable structure properties of these two entities that distinguish them from others are that they have wheels and have physical back supports. These two properties provide a concise description of the solution to the design problem. Another set of common observable properties that distinguishes them from all others also consists of two properties: has legs and lightweight. This description offers an alternative design to satisfy the specification.

In more complicated situations, design problems cannot be solved by just using existing knowledge codified in known entities as above. For example, assume that in addition to the previous specification, the chair is also required to be aesthetic. There is no chair in the set of entities that satisfies the specification. A *re-design* process can be invoked by taking the nearly good candidates and inventing new objects by adding additional observable attributes. In this case, there are three nearly good candidates:

(1) *movable* and *constrains back*: wheelchair (G) and office chair (F);

(2) *constrains back* and *aesthetic*: suspended chairs (B) and (C);

(3) *movable* and *aesthetic*: Scandinavian chair (E).

When new features are added into a design, they must be analysed for consistency with the other attributes according to the physical laws, etc.

A design *analysis* problem can also be performed as the inverse process of design synthesis, i.e. it starts with a description of a design to find out the objects that satisfy the description and then to derive the functional properties of the objects. For example, suppose that we have a design of a chair that has legs and has a hanger. We can find that entity (C) Suspended Chair 2 is the only entity that has this structure. It has the properties of being not movable, does not revolve, not easy to manufacture, but it is aesthetic and supports back. Of course, such analysis is only empirical. Further analysis of the design must be made upon the details of the design.

8.2 DESIGN SPACE OF ARCHITECTURAL ELEMENTS

To a certain extent, design is to 'find the right component of a structure' [3]. Therefore, it is of vital importance to understand the variety of components so that the right component can be found and used as well as the variety of ways that components can be put together. The structure of such varieties forms a space in which particular designs are elements. In this section, we consider the variety of software architectural elements and apply the theory of design space to such elements. Here, by software architectural elements, we meant both components and connectors. We systematically present knowledge about software architectural elements as a design space. To do so, we examine various observable properties of software architectural elements.

Notice that, software design has a fundamental difference from the designs of other physical artefacts. As discussed in Chapter 3, software systems are invisible; hence the notion of observable properties for physical artefacts does not make much sense for software. However, properties of software artefacts can be divided into two types: behaviour features and static features. They are similar to the functional features and observable properties, respectively. Therefore, we will first examine the behaviour features of various software architectural elements and then discuss the static features of software architectural elements.

8.2.1 Behaviour features

Behaviour features of an architectural element represent the dynamic behaviour of the element over time. The execution of an architectural element can be viewed as a series of contiguous temporal 'episodes'. Each episode is a continuous period of time in which the element is continuously active under at least one thread of control. Figure 8.2 illustrates the temporal view of the execution of a single architectural element in one episode. There are two threads of control flow through the element. The thread A begins at time t_1 and terminates at time t_2. The thread B starts at t'_1 and terminates at time t'_2. The figure also shows that data entering and leaving thread A via the arrows labeled d_1, and d_2, and entering and leaving thread B via d'_1 and d'_2. The time t_s and t_e are the instants when the episode starts and terminates, respectively.

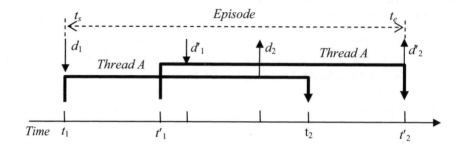

Figure 8.2 Illustration of the temporal view of architectural elements

The behaviour features of a software architectural element are concerned with the temporal relationships between the run-time events of the elements. For example, whether or not does the acceptance of data always happen at the same time when control is accepted? Whether or not a second thread of control can be accepted? And so on. For this reason, behaviour features are called temporal features in [4]. Questions like these fall into the following 6 groups. Different answers to such questions form various behaviour attributes.

(1) *Times of control acceptance.* Attributes in this group are concerned with when the acceptance of control can happen with respect to the start of the episode. Different answers to this question lead to the following attributes.

- *Non-executable* (*Not accept control*): The element does not accept control at any time, i.e. the element is not executable.

- *Accept control at start time*: The time t_1 that the element accepts control can be the start time of the system t_s.

- *Accept control during execution*: The time t_1 that the element accepts control can be any time after the system start time t_s.

(2) *Times of control transmission.* Attributes in this group are concerned with when the transmission of control can happen with respect to the end of the episode. Similar to the above, different answers to this question lead to a set of attributes.

- *Transmit control at termination*: The element may transmit control at the time t_e when the episode terminates.

- *Transmit control during execution*: The element may transmit control before the time t_e that the episode terminates.

(3) *Times of data acceptance.* Attributes in this group are concerned with when the acceptance of data can happen with respect to the start of the thread. Attributes in this group are:

- *Accept data at the beginning*: The element can accept data at the time t_1 when the thread starts.

- *Accept data during execution*: The element can accept data at a time after the start of the execution of the element.

- *Not accept data*: The element does not accept data at any time.

(4) *Times of data transmission.* Attributes in this group are concerned with when the transmission of data can happen with respect to the end of the thread. Attribute in this group are:

- *Transmit data at end*: The element may transmit data at the time t_2 when its execution terminates.

- *Transmit data during execution*: The element may transmit data before its execution terminates.

- *Not transmit data*: The element does not transmit any data.

(5) *Multiple threads.* The attributes in this group are concerned with acceptance or creations of multiple thread in one episode. The attributes are:

- *Multiple-entry* (*Accept multiple controls*): The element can accept more than one control at the same episode.

- *Forks*: The element may create a new thread of control, provided it accepts control.

(6) *State retention.* The attributes in this group are concerned with the relationship between multiple executions of the architectural elements, i.e. whether the state of one execution of the element can be passed to the next execution. The attributes are:

- *Retain state within thread*: The element retains state information over the same thread. That is, its behaviour depends on its state of previous invocation in the same thread.

- *Retain state between threads*: The element retains state information between different threads. That is, its behaviour depends on its state of previous invocation even in a different thread.

For example, let's analyse procedure's properties using the above attributes. Notice that, by procedures we meant multi-entry procedures because in most high-level programming languages, procedures are re-enterable.

- *None-executable* (*Not accept control*): False, because procedures are executable.

- *Accept control at start time*: True, because a procedure can accept control when the episode starts.

- *Accept control during execution*: False, because a procedure can only start when the episode starts.

- *Multiple-entry* (*Accept multiple controls*): True, as we assumed that the procedure can have multiple entries.

- *Transmit control at termination*: True, because a procedure can transmit control at the time t_e when the episode terminates if there is no other thread of control in the procedure.

- *Transmit control during execution*: False, because a procedure transmits only when it finishes execution and returns control to the caller.

- *Accept data at the beginning*: True, because a procedure can accept data as its parameters when it begins the execution.

- *Accept data during execution*: False, the only way a procedure accepts data is by parameters, which are transmitted at the beginning of the execution of the procedure.

- *Not accept data*: True, because a procedure that has no parameters does not accept any data at any time.

- *Transmit data at end*: True, because a procedure can transmit data through output parameters or call-by-reference parameters at the time when its execution terminates.

- *Transmit data during execution*: False, because the only way that a procedure transmits data is via output parameters or call-by-reference parameters, which transmit data when the procedure terminates.

- *Not transmit data*: True, because a procedure that has no parameters does not transmit any data.

- *Forks*: False, because a procedure does not create a new thread of control.

- *Retain state within thread*: True, because a procedure can retain state information over the same thread if the procedure has static local variables.

- *Retain state between threads*: False, because the values of static local variables of a procedure do not pass between different executions of the software.

The following table, Table 8.3, summarises the analysis of various software architectural elements against the behaviour attributes.

Table 8.3 Behaviour features of software architectural elements

Attributes / Elements of architecture	Non-executable	Accept control at start time	Accept control during execution	Multiple-entry	Transmit control at termination	Transmit control during execution	Accept data at the beginning	Accept data during execution	Not accept data	Transmit data at end	Transmit data during execution	Not transmit data	Forks	Retain state within thread	Retain state between threads
Single-entry procedure	–	+	–	–	+	–	+	–	+	+	–	+	–	+	–
Multiple-entry procedure	–	+	+	+	+	–	+	–	+	+	–	+	–	+	–
Object	–	+	+	–	+	–	+	–	+	+	–	+	–	+	+
Function	–	+	–	+	+	–	+	–	+	+	–	+	–	+	–
Multi-threaded single-entry procedure	–	+	+	+	+	+	+	+	+	+	+	+	–	+	+
Filter	–	+	–	–	+	–	+	+	–	+	+	–	–	+	–
Local process	–	+	–	–	+	+	+	+	+	+	+	+	+	+	–
Distributed process	–	+	+	–	+	+	+	+	+	+	+	+	+	+	–
Layer	–	+	+	+	+	+	+	+	+	+	+	+	–	+	+
Server process	–	+	–	–	+	–	+	+	+	+	+	+	+	+	–
Client process	–	+	–	–	+	–	+	+	+	+	+	+	+	+	–
Call back	–	+	–	–	+	–	+	–	+	+	–	+	–	+	–
Pipe	–	+	–	–	+	–	+	+	–	+	+	–	–	–	–
Remote procedure call	–	+	–	–	+	–	+	–	+	+	–	+	–	+	–
Procedure call	–	+	–	–	+	–	+	–	+	+	–	+	–	+	–
Shared memory	+	x	x	x	x	x	+	+	+	+	+	+	x	+	+
Global data	+	x	x	x	x	x	+	+	+	+	+	+	x	+	+
Unprotected file	+	x	x	x	x	x	+	+	+	+	+	+	x	+	+
Socket	–	+	–	–	+	–	+	+	+	+	+	+	–	–	–
Blackboard	–	+	–	–	+	–	+	+	+	+	+	+	–	+	+
Database	–	+	+	+	+	+	+	+	–	+	+	–	–	+	+
Semaphore object	–	+	–	–	+	–	+	–	–	+	–	–	–	+	+
Broadcast	–	+	–	–	+	–	+	–	–	+	–	–	–	–	–
Multicast	–	+	–	–	+	–	+	–	–	+	–	–	–	–	–
Process scheduler	–	+	–	–	+	–	–	–	+	–	–	+	–	+	+

8.2.2   Static features

Static features are those that do not relate to the run-time events [4]. They can be determined by the syntax and semantics of code of the element. They are mostly about the structure of architectural elements and its structural relationships to other elements. For example, where the data of the architectural elements come from and where are the data go to? Do the connections to other elements have directions? These features are not concerned with the events that happen at run-time. Similar to behaviour features, static features fall into seven groups.

(1) *Ports*. Attributes of this group are concerned with the connection ports of the architectural element. For example, how many ports the element can have? Are the ports directed or not? If the ports directed, what are the directions of the ports? The attributes are:

- *Multiple in ports*. The element can have multiple in ports, i.e. where control and data comes into the element.

- *Single in port*. The element can have only one in port.

- *Multiple out ports*. The element can have multiple out ports, where data and control go out of the element.

- *Single out ports*. The element can only have one out port.

- *Bi-direction ports*. The elements can have bi-direction ports, where data/control can come into the element and also go out of the element.

(2) *Binding time*. This feature is about when the ports of the element are bound to the sources and destinations of data and control. A port of the architectural element can be connected to other architectural elements at various times. Generally speaking, such binding can be determined at specification time, i.e. before the execution of the software. It can also be bound when the architectural element is invoked. It can also be determined during the execution of the element and can change in the course of the execution. These lead to the following attributes.

- *Binding at specification time*. The ports of the element can be bound to the sources and destinations of data/control at specification time.

- *Binding at invocation time*. The ports of the element can be bound to the sources and destinations of data/control at invocation time, i.e. when the element is invoked and becomes active.

- *Binding at execution time*. The ports of the element can be bound to the sources and destinations of data/control at execution time, i.e. after the element becomes active.

(3) *Associations*. This group of attributes is concerned with the features related to how other elements are associated to the ports. In particular, how many other elements can be associated to one port at the same time and how many during the lifetime of the element? The attributes are:

- *Multiple simultaneous connections*. The port can be associated to multiple elements at the same time.

- *One–one connection*. The port can only be connected to one element at a time.

- *Dynamic connection*. The port can be connected to different elements at different times during its life time.

- *Static connection*. The port can only be connected to one element during its life time. The connection once established, cannot be changed.

(4) *Life lines and control*. This group of attributes are concerned with the control of the element's life line and that of the connected elements. The attributes are:

- *Stable life*. The element never receives nor transmits control. Notice that, it does not mean that the element does not have control, instead, many types of architectural elements have control, but they never change their execution state by transmitting or receiving controls.

- *Blocking*. The element blocks the other elements to suspend their control when they are connected to this element.

- *Relinquish*. The element can give up its control.

(5) *Functionality*. This feature describes the functionality of the architectural element with regards to its processing of data. The attributes are:

- *Transformation*. The element receives data from other element, transforms and processes the data, and then, transmits the data to other elements. The main functionality of the element is the transformation of data.

- *Data source*. The element generates data and transmits data to other elements. It does not receive any data from other elements. Its main functionality is a data source.

- *Data sink*. The element receives data from other elements, but does not transmit to any other elements. Its main functionality is a data sink.

- *Data flow channel*. The element receives data from one or more elements and transmits them to other elements, but it does not make any modification of the data.

- *Control flow channel*. The element receives control from one element and transmits it to other elements.

(6) *Data scope*. Attributes of this group are concerned with the largest scope across which data can be passed by the architectural elements, provided that it accepts or transmits data. In other words, they are about the addresses from which data is received and transmitted. Attributes of this group are:

- *Virtual data address space*: The architectural element can only have data that come from and go to the same virtual address space.

- *Physical data address space*: The architectural element can have data that come from and go to the same physical address space, but may be in different virtual address space.

- *Distributed data address space*: The architectural element can have data that come from and go to different physical address spaces on different computers across a network.

- *No data scope*. The element never receives nor transmits data.

(7) *Control scope*. Attributes of this group are concerned with the largest scope over which control may be acquired and transferred, provided that the architectural element receives or transmits control. Similar to data scope, there are three attributes in this group.

- *Virtual control address space*: The architectural element can acquire and transfer control only within the same virtual address space.

- *Physical control address space*: The architectural element can acquire and transfer control within the same physical address space, but across different virtual address spaces.

- *Distributed control address space*: The architectural element can acquire and transfer control across different physical address spaces of the computers in a network.

For example, let's analyse the features of procedures as an architectural element. Notice that the 'ports' of a procedure are where the procedure starts execution and data is passed into the procedure (in port), and where the control of the procedure leaves the body of the procedure and data is passed back to the caller (out port). Therefore, we have that:

- *Multiple in ports*: False, a procedure in modern high level programming languages usually has a unique entrance.

- *Single in port*: True, see above.

- *Multiple out ports*: True, a procedure may have multiple points to leave the body. Therefore, there may be multiple output ports.

- *Single out ports*: False, see above.

- *Bi-direction ports*: False, the ports of a procedure are directed to one direction, either in or out.

- *Binding at specification time*: True, the entrance to a procedure and exit points out of a procedure are determined at specification time.

- *Binding at invocation time*: True, where the output ports, i.e. the return address of the procedure call, are determined at invocation time.

- *Binding at execution time*: False, the return address and the caller of the procedure cannot be changed after the procedure has started execution.

- *Multiple simultaneous connections*: False, because each execution of the body of a procedure binds to one caller.

- *One-one connection*: True, see above.

- *Dynamic connection*: True, because a procedure can be called by different callers during the life time of the system.

- *Static connection*: False, see above.

- *Stable life*: False, because a procedure receives control when it is called and it transmits back the control when it finishes the execution of its body.

- *Blocking*: True, because a call of a procedure means to pass the control to the procedure and suspend its own control until the procedure stops its execution and passes the control back.

- *Relinquish*: True, see above.

- *Transformation*: True, a procedure can receive data as parameters from the caller, transform the data and then transmit the processed data back to the caller also using parameter passing.

- *Data source*: True, because a procedure can be used to generate data without receiving data.

- *Data sink*: True, because a procedure can be used to receive data without transforming and passing it back.

- *Data flow channel*: False, a procedure alone cannot be used as data channel because the mechanism of parameter passing is only between the procedure and the same caller. Notice that, procedures can be used in combination with other architectural elements, such as globally shared variables, to implement data channels.

- *Control flow channel*: False, for the similar reason as above.

- *Virtual data address space*: True, because the parameters of a procedure must be within the same virtual address space.

- *Physical data address space*: False, see above.

- *Distributed data address space*: False, see above.

- *No data scope*: False, because a procedure can have data parameters.

- *Virtual control address space*: True, a procedure call must be within the same virtual address space.

- *Physical control address space*: False, see above.

- *Distributed control address space*: False, see above.

The following table, Table 8.4, summarises the analysis of various architectural elements against structure attributes defined above.

Table 8.4 Structural features of software architectural elements

Element of architecture / Structure attributes	Multiple in ports	Single in port	Multiple out ports	Single out ports	Bi-direction ports	Binding at specification time	Binding at invocation time	Binding at execution time	Multiple simultaneous connections	One–one connection	Dynamic connection	Static connection	Stable life	Blocking	Relinquish	Transformation	Data source	Data sink	Data flow channel	Control flow channel	Virtual data address space	Physical data address space	Distributed data address space	No data scope	Virtual control address space	Physical control address space	Distributed control address space
Single-entry procedure	−	+	+	+	−	+	+	−	−	+	+	−	−	+	+	+	+	+	−	−	+	−	−	−	+	−	−
Multiple-entry procedure	−	−	+	+	−	+	+	−	−	+	+	−	−	+	+	+	+	+	−	−	+	−	−	−	+	−	−
Object	+	+	+	+	−	+	+	+	−	+	+	−	−	+	+	+	+	+	−	−	+	−	−	−	+	−	−
Function	−	+	+	+	−	+	+	−	−	+	+	−	−	+	+	+	+	+	−	−	+	−	−	−	+	−	−
Multi-thread single-entry procedure	−	+	+	−	−	+	+	−	−	+	+	−	−	+	+	+	+	+	−	−	+	−	−	−	+	−	−
Filter	−	+	−	+	−	−	+	−	−	−	−	+	+	−	−	+	+	+	+	−	+	+	−	−	−	−	−
Local process	+	+	+	+	+	+	+	+	+	+	+	+	+	−	+	+	+	+	+	+	+	−	−	+	+	−	−
Distributed process	+	+	+	+	+	+	+	+	+	+	+	+	+	−	+	+	+	+	+	+	+	+	+	−	+	+	+
Layer	+	+	+	+	+	+	+	−	−	+	−	+	+	+	+	+	+	+	+	+	+	−	−	−	+	−	−
Server process	+	+	+	+	+	+	+	+	+	+	+	+	+	−	+	+	+	+	+	+	+	+	+	−	+	+	+
Client process	+	+	+	+	+	+	+	+	−	+	+	+	+	−	+	+	+	+	+	+	+	+	−	−	+	+	−
Call back	−	+	+	+	−	+	+	−	−	+	+	+	−	+	+	+	+	+	+	+	−	−	−	−	+	−	−
Pipe	−	+	−	+	−	+	+	−	−	+	−	+	+	−	−	−	−	−	+	−	+	+	−	−	−	−	−
Remote procedure call	−	+	+	+	−	+	+	−	−	+	+	−	+	+	+	+	+	+	−	−	+	+	+	−	+	+	+
Procedure call	−	+	+	+	−	+	+	−	−	+	+	+	−	+	+	+	+	+	−	−	+	−	−	−	+	−	−
Shared memory	+	−	+	−	+	+	−	−	+	+	+	+	+	−	−	−	+	+	+	−	+	+	−	−	−	−	−
Global data	+	−	+	−	+	+	−	−	+	+	+	+	+	−	−	−	+	+	+	−	+	−	−	−	−	−	−
Unprotected file	−	+	−	+	+	+	+	+	+	+	+	+	+	−	−	−	+	+	+	−	+	+	+	−	−	−	−
Socket	−	+	−	+	−	+	+	−	−	+	+	+	+	+	+	−	−	−	+	−	+	+	+	−	−	−	−
Blackboard	+	+	+	+	+	+	+	+	+	+	+	+	+	+	+	−	+	+	+	−	+	+	+	−	+	+	+
Database	−	+	−	+	+	+	+	+	−	+	+	+	+	−	+	−	+	+	+	−	+	+	+	−	−	−	−
Semaphore object	−	+	−	+	−	+	+	−	−	+	+	−	+	−	+	−	−	−	−	−	−	−	−	+	+	+	−
Broadcast	−	+	−	+	−	+	+	−	+	−	+	+	+	+	−	+	−	+	−	−	−	−	+	+	+	+	+
Multicast	−	+	+	−	−	+	+	−	−	+	+	+	+	+	−	+	−	+	−	−	−	−	+	+	+	+	+
Process scheduler	+	+	+	+	−	+	+	+	+	+	+	+	+	+	−	−	−	−	−	+	−	−	−	+	+	+	+

8.3   DESIGN SPACE OF ARCHITECTURAL STYLES

In this section, we re-examine the software architectural styles presented in the previous chapters using the theory of design spaces. We will first discuss the structural and behavioural features of software architectural styles that distinguish one style from another. We will then discuss how various architectural styles can be classified by the structural and behavioural features.

8.3.1   Characteristic features of architectural styles

The structural feature of an architectural style is related to the structure of software systems in the style. These features include:

- *Constituent parts:* What are the allowable kinds of components and connectors of the style? For example, in the pipe-and-filter style, components must be filters and connectors must be pipes.

- *Control topology:* What geometric form does the control flow for the systems of the style take? For example, in the main-program-and-subroutine style, components must be organised into a hierarchical structure.

- *Data topology:* What geometric form does the data flow for the systems of the style take? For example, in the batch sequential processing style, components are organised in a linear sequence structure that data are passed from one component to the next.

- *Control/Data interaction topology:* Are the topological structures of control topology and data topology substantially isomorphic? For example, for all systems in the batch sequential processing style, the topological structure from the control-flow point of view is identical to the structure from the data-flow point of view. In the main-program-and-subroutine style, from the control point of view, the components are organised hierarchically. However, from the data flow point of view, the system can be in any structure because data can flow between components through shared data stores without any restrictions. Therefore, the control topology and data topology are not isomorphic.

- *Control/Data interaction direction:* If the control and data topologies of the systems of the style are the same, does the control flow in the same directions as the data flows or the opposite? In the batch sequential processing style, data is passed from one component to another in the same direction that control is passed between the components. However, in the client and server style, control is passed opposite to the direction in which data is passed between components.

The behavioural features of an architectural style are properties that are related to the dynamic behaviour of the systems. They include the following.

- *Synchronicity:* How dependent are the components' actions upon each other's control state? The synchronicity between two components can be any one of the following.

  - *Lockstep*: one component's state implies the other component's state. For example, in batch sequential processing style, a component will not execute until its predecessor finishes execution.

  - *Synchronous*: components synchronise at certain states to make sure they are in the synchronised states at the same time in order to cooperate, but the relationships on other states are not predictable. For example, in a synchronous communication between component A and B, the component A must be in the state of sending data and the component B must be in the state of receiving data at the same time. If component A is in the sending state but B is not in the receiving state, component A must wait until B comes to the receiving state. On the other hand, if B is in the receiving state while A is not in the sending state, B must wait for A. After the communication, the components can do whatever they like.

  - *Asynchronous*: components are not synchronised at any state, however the state of a component may affect the other components' behaviour. For example, in asynchronous communication between two components C and D, component C can perform the action of sending data without waiting for component D to be in the receiving state. When component D comes to the state of receiving data, what has been sent by component C will be received by D.

  - *Opportunistic*: two components work completely independently from each other in parallel.

- *Data access mode:* How is data made available throughout the system? It can be *passed* from one component to another, such as in a message passing style. It can also be *shared* by making it available at a place accessible to all sharers. If a component copies the data from a public store, modifies it and then reinserts it back to the public store, the data access mode is *copy-out-copy-in*. In some styles, data are *broadcast* or *multicast* to specific recipients.

- *Data flow continuity:* How continuous is the data flow throughout the system? A continuous data flow system has fresh data available all the time. A sporadic data flow system has new data generated at discrete times. Data transfer between components can also be *high volume* in data intensive systems, or *low volume* in computation intensive systems.

- *Binding time:* When the names are bound to the entities for control and data transfer. That is, when the identity of a partner in a control or data transfer is established. It can be at *code-time*, i.e. when the programmer writes the source code. It can be at *compile-time*, i.e. when the source code is compiled into object code. It can be at *invocation-time*, i.e. when the operating system initialises the execution of the system. It can also be at *run-time*, during the execution of the system.

8.3.2 Classification of styles

A software architectural style can be defined by the characteristic features discussed above.

For example, consider the pipe-and-filter style. For structural features, the constituent parts of the style are filters as the components, which are transducers, and pipes as the connectors, which are data streams. Both the control topology and data topology can be any directed graphs, however they are identical. In particular, if the system is implemented in Unix shell, it must be linear, i.e. it must consist of a number of text input/output programs as filters linearly connected using the operator '|' as connector. The data flow and control flow directions are the same. For behaviour features, the components can execute in parallel and their synchronicity is asynchronous. The data access mode is that data are passed from one component to another, rather than copied or shared. Data flows are sporadic and can be in high volume. The binding time can be as late as at invocation time when the system is initialised by the operating system.

Using a design space, we can recognise if a style is a sub-style of another. If for characteristic features, style A's values on the feature is a subset or special case of the value of style B on the same feature, we can say that A is a sub-style of B. For example, abstract data type is a sub-style of call-and-return style.

Table 8.5 below summarises the structural features of various software architectural styles discussed in the previous chapters.

Table 8.5 Structural features of architectural styles

Style	Components	Connectors	Control topology	Data topology	Interaction topology	Interaction direction
Data flow	Processing elements	Data flows	Arbitrary	Arbitrary	Identical	Same
Pipe-and-filter	Filters (Transducers)	Pipes (data streams)	Directed graphs	Directed graphs	Identical	Same
Batch sequential processing	Phases (Stand-alone programs)	Batch data (e.g. files)	Linear	Linear	Identical	Same
Independent components	Processes, Modules	Communication protocols	Arbitrary	Arbitrary	Possible	Either
Event-based implicit invocation	Processes and event handler	Events	Arbitrary	Arbitrary	Identical	Same
Communicating processes	Processes	Message protocols	Arbitrary	Arbitrary	Identical	Same
Call-and-return	Procedures (subroutines) and Data stores	Procedure calls and Data accesses	Arbitrary	Arbitrary	Not always	Any
Layered systems	Layers (sets of procedures)	Procedure calls	Hierarchical	Hierarchical	Often	Any
Abstract data type	Managers (abstract data types)	Procedure calls	Arbitrary	Arbitrary	Identical	Same
Object-oriented	Managers (objects/ classes)	Procedure calls	Arbitrary	Arbitrary	Identical	Same
Data-centred	Data store and Computation clients	Data access, Data queries	Star	Star	Possible	Opposite, if structures are identical
Virtual machine	Data memory, State memory, Program memory, Interpretation engine	Data paths	Fixed	Fixed	No	Not applicable

Table 8.6 below summarises the behavioural characteristic features of various software architectural styles.

Table 8.6 Behavioural features of architectural styles

Style	Synchronicity	Data access mode	Data flow continuity	Binding time
Data flow	Asynchronous	Passed	Sporadic or Continuous, Low or High volume	Any
Pipe-and-filter	Asynchronous	Passed	Sporadic	Code, Compile, Invocation
Batch sequential processing	Lockstep (sequentially)	Passed, Shared	Sporadic High volume	Any
Independent components	Synchronous, Asynchronous	Any	Sporadic low volume	Any
Event-based implicit invocation	Asynchronous	Multicast	Sporadic low volume	Any
Communicating processes	Any except sequential	Message	Sporadic low volume	Any
Call-and-return	Lockstep	Passed, Shared	Sporadic low volume	Any
Layered systems	Lockstep	Passed	Sporadic low volume	Any
Abstract data type	Lockstep (sequential)	Passed	Sporadic low volume	Code, Compile
Object-oriented	Lockstep (sequential)	Passed	Sporadic low volume	Code, Compile, Run-time
Data-centred	Asynchronous	Shared, Passed, Multicast	Sporadic low volume	Code
Virtual machine	Lockstep (sequential)	Shared	Continuous	Code

SUMMARY

Generally speaking, a *design space* represents a domain knowledge related to the design of a set of artefacts that have the same main functional characteristics, but these artefacts have various other functional and structural features. A design space normally divides the features associated to each artefact into two groups: functional properties and structural features. This manifests two types of knowledge. Firstly, it provides the knowledge about what is the variety of the designs in the domain in terms of what are valid combinations of the functional and structural properties. Secondly, it represents the relationships between functions and structures in the specific domain of design. A design space represented in such a way enables designers to solve both synthesis and analysis design problems. A *synthesis design problem* is to find the appropriate structure of a system so that certain functional requirements are met. An *analysis design problem* is to find out the properties of a design when the structure of the design is provided, at least partially provided.

The general theory of design space can be applied to software design in the study of the variety of software architectural elements. The domain knowledge of software architectural elements can be represented and described through a set of static properties and a set of behaviour properties. *Behaviour properties* characterise architectural elements through their run-time behaviours. They are defined in terms of the temporal relationships between various run-time events, such as the acceptances and transmissions of control and data. These features are similar to the functional features of physical artefacts. *Static properties* represent the architectural element's characteristics that are not related to run-time events. They are similar to the structural features of physical artefacts. The variety of software architectural styles also forms a design space, where *static* and *behavioural* features provide a classification of software architectural styles.

FURTHER READING

The theory of design spaces is based on Yoshikawa's work on mathematical theory of design, which was developed in Japan in the 1970s and first presented in English in 1981 [1]. The theory was further developed by Yuzuru Kakuda and Makoto Kikuchi and their colleagues; see for example, [2]. Although the theory may be still far from mature to capture all aspects of design, it presents a good starting point towards a mathematical foundation of the scientific discipline of design. Here, this chapter is only an informal introduction to the basic ideas of the theory, rather than the mathematical treatment of the subject. An introduction to the theory and a critical review of recent developments in the direction can be found in [5].

The design space of software architectural elements is based on Kazman, Clements, Abowd and Bass's work on classification of software architectural elements [4]. Another important work on the classification of software architectural elements is by Melta, Medvidovic and Phadke [6], which is devoted to connectors. The design space of software architectural styles is based on Shaw and Clements's work on the classification of software architectural styles [7].

EXERCISES

(8–1) In Yoshikawa's theory of design space, what is a functional property of an object? What is an observable property?

(8–2) What is a design synthesis problem? Describe the process of solving a design synthesis problem by using a design space.

(8–3) What is a design analysis problem? Describe the process of solving a design analysis problem by using a design space.

(8–4) What is an episode of an architectural element during the execution of a software system?

(8–5) Use attributes in the groups of the times of control acceptance and transmission to analyse the following architectural elements: filters, pipes, layers, and blackboard.

(8–6) Use the attributes in the groups of times of data acceptances and transmissions to analyse the following architectural elements: functions, procedures, shared memory, unprotected files, and databases.

(8–7) Use the attributes in the groups of multiple thread and state retention to analyse the following architectural elements: local processes, distributed processes, server processes, client processes, and process schedulers.

(8–8) What is a port of a software architectural element?

(8–9) For each of the following static features, give an example of architectural elements that have the feature:

(i) multiple in ports, (ii) single out port, (iii) bi-direction ports.

(8–10) What is the binding time of a port of a software architectural element? How many possible different binding times are there? For each possible binding time, give an example of software architectural elements that have such a port.

(8–11) Use the static features in the groups of associations and life lines and control to analyse the following software architectural elements: filters, pipes, layers, and blackboards.

(8–12) Use the static features in the group of functionality to analyse the following software architectural elements: procedures, functions, shared memories, global data, process schedulers, and objects.

(8–13) For each pair of the architectural elements given below, what are the static features that distinguish one from the other?

(i) local processes and distributed processes;

(ii) procedure calls and remote procedure calls;

(iii) single entry procedures and multiple entry procedures;

(iv) client processes and server processes;

(v) filters and pipes.

(8–14) For each set of behaviour properties listed below, find the architectural elements that have the properties, and then discuss if these architectural elements have common static features.

(i) Accept control at start time, transmit control at termination, accept data at the beginning, transmit data at termination, not accept data during execution, not transmit data during execution;

(ii) Forks, and retains states within thread;

(iii) Transmit data during execution, do not transmit control during execution, do not fork, and do not retain state between threads.

(8–15) An architectural element has the following known static properties. It can only have a single in port, but may have multiple out ports, and no bi-direction ports. Its ports have dynamic connections, but not static connections. It is a transformation, but, neither data flow channel, nor control flow channel. Its execution blocks the element connected to its in port. What are the behaviour properties that it must have?

(8–16) Discuss the structural and behavioural features of the following architectural styles

- Batch sequential processing   - Abstract data type

- Virtual machine   - Event-based implicit invocation

- Main-program-subroutine with shared data

(8–17) Discuss why, from the structural and behavioural features point of view, layered systems, main-program-subroutine, abstract data type and object-oriented styles can be considered as sub-styles of call-and-return.

REFERENCES

1 Yoshikawa, H., General design theory and a CAD system, in Sata, T. and Warman, E. editors, *Man-Machine Communication in CAD/CAM, Proceedings of the IFIP WG5.2-5.3 Working Conference*, 1980, Tokyo, Japan, pp35–57, North-Holland, 1981.

2 Kakuda, Y. and Kikuchi, M., Abstract design theory, *Annals of the Japan Association for Philosophy of Science*, 2001.

3 Alexander, C., *Notes on the Synthesis of Form*, Harvard University Press, Cambridge, Mass., 1964.

4 Kazman, R., Clements, P., Abowd, G. and Bass, L., Classifying architectural elements as a foundation for mechanism matching, *Proc. of COMPSAC'97*, Washington DC, August, 1997.

5 Reich, Y., A critical review of general design theory, *Researches in Engineering Design*, Vol. 7, No. 1, pp1–18, 1995.

6 Melta, N. R., Medvidovic, N. and Phadke, S., Towards a taxonomy of software connectors, in *Proc. of ICSE'2000*, Limerick, Ireland, 2000, pp178–187.

7 Shaw, M. and Clements, P., A field guide to boxology: Preliminary classification of architectural styles for software systems, in *Proc. of COMPSAC'97*, Washington, DC, August 1997.

9 Scenario-Based Analysis and Evaluation

In previous chapters, we studied how to create software architectural designs. From this chapter, we study how to evaluate, compare and analyse software architectural designs. In particular, we will learn two approaches to the analysis and evaluation of software architectural designs: scenario-based and model-based approaches. In this chapter, we study the principles underlying scenario-based architectural analysis methods. The objectives of this chapter are:

- To study the concept of scenario in the general context of software analysis and design as well as in the more specific context of evaluation and analysis of software architectural designs;

- To study how functional and non-functional software requirements, especially quality requirements, can be specified as scenarios;

- To study how to analyse and evaluate a software system's quality against a well-specified scenario.

The chapter is organised as follows. Section 1 discusses the concept of scenarios. Section 2 discusses the uses of scenarios in the specification of software modifiability requirements and the evaluation of software modifiability based on architectural designs. Section 3 discusses the uses of scenarios in the specification of performance requirements and the evaluation and analysis of software performances. Section 4 is devoted to software reusability.

9.1   THE CONCEPT OF SCENARIO

As seen in Chapter 2, software quality attributes are normally expressed using words such as maintainability, security, performance, reliability, and so forth. These words provide convenient ways for describing and communicating many common recurring problems in software. Many quality attributes are defined in this way in software engineering standards.

However, most software quality attributes are too complex and amorphous to be evaluated on a simple scale. For example, a design of a system for extracting keyword frequency vectors from text files may demonstrate different behaviours in modifiability with respect to changes in usage, data representations and functionality. The point, of course, is that quality attributes do not exist in isolation but rather have meaning only within a context, such as modifiable with respect to changes in data representation, secure with respect to a specific threat, useable with respect to a specific user class, efficient with respect to its utilisation of a specific resource, and so forth. A statement such as 'this system is highly maintainable' carries little operational meaning. Therefore, software systems must be evaluated in contexts that are explicitly specified.

This notion of context-based evaluation of quality attributes has led us to the use of scenarios as the descriptive means of specifying and evaluating quality attributes.

Generally speaking, a *scenario* is a set of situations of common characteristics that might reasonably occur in the interactions between stakeholders and a system. However, not an arbitrary set of situations of the interactions between stakeholders and the system form a scenario. To be a scenario, the set of situations should have common characteristics on the following aspects.

- *Participating Stakeholders*: The situations in a scenario must all involve a specific subset of stakeholders in the interactions with the systems.

For example, consider a software system for banking. A typical scenario is that a customer of the bank withdraws money from his/her own bank account. All situations in this scenario involve the account holder, i.e. a specific sub-type of the stakeholder user.

- *Operation condition*: The situations in a scenario must occur under a certain operational condition and/or in a certain state of the system.

For example, in the withdrawal money scenario, the condition is that the user involved in the interaction must own an account in the bank. If the user does not own an account, the situation would not belong to the withdrawal money scenario, but probably a scenario called hacking, or stealing.

- *Interaction purpose*: The situations of a scenario must occur when the stakeholders interact with the systems for the same purpose.

For example, the purpose of the withdrawal money scenario is to withdraw cash from the bank account. With the same properties that the stakeholder is a customer of the bank and owns an account in the bank, there are other scenarios that have different purposes of the interactions. For instance, one may deposit money into the account, or check the balance of the account, etc. All situations in the withdrawal money scenario should have the purpose, i.e. to get cash from the account.

The concept of scenario has been used widely in computer science and engineering, especially in requirements engineering. For example, in object-oriented analysis and design methodology, it is used with the concept of use cases to specify users' functional requirements. However, in requirements engineering, they have been used primarily in connection to the run-time behaviour of the system to characterise the interactions between the system and its users as well as other actors in the run-time environment.

In the application of scenarios to the analysis of software architectural designs, scenarios encompass other interactions with the system as well, such as a maintainer carrying out a modification. The actors involved in a scenario are not only the run-time end users and equipment in the environment, but also other types of stakeholders. As discussed in Chapter 1, there are a number of types of stakeholders involved in various stages of software development. Different types of stakeholders are often concerned with different aspects of the system, even if they want to achieve the same objectives. For example, consider the following two scenarios:

- *Scenario* 1: An end user wants to change the background colour of the windows of the users' interface.

- *Scenario* 2: A programmer wants to change the background colour of the same software's windows.

Scenario 1 above is concerned with the quality attribute of the adaptability of the user-computer interface, i.e. how easy to adapt the human-computer interface to suit the user's personal preferences without changing the code of the system. In contrast, scenario 2 is concerned with the modifiability of the system, i.e. how easy to modify the software, possibly by changing the code of the system.

Scenarios are often classified into *generic scenarios* and *concrete scenarios*. A generic scenario serves as a representative for an entire class of situations. This class consists of all interactions for which the system under consideration responds in exactly the same way. A generic scenario usually contains some parameters that can be replaced with concrete values. For example, scenario 1 above is a generic scenario that contains a parameter 'end user', which can be replaced by various particular users, such as John, Smith, Hong, etc. There is also another parameter in scenario 1, i.e. the back colour of the window that the user wants to change to, which can be blue, white, pink, etc. Concrete scenarios can be considered as instances of generic scenarios. The following examples are the concrete scenarios of scenario 1. Under most system designs, these scenarios are essentially equivalent.

- *Scenario* 3: User John changes the background colour on all windows to blue.

- *Scenario* 4: User Smith changes the background colour on all windows to black.

Concrete scenarios and generic scenarios can play different roles in the system analysis and each has its own strength and weakness. Concrete scenarios often have the advantages that they are easy to understand and easy to use in order to find out the responses from the system. Generic scenarios are slightly more abstract than concrete scenarios. However, since the interactions between the system and the stakeholders in the set of concrete scenarios of a generic scenario are equivalent, a generic scenario can represent the interactions more generally. Hence, the results of the analysis on a generic scenario apply to all its concrete scenarios. Therefore, analysing a system's responses and features using a generic scenario is equivalent to repeating the same analysis process on a number of concrete scenarios, which is often unnecessary.

In addition to specifying functional requirements in the form of a set of scenarios, which has been a standard practice in requirements analysis, scenarios can also be used to specify non-functional requirements. It is thus easy to imagine that a set of scenarios of potential changes to be made to a system would specify the modifiability of the system. Similarly, a set of specific threat actions would clarify what is required for security, and so on. The following sections discuss how to use scenarios to specify various attributes of software quality and how to evaluate and analyse software architectural designs against such scenarios.

9.2   SCENARIOS FOR EVALUATING MODIFIABILITY

The modifiability of a software system is the easiness to modify the system to meet the changes in the environment, requirements or functional specifications of the systems. Modifiability requirements can be best specified by a set of scenarios that require changes to the system with various purposes. The stakeholders involved in such scenarios are usually developers, who will modify the system somehow. The purposes or motivations of such scenarios can be classified into a number of categories, which are discussed in the following sub-sections.

9.2.1   Changes of users' functional requirements

The changes in users' requirements are perhaps one of the hardest things to predict in software development. However, such changes often fall into two types: the *enhancement of system's functionality* and the *amendment of system's functionality*.

The enhancement of system's functionality is to include a new function into an existing system. For example, an old version of a word processor that does not have a spelling check facility is required to provide spelling check. Adding a spelling checker into the system enhances the system's functionality. A new functionality can be represented as a generic scenario that involves users as the stakeholder and an interaction with the system that is not implemented by the existing system.

For example, consider the Keyword Frequency Vector extraction system discussed in the case study in Chapter 8. In the discussion of the modifiability of the architectural designs, we considered the situation when the system is required to produce keyword frequency vectors that synonyms are to be treated as the same word to calculate the frequencies of the keywords. This functionality that may cause a modification to the system can be represented as a scenario as follows.

- *Scenario* 1: The user inputs a text file and the system produces a keyword frequency vector in the form of sequence of keywords and their number of occurrences in the text file. In the keyword frequency vector, small words are removed and synonyms are treated as the same word in the calculation of the frequency that word occurs in the document.

The amendment of system's functionality is to change or remove the existing functions of the system. A particular type of change to the existing functions of a system is to change the way that a function is delivered.

The functions of a system can often be delivered to the user in a number of different ways. For example, the spelling check function of a word processor can be delivered as a function that is only invoked when the user explicitly calls the function, such as by pressing a button or selecting a menu item. It can also be delivered without explicit user's command, but automatically invoked when the user enters text in the editing window. The users may want to change the way that a function is delivered or invoked, or to provide a number of alternative ways in the same system. For example, the earliest versions of Microsoft's Word only have the explicit invocation way of delivering the spelling check function. More recent versions of Microsoft's Word have both ways of implicit and explicit invocations.

Generally speaking, a function can be delivered in at least 4 different ways according to whether the functionality is delivered incrementally or as a whole, and if the invocation is explicit or implicit. For example, the spelling check function in an email application can be delivered in various ways as shown in Table 9.1.

Table 9.1 Ways of delivery of spelling check in email applications

	Processing as a whole	Incremental processing
Explicit invocation	The interface of the software contains a button or menu item for spelling check. The spelling of the whole email text in the editing window is checked when the user clicks the button or selects the menu item. All misspelled words are marked somehow, for example, underlined, after the spelling check is finished. The user can then correct the misspelled words.	The interface of the software contains a button or menu item for spelling check. The spelling of the whole email text in the editing window is checked when the user clicks the button or selects the menu item. The misspelled words in the editing window are displayed to the user one by one, for example in a popup window, possibly together with recommendations for correctly spelled words.
Implicit invocation	The spelling checker is invoked implicitly and it checks the whole text in the editing window. Such invocation is triggered by certain events, such as when the 'send email' function is invoked.	The spelling check is invoked implicitly and it processes the spelling check incrementally. For example, it may check each word while the user types a message into the window. In this case, the trigger event of the invocation of the spelling check is type in words.

In Table 9.1, the columns are the different ways information is processed. The *processing as a whole* approach takes the whole input data and delivers the results of the processing to the users as a whole. The *incremental processing* approach usually reads the input data piece by piece and processes the data incrementally. The results are also delivered to the user piece by piece. The rows in the table are the invocation mechanisms. *Explicit invocation* requires the user to explicitly issue a command through the users' interface, such as click on a button, select a menu item, type in a command, etc. *Implicit invocation* usually is associated with certain types of events, such as the completion of a task, the start of a new task, a certain keyboard or mouse activity, even user's inactiveness for a period of time, etc. When such an event happens, the function is invoked.

9.2.2 Changes of hardware environment

With the rapid development of computer hardware and network technology, the hardware platform on which a software system executes is often changed to upgrade the computer's processing power. In some cases, changes in hardware platform results in the migration from one type of platform to another in order to take the advantages of the new platform. The following are some of the typical scenarios in hardware environment changes.

- *Scenario 1*: The computer that the software system is executing on is upgraded to a more powerful one with larger memory space and high processing speed, but completely compatible with the existing one.

- *Scenario 2*: The computer that the software system is executing on is changed to a new computer, which is a product from a different manufacturer. The hardware of the new computer is not compatible with the existing one.

Scenario 1 above only involves the upgrading of the hardware, which usually does not affect the software system. However, moving from one computer to another may still cause problems and disruption to the services that the software provides. In addition to the amount of efforts required to install the software on the new hardware platform, one should also consider whether the system can actually benefit from the new hardware's capability. In some cases, one may not be able to benefit from the new hardware. Instead, it may have adverse effects. For example, game software designed to play on the PC AT platform often assumes a certain CPU speed and display screen resolution. When the same program is installed on a more powerful PC with much higher CPU speed and higher screen resolution, it could become unplayable, because the screen display changes too fast for the users to catch the information and to respond with appropriate input. The text designed to be displayed on a low resolution screen also becomes too small to be legible on a high resolution screen. In such cases, the modification of the code becomes necessary even if the hardware is compatible. How much effort is required for such modifications is concerned with the maintainability of the software. Scenario 2 involves the transportation of the software from one computer to another, which is related to the portability of the system. The same considerations discussed for scenario 1 also apply.

- *Scenario 3*: A new computer is added into the network as an additional server to improve the system's performance. The new server is of the same type as the existing ones.

- *Scenario 4*: A new computer is added into the network as an additional server. It is of different type from the existing one.

Both scenario 3 and 4 involve the installation of an additional computer into the network to share the load with existing hardware. This often involves the modifications of the software system through new deployment of the code to different computer hardware, or modification of the code in order to be executed on new hardware, or configuration of the parameters of the system to allow it to dynamically load tasks to the new hardware, or a combination of these. Scenario 3 will not change the homogeneity of the network architecture, while scenario 4 will inevitably result in heterogeneous network architecture. Hence, in scenario 4, one may expect more modification cost than in scenario 3.

- *Scenario 5*: The computer network is upgraded from 10M Ethernet to 100M Ethernet.

- *Scenario 6*: The computer network is added with some wireless connections so that notebook computers and handheld computing devices can be connected into the system from the wireless network ports.

Scenario 5 and 6 are concerned with network capability and functionality. A well-designed software system should not be severely affected by such upgrade of the infrastructure while users expect improvement in system's performance. However, attention must be paid to the consequences in security issues due to the use of wireless connections in scenario 6. This may result in the change of the software's design and implementation.

9.2.3 Changes of software environment

Changes in software environment include the changes of the system software, such as the operating system, database management system, middleware, network and communication packages, etc. Changes of such supporting software systems may have a significant effect on the application software. The following are some examples of such scenarios.

- *Scenario 1*: Upgrade operating system from Windows 98 to Windows NT;

- *Scenario 2*: Change of the operation system from Windows to Linux;

- *Scenario 3*: Upgrade the database management system Oracle 4 to a higher version Oracle 6;

- *Scenario 4*: Change the database management system from Oracle to Microsoft's Access.

- *Scenario 5*: Change the middleware of the system from CORBA to DCOM.

Another type of change in software environment is the changes in the software systems that the application interoperates with. For example, suppose that a graphic editor that enables the user to draw various types of diagrams is designed to interoperate with a particular word processor. To change the word processor that the graphic editor is supposed to interact with is a change of the graphic editor's software environment. The following are examples of such scenarios.

- *Scenario 6*: A web-based application that links to a specific website that provides an online map. The website that provides the online map changes its web address, and/or the way online maps are requested.

- *Scenario 7*: A shopbot software agent helps the users to compare the prices of books that online bookstores on the web offer for online shopping. An online bookstore that the shopbot links to changes its format of messages in the way that the prices of books are requested.

9.2.4 Changes of software components

With the rapid development of software component technology and availability of COTS (Components Off-The-Shelve) components and shareware, more and more software developers use third-party software components to reduce development costs and speed up development processes. In house components are also becoming more and more widely reused in software development. Such components often evolve for many reasons, such as bugs fixed. An application software system often needs to be modified due to the changes to the components either to take advantage of the availability of better components or forced to make modifications because, say, the component provider is no longer able to provide the support, or a free component is no longer free, etc. The following are some examples of such scenarios.

- *Scenario 1*: The representation of data produced by a new version of a third party component is changed.

- *Scenario 2*: The representation of the data required by a new version of a third party component is changed.

- *Scenario 3*: The format of messages sent to and received from a new version of a third party component is modified.

- *Scenario 4*: The interaction protocol to access a new third party component is different from the original third party component. The protocol determines the sequences of messages sent to and received from the component.

In the above scenarios, modifications are inevitable to be made to the software systems that use the modified component. In many cases, a component is upgraded or replaced with a new version that is compatible with the old version after bugs are fixed. In such cases, usually there is no modification to be made to the software system. Theoretically speaking, the main effort and cost of using the new one is installation. However, it could also end up with a huge effort and cost of integration and regression testing to install the new component.

9.2.5 Evaluation of modifiability

To evaluate the modifiability of an architectural design in a particular scenario, the components and connectors that must be modified, and/or added into the system must be identified. The efforts and cost that are required to perform the modification should also be estimated. In some cases, the architectural style may need to be modified, which may cause more fundamental changes to the system.

For example, consider the Keyword Frequency Vector extraction system discussed in Chapter 8. To modify the design in Main-Program-Subroutine with shared data style, we need to modify the component Reduce so that for each word it not only returns the normal form of the word, but also the standard synonym of the word. It must also modify the dictionary so that each word is associated with a standard synonym. The efforts required to modify the Reduce component's code is probably not very large, say, about 1 man-month. However, the modification of the dictionary may need more efforts if the information about the synonyms is to be added into the dictionary. It may probably cost about 5 man-months. Therefore, a rough estimate of the efforts required to implement this change is 6 man-months.

9.3   SCENARIOS FOR EVALUATING PERFORMANCE

The performance of a software system is the efficiency with which the system uses the computation resources, especially the efficient uses of the CUP, i.e. the time efficiency, and the memory, i.e. the space efficiency, etc. There are a number of measurements of a software system's performances. For example, *response time* is a measurement of system's time efficiency according to how fast the system responds to each stimulus event or input data. *Throughput* is another often used performance measurement of computer systems. It is concerned with the maximal amount of input/output the system can process within one unit period of time. Another commonly used time efficiency measurement is the computational complexity, which is a function from the complexity measurement of the input data (i.e. the size of the input data) to the required time to process the input. An example of this kind of efficiency statement is that, to process a sequence of N input values, the software needs N^2 seconds, where N is any positive integer. Space efficiency is often measured by the amount of internal memory and secondary data storage space, e.g. disk spaces, required to process the input data.

9.3.1   Specification of operational profiles

In the analysis of a software system's performance, software designers, and users alike, are concerned with not only how the system will perform in normal average situations, but also in worst cases and in best cases. To specify the performance requirements, the scenarios must state what the average situations are, what the worst situations and the best situations are. A situation may also occur with certain frequency and probability. Such information will also be useful in the evaluation of a system's performance. The following are some examples of scenarios for specifying performance requirements.

- *Scenario* 1: The website of a newspaper is expected to have about 5000 users browsing its web pages simultaneously at peak hours, which usually occur from 12:00 pm to 2:30 pm every working day.

- *Scenario* 2: The website of a newspaper is expected to have about 200 new HTML files posted on its website for updating during the peak hours, which usually occurs from 11:30 am to 12:30 am everyday.

Both scenario 1 and scenario 2 are for the same website. However, they describe different usages of the system by different types of users. Such scenarios describe the maximal system load. They can be used to find out whether the system can handle such a workload and the response time in such scenarios.

- *Scenario* 3: A software system used to collect and process data in wind tunnel experiments is connected to 100 to 500 pressure sensors. The software will take readings from each sensor every $2\mu s$ during the process of a wind tunnel experiment, which usually lasts no more than 10 minutes.

- *Scenario* 4: A room temperature control system is usually connected to 10 to 100 temperature sensors depending on the size and structure of the building. These sensors are grouped into a number of sets according to the rooms they are in. The system reads the temperature readings from each sensor every 2 minutes and calculates each room's temperature. When the room's temperature is lower or higher than the room's set temperature by a certain degree, the air conditioner of the room must be switched to heat or cool or off within 10 seconds.

- *Scenario* 5: In the room temperature control system described in scenario 4 above, each room has a temperature setting, which can be changed according to the goods stored in the room. On average, a room temperature setting changes once in the period of 3 months. Once a new setting is made, the switch of the air conditioner should be reset immediately after a delay of 20 seconds.

Scenarios 3, 4 and 5 above are typical usage scenarios of real-time systems, which have periodical events and sporadic events. Scenario 3 and scenario 4 are the average scenarios of periodical events, which occur in a more or less fixed frequency periodically. Scenario 5 is an average scenario of sporadic events, which does not occur with a fixed frequency.

- *Scenario* 6: The email application software is expected to send and receive text messages of a length up to 5000 characters, but a message may have attachment files of a size up to several megabytes.

- *Scenario* 7: The word processor is expected to be used to edit and format files of a length about 2,000 words to 20,000 words. However, in extreme cases, the file's size could reach 5,000,000 words. A file may also contain data from other office applications, such as drawings, charts, and photos, etc.

Scenario 6 and scenario 7 specify the size and complexity of the input data. They are valuable to evaluate how long the system needs to process such data and how large a space is required. For example, suppose that a component that fulfils the spelling check functionality of the word processor in scenario 7 takes 0.001 second to check the spelling of each word on average. It will take about 2 to 20 seconds to check the text in a file on average.

9.3.2 Evaluation and analysis of performance

To evaluate the performance of an architectural design in a particular scenario, the information about the performances of each component and connector must be available.

For example, consider the Keyword Frequency Vector extraction system discussed in Chapter 8. To evaluate the performance of the architectural design in the pipe-and-filter style on the following scenario, we must know the time required by each processing component (i.e. the filters) to process each data element and the time delay by the connectors (i.e. the pipes).

- *Scenario* 8: On average, a text file to be processed by the Keyword Frequency Vector extraction system consists of N characters. The average length of the words is about 6 characters. Among the words, there are about 40% small words that should be removed from the frequency calculation, and the number of different keywords is only about 1% or less of the total number of words.

Assume that the components and connector have the following performance parameters[1].

- The Input filter processes each character in 5 units of time.

- The Delete Small Words filter takes 20 units of time to decide whether the word should be deleted from the stream or output to the stream.

- The Reduce Word to Original Form filter takes about 30 units of time to process each word.

- The Sort Words Alphabetically component uses an insert sorting algorithm to sort the words into alphabetical order. For each word it takes about 3 $log(n)$ units of time to insert it into the list, where n is the length of the list of words.

- The Statistics of Frequency filter processes each word in 10 units of time.

- The Sort According to Frequency also uses an insert sorting algorithm and takes $3log(n)$ time units to insert a keyword-frequency pair into the keyword frequency vector of n elements.

- The Output component processes each element in 1 unit of time.

---

[1] Notice that the parameters given in this example are for illustration of the analysis and evaluation process only. It does not reflect the real performance of a system.

- There is a delay of about 10 units of time on all pipes in the system.

Figure 9.1 illustrates the performance parameters of the architectural design in the pipe-and-filter style.

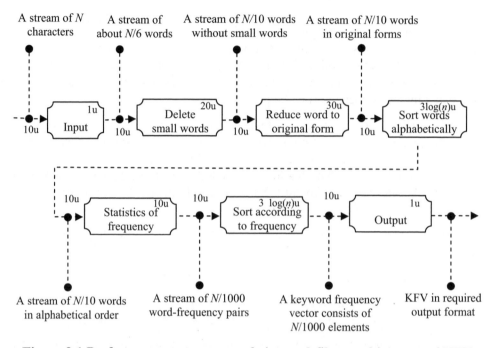

Figure 9.1 Performance parameters of pipe-and-filter architecture of KFV

Assume that the input stream of characters is always ready for the Input filter. The Input filter will then produce words on its output stream at an average rate of 6 units of time per word. The first word produced by the Input filter will be 6 units later after the start execution of the system. The whole stream of characters will be processed by the Input filter in about N units of time, where N is the length of the stream, i.e. the number of characters in the document. The earliest time that the Input filter can finish processing of N characters is therefore, N units of time after it started computation.

The Delete Small Words filter will start 10 units of time later after the Delete filter output the first word. That is, it will start computation after about 16 units of time after the whole system started execution. It will then take about 20 units to process each word. Since the processing rate of the Delete filter is slower than the upstream (i.e. the Input filter), the input to this filter can be considered always ready. Consequently, it will produce output on its output stream at an average rate of 28 units per word. The earliest time that it can produce a word to its output stream is 36 units of time after the whole system started. It will take about $20 \times N/6$

units of time to finish the process of all words, which are $16 + 20 \times N/6$ units after the whole system started computation.

Similarly, the Reduce Word filter can start the computation at the earliest time of 46 units of time after the whole system started, and process each word using 30 units. It will produce the words on its output stream at an average rate of 30 units of time per word. It starts the computation at the earliest after 46 units after the whole system started. The earliest time that it can produce the first output on its downstream is 76 units of time after the system started. It needs $30 \times N/6 \times 60\%$ time units to complete the process of the whole stream.

The Sort Words filter collects the input from the upstream from the Reduce Words filter and gradually builds up an alphabetically sorted list of words and when the whole list of words are processed, it starts output. At the beginning, the processing time is faster than the rate that words are produced by the upstream. However, when the list of words that it collected is large enough, i.e. when the length of word list n satisfies the condition $log_2(n) > 30/3 = 10$, i.e. when $n > 2^{10}$, it takes longer time than the rate the words become available. So the total time need to process the whole stream of words is $30K + 3 \sum_{n=K+1}^{N/10} \log(n)$, where $K = N/10$, if $N < 10 \times 2^{10}$; otherwise, $K = 2^{10}$. After the sorting, the filter can now produce the whole stream to its output port. It will take the same amount of time to clear off the stream by the downstream filter.

The Statistics filter will start the computation when the data is available on its upstream, which will be 10 time units later after the Sort Words filter starts to produce the words. It takes N (i.e. $10 \times N/10$) units of time to process the whole stream of words. Until all the words in the upstream are processed, it produces the sequence of keywords-frequency pairs on its downstream output. Therefore, it will start producing outputs at $86 + 30K + 3 \sum_{n=K+1}^{N/10} \log(n) + N$ units of time after the system started computation.

The keyword-frequency pairs generated from a text file are then processed by the Sort KFV filter according to the frequency which will take $3 \log(n)$ time units to process each element, where n is the number of keyword-frequency pairs already processed by the filter and stored in the filter. Since the whole stream of the input is available at the same time, the time the Sort KFV component needs to process the whole stream is $3 \sum_{n=1}^{N/1000} \log(n)$ units.

The Output filter will finally then take $N/1000$ units of time to produce the whole keyword frequency vector in the format required for output.

Table 9.2 summarises the analysis made above.

Table 9.2 Analysis of the computation times in pipe-and-filter architecture

Component	Start time	Time to produce the first output	Output rate (time units per word / element)	Total number of output	Time to finish the last output
Input	0	6	6	$N/6$	N
Delete	16	36	28	$N/10$	$16 + 20 \times N/6$
Reduce	46	76	30	$N/10$	$76 + 3 \times N$
Sort Words	86	T_1	–	$N/10$	T_1
Statistics	T_1+10	T_2	–	$N/1000$	T_2
Sort KFVs	T_2+10	T_3	–	$N/1000$	T_3
Output	T_3+10	T_3+10+1	1	$N/1000$	T_4

where $\quad T_1 = 86 + 30K + 3 \displaystyle\sum_{n=K+1}^{N/10} \log(n)$,

$$T_2 = T_1+10+10\times(N/10) = T_1+10+N,$$

$$T_3 = T_2+10+3 \sum_{n=1}^{N/1000} \log(n),$$

$$T_4 = T_3+10+N/1000.$$

Therefore, it is easy to see that

$$T_4 = 116 + 30K + \left(1 + \frac{1}{1000}\right)N + 3\left(\sum_{n=1}^{N/1000} \log_2(n) + \sum_{n=K+1}^{N/10} \log_2(n)\right), \qquad (*)$$

where $\quad K = \begin{cases} N/10, & \text{if } N < 10 \times 2^{10} \\ 2^{10}, & \text{otherwise} \end{cases}$.

In other words, the whole process of processing a text file of N characters in the scenario will take about the number of T_4 time units given in equation (*). This gives the time efficiency of the architectural design.

9.4 SCENARIOS FOR EVALUATING REUSABILITY

Software reuse refers to the use of a software artefact produced in one process of software development in another project. Such software artefacts are not limited to the code of a software component, but also the architectural designs, test scripts, requirements documents, etc. just to mention a few. The reusability of a software artefact is therefore the easiness of reusing the artefact across the boundary of software products and/or software engineering projects. Similar to the statement 'the software is highly maintainable', a statement like 'this component is highly reusable' bears little operational meaning. The best way to specify reuse requirements needs to explicitly specify the context in which the artefact is to be reused. Scenarios can be employed to specify such contexts.

For example, suppose that a word processor is to be designed and implemented with a functionality of spelling check. A context of reusability requirements for the design of the word processor is that a software system is going to be developed for editing, receiving and sending emails. One of the functionalities of the email software is to perform a spelling check on the text messages entered by the user. In this context, we would expect the design of the word processor to have a relatively independent component that implements spelling check so that it can be reused by the email software. If this function is implemented with code spread all over the system and imbedded in various other components, the reusability in that context is poor, though we may still be able to reuse some parts of the word processor's spelling check functionality, such as the dictionary of correctly spelled words. Several types of reuse context scenarios can be identified. The following discusses a few of such types.

The first type is to reuse across the boundary of software products in the same application domain. These applications often have certain common functional and non-functional requirements. The following is such an example.

- *Scenario* 1: The software to be developed belongs to the office applications domain, and other products of the same domain are planned to be developed in the future.

In scenario 1, a number of software products are planned to develop in the application domain of office automation. The common features of this group of applications include that, first, they are all required to have a good interactive human-computer interface to support the user to enter various types of information and to view such information. Second, they are all required to handle a number of files at the same time and to store these files in a well organised way. Third, they must be easily fitted into various user's organisational environments, which may vary in many different aspects, such as the workflow for documents to be generated, reviewed and approved for certain actions to be taken, the security policies for who can view the documents and on what conditions, etc. and the document templates for various tasks and purposes. Third, they must be able to be connected to various office devices, such as printers, photocopier, fax machine, mail sorting machines, telephone switch, etc. and various special software applications such as graphical design tools.

- *Scenario* 2: The software to be developed is a real-time control of rapid moving machinery. At the time of software architectural design of the project, another customer is negotiating with the developer to develop a software system to control a big warehouse's temperature.

In this scenario, both the software being developed and the software under negotiation are real-time control systems. Although they belong to different application domains, they have the common features of real-time systems, that is, the system constantly senses the state of the system and makes decisions for what actions to be taken to control the system, although the devices that sense the system state and activate the control actions can be quite different. A common function of such systems is the scheduler that schedules the real-time processing of a variety of tasks, which usually include data collection, data processing, multi-criteria decision making and control activation, etc.

Software reuse often occurs within one company that develops a series of products of the same kind. These products have very similar functionalities, but often require to be tailored according to the customer's special needs. The following are some examples.

- *Scenario* 3: A software development company is specialised in developing customer relationship management systems (CRM) automated call centres. Their customers come from various sectors of industry and public services, such as energy providers, satellite and cable TV programme providers, communication providers, banks, mortgage lenders, etc.

CRM systems have a number of common functions. For example, a CRM system is usually required to prompt the call centre's staff to ask a certain number of questions in certain sequences, to record the information provided by the caller and to display the information recorded in a database about the caller and previous services and transactions. It is also required to prompt appropriate questions according to the caller's answers to previous questions, and issue certain actions accordingly. Although the clients of the software developer vary one from another in terms of client's business requirements, such differences only have impacts on the details of the information to be recorded and processed by the CRM system, such as the questions to be prompted on the screen.

- *Scenario* 4: A software development company is specialised in developing printer drivers for various makes and models of printers to be installed on various computer hardware and software platforms.

In this scenario, for each printer, a series of software products is required for running on different computer hardware and software platforms. For example, the drivers for PC with Windows 98, Windows 2000 and Windows NT operating systems, and for various operating systems running on Mac, and Sun Workstations, etc. Similarly, for each hardware and software platform, a number of different drivers of various printers are also required. Therefore, two sub-scenarios can be derived from scenario 4 as follows.

- *Scenario* 4A: A number of printer drivers for various makes and models of printers are required to be developed to be installed on a specific computer hardware and software platform.

- *Scenario* 4B: A number of printer drivers are required to be developed for a specific model of printer to be installed on various computer hardware and software platforms.

Scenario 4A is a typical scenario in which a number of software products are to be developed for a number of devices of the same kind but used in different environments. Scenario 4B is a typical scenario in which one device is to be used in different environments. A printer driver developed for one specific model of printer to be running on a specific operating system may need to be reused on both scenarios. However, the reusability could be different in these scenarios.

SUMMARY

A scenario is a set of situations of common characteristics that might reasonably occur in the interactions between stakeholders and a system. These common characteristics must define (a) a specific subset of stakeholders who participate in the interactions with the system, (b) a specific condition under which the interactions take place, and (c) a specific purpose that the stakeholder(s) carry out the interaction.

Scenarios can be concrete, in which the stakeholders, the condition and the purposes of the interactions as well as all the data involved in the interactions are all given as concrete instances. Scenarios can also be generic, which contain parameters of the data, and the stakeholders, the interaction conditions and purposes are abstract rather than concrete instances.

Software functional requirements can be specified by a set of scenarios that only involve the users of the system as the participants of the scenarios and the purposes of interactions are the uses of the system.

Non-functional requirements can often be specified using scenarios that usually have other types of stakeholders as participants, such as developers, etc. In this section, we examined how scenarios can be employed to specify some quality requirements including modifiability, performance and reusability. Modifiability requirements can be specified by a set of scenarios that demand modifications to the system, such as changing the hardware and/or software environments of the system, the enhancement and amendment of functional requirements, and changing the software components. Performance requirements can be specified by a set of scenarios that defines various operational profiles of the system, such as worst operational conditions and average operational conditions, etc. Reusability requirements can be specified by a set of scenarios that define the context in which components of the system may be used, such as across a number of systems in the same application domain, in the context of a family of products tailored to meet the specific requirements of different customers, etc.

The main reason for using scenarios in the specification of software quality requirements is that they can provide the specific contexts in which designs of a software system can be evaluated. Given a quality requirement specified by a well defined scenario, the basic means of evaluation and analysis of an architectural design against the scenario is to find out the interactions between the stakeholder(s) and the system in that scenario and to determine if the interaction meets the expected requirement. For modifiability, we identify what modifications need to be carried out in the scenario and to estimate the efforts and costs that will incur to carry out the modification. For performance, we calculate how much resource will be used by the system in the operation scenario in terms of the time and space and to determine whether the uses of resources meet our expectation. For reusability, we identify which part of the system can be used in the production of other systems specified by a scenario.

FURTHER READING

The uses of scenarios in the evaluation and analysis of software architectural designs have been investigated intensively in the past decade. It is recognised as the most mature approach to the analysis and evaluation of software architectural designs. A survey of current state of art in the research on the evaluation of software architecture can be found in [1].

The first systematic scenario-based method for analysing and evaluating software architecture is perhaps the SAAM method [2, 3, 4], which will be studied in the next chapter. SAAM method was originally proposed to analyse modifiability of software systems based on information presented in architectural designs. It has been explored for the evaluation and analysis of software quality attributes related to the modifications, such as portability, extensibility, integratability, etc. as well as functional coverage, performance and reliability. Scenario-based methods for analysing various software quality attributes at architecture level have also been studied by Jan Bosch, Per Olof Bengtsson for maintainability [5], by Per Olof Bengtsson, Nico Lassing, Jan Bosch and Hans van Vlient for modifiability [6, 7], and Per Olof Bengtsson and Jan Bosch for scenario-based architecture reengineering [8]. Rick Kazman, Jeromy Carriere and Steven Woods [9] investigated how to elicit scenarios in a systematic way and presented a software tool to support the management of scenarios in architecture analysis.

In a wider context, scenarios are employed in requirements engineering to elicit software requirements, see for example [10], but mostly for functional requirements. In particular, use cases and scenarios play a significant role in object-oriented analysis and design methodology largely due to Jacobson's work [11]. Scenarios can also be used in the validation and testing of software requirements; see for example [12, 13].

EXERCISES

(9–1) From each of the following sets of concrete scenarios, derive a generic scenario that contains the concrete scenarios as its instances.

(a) {(1) User John sets the font size of the text displayed on the window to 12 point, (2) User Howard sets the font size of the text displayed on the window to 10 point}.

(b) {(1) The middleware used to build the software system is to be changed to CORBA, (2) The middleware used to build the software system is to be changed to DCOM}.

(c) {(1) The operation of the software takes input from a text file that contains 1K bytes of characters, (2) The operation of the software takes input from a text file that contains 2K bytes of characters, (3) The operation of the software takes characters from keyboard as input}.

(9–2) For each of the following generic scenarios, derive some concrete scenarios as its instances by following the steps given below:

(i) Identify the parameters contained in the scenario;

(ii) Give some instant values of the parameters;

(iii) Substitute the instant values into the generic scenarios to replace the parameters.

The generic scenarios are:

(a) The computer that the software system is executing on is upgraded to a more powerful one with larger memory space and high processing speed, but completely compatible with the existing one.

(b) A new computer is added into the network as an additional server to improve the system's performance. The new server is of the some type as the existing ones.

(c) A web-based application that links to a specific website that provides an online map. The website that provides the online map changes its web address, and/or the way online maps are requested.

(d) The database management system used to implement a software application is upgraded to a new version;

(e) The operating system on which the software system executes is upgraded to a new compatible version;

(f) The operating system on which the software system executes is changed to a new incompatible one.

(9–3) Consider the following scenario used in section 9.3.2 to analyse the architectural design of Keyword Frequency Vector extraction system in the pipe-and-filter style.

Scenario:

On average, a text file to be processed by the Keyword Frequency Vector extraction system consists of N characters. The average length of the words is about 6 characters. Among the words, there are about 40% small words that should be removed from the frequency calculation, and the number of different keywords is only about 1% or less of the total number of words.

(i) Use the same scenario to analyse the architectural design in the main-program-subroutine with shared data style given in Chapter 8;

(ii) (a) Identify the concrete values in the description of the scenario;

(b) Replace the concrete values with parameters in the scenario description and derive a generic scenario.

(c) Use the generic scenario to evaluate the architectural design in the pipe-and-filter style.

(9–4) For each of the following scenarios, discuss which quality attribute (s) is/are associated to the scenario.

(a) The software is required to present the same information to the user(s) but in different presentations, such as in different font, colour, and sizes;

(b) The time budget for initialisation is reduced from 5 minutes to 90 seconds.

(c) The maximal number of simultaneous accesses to the system increases from 50 users to 1000 users;

(d) The software should allow the user to set their own presentation preferences, such as the font and size of the text displayed on the screen and the windows' background colour.

(e) The system should respond to user's input within 1 second.

(f) Search, browse, and order submission should not be down for more than 1 hour per week due to either system failure or backup operations.

REFERENCES

1 Dobrica L. and Niemela, E., A survey on software architecture analysis methods, *IEEE Transactions on Software Engineering*, Vol. 28, No. 7, pp638~653, July 2002.

2 Kazman, R., Abowd, G., Bass, L. and Clements, P., Scenario-based analysis of software architecture, *IEEE Software*, November, 1996.

3 Bass, L., Clements, P. and Kazman, R., *Software Architecture in Practice*, Addison Wesley, 1998.

4 Clements, P., Kazman, R. and Klien, M., *Evaluating Software Architectures: Methods and Case Studies*, Addison Wesley, 2002.

5   Bosch, J. and Bengtsson, P., Assessing optimal software architecture maintainability, fifth European Conference on Software Maintainability and Reengineering, September 2000.

6   Bengtsson P. O. and Bosch, J., Architecture Level Prediction of Software Maintenance, *Proc. Third European Conf. Software Maintenance and Reengineering*, pp.139–147, Mar. 1999.

7   Bengtsson, P., Lassing, N., Bosch, J. and van Vlient, H., *Analyzing software architectures for modifiability*, Technical Report HK-R-RES-00/11-SE, Hogskolan Karlskrona/Ronneby, 2000.

8   Bengtsson, P. and Bosch, J., Scenario-based software architecture reengineering, *Proc. Fifth Int'l Conf. Software Reuse (ICSR 5)*, 1998.

9   Kazman, R., Carriere, S. J. and Woods, S., Toward a discipline of scenario-based architectural engineering, *Annals of Software Eng.*, Vol. 9, 2000.

10   Sutcliffe, A., Scenario-based requirements analysis. *Requirements Engineering Journal*, Vol. 3, No. 1, pp8–65, 1998.

11   Jacobson, I. *et al.*, *Object-Oriented Software Engineering: A Use Case Driven Approach*, Addison Wesley, 1992.

12   Zhu, H., and Jin, L., Scenario analysis in an automated tool for requirements engineering, *Requirements Engineering Journal*, Vol. 5, No.1, pp2–22, June 2000.

13   Zhu, H., Jin, L., Diaper, D., Software requirements validation via task analysis, *Journal of System and Software*, March 2002, Vol. 61, Issue 2, pp145–169.

10 Analysis and Evaluation of Modifiability: The SAAM Method

In the previous chapter, we studied the concept of scenarios and the basics of specifying quality requirements in scenarios. We have seen how to analyse a software architectural design against one scenario. However, questions remain, such as how to systematically elicit quality requirements and represent such requirements in a set of scenarios, and how to evaluate and analyse architectural design against a set of scenarios, which may have interactions between them. This chapter addresses these questions by presenting the SAAM method for evaluating and analysing modifiability based on information presented in architectural designs. SAAM is the acronym of Software Architecture Analysis Method. It was proposed by a group of computer scientists at the Software Engineering Institute of Carnegie Mellon University largely due to the work by Len Bass and Gregory Abowd [1, 2]. It is believed to be the first documented and widely known software architecture analysis method. It is a scenario-based analysis method. The objectives of the chapter are:

- To further study how to elicit modifiability requirements and to represent them in a set of scenarios;

- To study how to analyse and evaluate architectural designs against a set of scenarios that represent modifiability requirements;

- To learn how to apply the SAAM method.

The chapter is organised as follows. Section 1 discusses the input and output of SAAM analysis. Section 2 is an introduction to the process of SAAM analysis. We will illustrate the method by an example. Section 3 uses the case study of a Keyword Frequency Vector extraction system to give a complete example of applying SAAM in the evaluation and analysis of modifiability.

10.1 THE INPUT AND OUTPUT

SAAM can be applied to two different analysis and evaluation tasks. One is to compare two or more candidate designs to see which one satisfies its quality requirements better. The other is to evaluate a single design to point out the places where that architecture fails to meet its quality requirements and in some cases to show obvious alternative designs that would work better.

To achieve these objectives, the SAAM method requires two types of input. The first is a description of the architectural design or a set of designs that are under analysis and evaluation. SAAM does not require any specific description of the architectural designs as far as the designs are understood by all the people involved in the analysis. It does not require the description of the architectural designs in any specific level of details. However, if more detailed descriptions of the architectural design/designs are necessary, the SAAM process makes their need clear as it progresses.

The second input is the quality requirements that the system is intended to achieve. SAAM is a scenario-based method for analysing architectures. As discussed in the previous chapter, a scenario is a short description of a set of typical situations in the interactions with the system. A scenario provides a specific context for the evaluation of software quality. Quality requirements must be represented in the form of a set of scenarios before it can be applied to the analysis and evaluation of the architectural designs. Therefore, SAAM takes a serious activity to elicit quality requirements and to translate such requirements into an agreed set of scenarios to represent quality requirements. This agreed set of scenarios is used as the benchmark to compare and contrast different candidate architectures to determine the extent to which the candidate architecture supports each scenario or must be modified to support it. This set of scenarios is the first intermediate result of SAAM analysis and evaluation process. These scenarios must also be weighted according to their importance and priority to be met. When such a set of weighted scenarios exists before the start of the SAAM process, it is the input.

SAAM provides a means to characterise how well an architectural design responds to the demands placed on it by each scenario. The results of such analysis on each scenario form the second intermediate output of the analysis process. It is the base for further analysis of the interactions between the scenarios.

SAAM measures, among other things, how many scenarios cause changes to the same architectural components; this is called *clustering*. However, in no case are absolute numbers on some mythical scale of 'architectural excellence' produced. SAAM is predicated on the principle that there is no such scale. An architecture's suitability depends entirely on the context in which it is being developed. Recall Mayall's principles of design discussed in Chapter 1, such context will inevitably change as time goes by.

If a single architecture is evaluated, the SAAM indicates places where the architecture fails to meet the quality requirements. It provides the information for how to improve the design. If more than one architectural design is evaluated, the method can also produce a relative ranking on the candidates being compared. This provides relatively objective information to support the design decisions to take which candidate for further development.

10.2 THE PROCESS

As shown in Figure 10.1, the process of applying the analysis method SAAM consists of a number of activities.

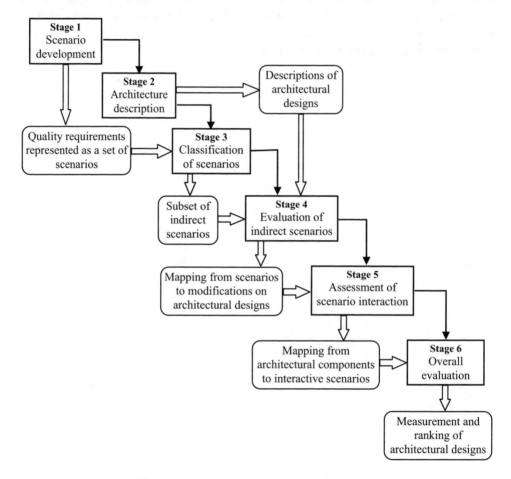

Figure 10.1 Activities in SAAM analysis

In the sequel, we will use an example, Keywords in Context index system, to illustrate the analysis process. The specification of the problem is given in Figure 10.2.

A KWIC index system is primarily used to create an index that is quickly searchable because every keyword can be looked up alphabetically even if it does not appear at the beginning of the original index phrase. Its practical instances are widely used by computer scientists. For example, the 'permuted' [sic] index for the

Unix Man pages is essentially such a system. In 1972, David Parnas [3] used this problem to demonstrate the use of information-hiding as a design discipline. In the 1990's, Mary Shaw and David Garlan [4] used this example to illustrate the effect of changes on software design. Here, we take two designs of the system as examples to show how SAAM is applied to software architectural designs.

Keyword in Context Index System (KWIC):

The Functional Requirements

The keyword in context (KWIC) index system accepts an ordered sequence of lines of text. Each line is an ordered sequence of words, and each word is an ordered sequence of characters. A line may be 'circularly shifted' by repeatedly removing the first word and appending it at the end of the line. The KWIC index system outputs a listing of all circular shifts of all lines in alphabetical order.

The following is an example of the input and output from a KWIC system.

Input: Sequence of lines

An Introduction To Software Architecture

Keyword In Context

Output: Circularly shifted, alphabetically ordered lines

An Introduction To Software Architecture

Architecture An Introduction To Software

Context Keyword In

In Context Keyword

Introduction To Software Architecture An

Keyword In Context

Software Architecture An Introduction To

To Software Architecture An Introduction

Figure 10.2 Functional requirements of the KWIC index system

10.2.1 Development of scenarios

The set of scenarios used in the analysis of software architecture should represent the kinds of activities that the system must support and the kinds of changes that will be made to the system in the future as expected or foreseen. In developing these scenarios, it must capture all important uses of the system from all stakeholders and users of the system in concern of all quality attributes that the system is to satisfy. Thus, scenarios will represent tasks relevant to different stakeholders such as end user, customer, marketing specialist, system administrator, maintainer, and developer.

Systematically identifying all important scenarios is not an easy task. A good approach to the identification task is to consider various stakeholders and their interaction with the system. SAAM, therefore, emphasises the involvement of peoples who represent various stakeholders in scenario elicitation. It is suggested that they meet at a workshop to elicit and document the scenarios and to agree on weighting on the importance of the scenarios. Such a brainstorming workshop serves as the base of SAAM analysis.

Generally speaking, the identification of scenarios belongs to requirements engineering, rather than design. The including of scenario elicitation is due to the current practice of requirements engineering not providing the required scenarios that represent quality requirements. If detailed quality requirements are available, scenarios should be identified and described according to the requirements.

For example, in the case study on the architectural designs of the KWIC index system, Mary Shaw and David Garlan [4] are concerned with the set of quality issues given in Figure 10.3. From these quality concerns, we can identify the following scenarios related to modifiability.

- *Scenario 1.* To operate in the batch fashion: line shifting is to be performed on all lines after they are read;

- *Scenario 2.* To operate in the incremental fashion: line shifting is to be performed on each line as it is read from the input device;

- *Scenario 3.* To eliminate noise words in the shifted lines;

- *Scenario 4.* To change the internal representation of the lines (e.g. compressed or uncompressed);

- *Scenario 5.* To change the internal representation of intermediate data structure (e.g. either store the shifted lines directly or store an index to the shifted words);

- *Scenario 6.* To operate in the on demand fashion: line shifting is to be performed when the alphabetisation requires a new set of shifted lines;

- *Scenario 7.* To operate interactively on the input: to allow the user to insert and delete lines from the original list of lines.

- *Scenario 8.* To operate interactively on the output: to allow the user to insert and delete lines from the circular shifted lists.

Whether a scenario is to be used in the SAAM analysis depends on whether the scenario is considered as important.

The KWIC Index System: Quality Concerns

The software that calculates keywords in context should also be efficient in both space and time. Its components should serve as reusable entities. It should be able to support the following changes in the future.

1. *Changes in the processing algorithm*: For example, line shifting can be performed on each line as it is read from the input device, on all the lines after they are read, or on demand when the alphabetisation requires a new set of shifted lines.

2. *Changes in data representation*: For example, lines, words, and characters can be stored in various ways. Similarly, circular shifts can be stored explicitly or implicitly (as pairs of index and offset).

3. *Enhancement to system function*: For example, modify the system to eliminate circular shifts that start with certain noise words (such as a, an, and, etc.), change the systems to be interactive, and allow the user to delete lines from the original lists (or from the circular shifted lists).

Figure 10.3 Quality concerns of KWIC

10.2.2 Description of candidate architecture

The candidate architecture or architectures should be described in an architectural notation that is well understood by the parties involved in the analysis. These architectural descriptions must indicate the system's computation and data components as well as all relevant connections. Accompanying this description of the architecture is a description of how the system behaves over time, or a more dynamic representation of the architecture. This may take the form of a natural language specification of the overall behaviour or some other more formal and structured specification.

For the KWIC index system, four architectural designs have been proposed in the literature and investigated by Mary Shaw and David Garlan in their case studies. Here, we use two of them, the shared data architecture and the abstract data type architecture, as the examples to illustrate the subsequent analysis activities.

The architectural design of the KWIC index system in the main-program-subroutine with shared data style is depicted in Figure 10.4. It decomposes the system according to the four basic functions performed by the system: input, shift, alphabetise and output. These computational components are coordinated as subroutines by a main program that sequences through them in turn. Data is communicated between the components through shared storage ('core storage'). Communication between the computational components and the shared data is an unconstrained read-write protocol. This is possible because the coordinating program guarantees sequential access to the data.

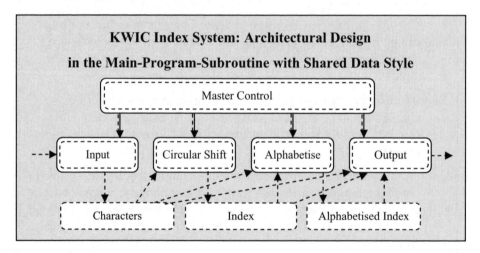

Figure 10.4 Design of KWIC in shared-memory architecture

This solution allows data to be represented efficiently, since computations can share the same storage. The original input of the sequence of lines of characters is stored in the shared data storage Characters. A circular shift of a line is represented by a pair of indexes <line, character> and stored in the data storage Index. For each pair of indexes <line, character>, the line is an integer that gives the position of the first character of the line in the data storage Characters. The character is an integer that gives the position of the first character of the shifted line. This representation avoids the duplication of all the characters in the original input. Alphabetised Index is an array of integers. Each integer points to a circular shifted line in the Index. The solution also has a certain intuitive appeal, since distinct computational aspects are isolated in different modules.

However, as Parnas argued, it has a number of serious drawbacks in terms of its ability to handle changes. In particular, a change in the data storage format will affect almost all of the modules. Similarly, changes in the overall processing algorithm and enhancements to system function are not easily accommodated. Finally, this decomposition is not particularly supportive of reuse.

The architectural design in abstract data type style decomposes the system into a similar set of five modules, as shown in Figure 10.5. However, in this case data is no longer directly shared by the computational components. Instead, each module provides an interface that permits other components to access data only by invoking procedures in that interface.

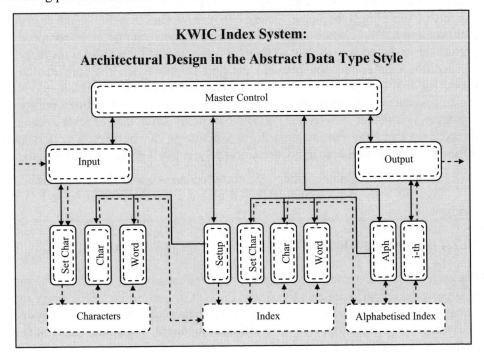

Figure 10.5 Abstract data type architecture

This solution provides the same logical decomposition into processing modules as the first. However, it has a number of advantages over the first solution when design changes are considered. In particular, both algorithms and data representations can be changed in individual modules without affecting others. Moreover, reuse is better supported than in the first solution because modules make fewer assumptions about the others with which they interact.

On the other hand, as pointed out by Garlan, *et al.*, the solution is not particularly well suited to certain kinds of functional enhancements. The main problem is that to add new functions to the system, the implementers must either modify the existing modules – compromising their simplicity and integrity – or add new modules that lead to performance penalties. The following sub-sections will show how these drawbacks of the designs can be revealed by applying SAAM.

10.2.3 Classification of scenarios

There is an important distinction between two types of scenarios. Recall that a scenario is a brief description of some anticipated or desired use of a system. The system may directly support that scenario, meaning that anticipated use requires no modification to the system for the scenario to be performed. This would usually be determined by demonstrating how the existing architecture would behave in performing the scenario (rather like a walk-through simulation of the system conducted in terms of the architectural constructs). If a scenario is not directly supported, there must be some changes to the system that we could represent architecturally. This change could be a change to how one or more components perform an assigned activity, the addition of a component to perform some activity, the addition of a connection between existing components, or a combination of these. The first type of scenario is referred to as direct scenario, and the second as indirect scenario. It is worth noting that a scenario is direct or indirect only with respect to a particular architecture. A candidate architecture may execute a scenario directly; another may require modification before it can be executed. It is such differences that enable us to apply scenario analysis to assess architectural design.

For the KWIC example, among the eight scenarios given above, only scenario 1 is direct for both of two candidates. All others are indirect with respect to the candidates.

10.2.4 Scenario evaluation

For each indirect scenario, the changes to the architecture that are necessary for it to support the scenario must be listed, and the cost of performing each change must be estimated. A modification to an architecture means that either a new component or connection is introduced or an existing component or connection requires a change in its specification.

For example, for the scenario 2 of the KWIC example, i.e. the scenario of operation in an incremental fashion, the following modifications on the shared data architecture must be made to support it.

(1) *Modification of the Input component*: The Input component must be modified so that after reading each line from the input device, it must pass the control back to the master control component.

(2) *Modification of the Master Control component*: The control component must be modified so that it repetitively calls the subroutines Input, Circular Shift and Alphabetise rather than just once.

(3) *Modification of the Alphabetiser component*: The Alphabetiser must now use an incremental sorting algorithm so that circular shifted lines can be added into sorted lines incrementally.

By the end of this stage, there should be a summary table that lists all scenarios (direct and indirect). For each indirect scenario, the effect or set of changes that the scenario has on the architecture should be described. A weighting of the difficulty must also accompany this stage. Usually, this weighting is coarse grained, based on the understanding of the architecture. A tabular summary is especially useful when comparing alternative architectural candidates because it provides an easy way to determine which architecture better supports a collection of scenarios.

For example, Table 10.1 shows the evaluation of shared data architecture by using the scenarios 1 to 5. The completion of the form for scenarios 6, 7 and 8 is left as an exercise for the readers.

Table 10.1 Evaluation of shared data architecture for KWIC

Scenario			Modification	
No	Description	Type	Component	Change
1	To operate in the batch fashion	Direct		
2	To operate in the incremental fashion	Indirect	Input	To yield control after reading each line
			Master Control	To call subroutines repetitively rather than just once
			Alphabetiser	To use an incremental sorting algorithm
3	To eliminate noise words in shifted lines	Indirect	Circular shift	To eliminate shifted sentences beginning with a noise word
4	To change the internal representation of lines	Indirect	Input	To modify the implementation according to the new data representation
			Circular shift	
			Alphabetiser	
			Output	
5	To change the internal representation of intermediate data structure	Indirect	Circular shift	To modify the implementation according to the new data representation
			Alphabetiser	
			Output	

10.2.5 Revealing scenario interaction

When two or more indirect scenarios require changes to a single component of a system, they are said to *interact* on that component. Scenario interaction is important to highlight because it exposes the allocation of functionality to the product's design. The interaction of semantically unrelated scenarios explicitly shows which system modules are computing semantically unrelated functions. Areas of high scenario interaction reveal potential poor separation of concerns in a system component. Thus, areas of scenario interaction indicate where the designer should focus subsequent attention.

The amount of scenario interaction is related to metrics such as structural complexity, coupling, and cohesion. High interaction among scenarios that are fundamentally different corresponds to low cohesion and suggests high structural complexity. High interaction among fundamentally similar scenarios signals high cohesion. Therefore, scenario interaction is likely to be strongly correlated with the number of defects in the final product.

Figure 10.6 gives the interactions between the first 5 scenarios on various components of the shared data architecture. In the diagram shown in Figure 10.6, the components that need modifications in a scenario is marked on the right upper corner with the number of the scenario.

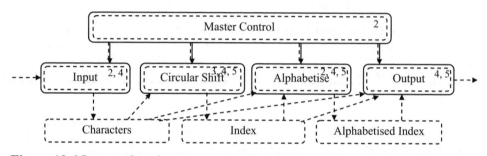

Figure 10.6 Interactions between scenarios on shared data store architecture

Compared with the interactions between the first 5 scenarios in the abstract data type architecture shown in Figure 10.7, we can see that the abstract data type architecture is superior to the shared data architecture because the latter has more scenario interaction. It has two components involved in interactions among three scenarios, which are semantically different to achieve modification to satisfy all the requirements contained in the scenarios.

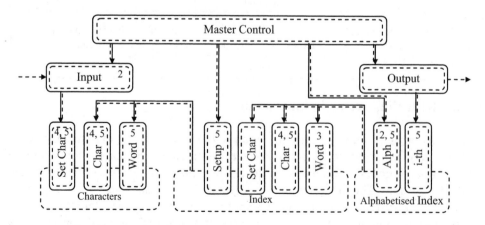

Figure 10.7 Interactions between scenarios on abstract data type architecture

10.2.6 Overall evaluation

If architectures are being compared, a weight should be assigned to each scenario and scenario interaction in terms of their relative importance. The weighting should be used to determine an overall ranking of the candidate architectures.

The purpose of assigning weights is to resolve the situation in which the first candidate architecture scores well on one half of the scenarios, and the second candidate architecture scores better on the other half. Assigning weights is a subjective process involving all stakeholders. Rather than offering a single architecture metric, SAAM produces a collection of small metrics, a set of per-scenario analysis. It is left to the users of SAAM (i.e. the analyst) to determine which scenarios are most important to them so that they can resolve cases in which the candidates outscore one another on different scenarios.

The following table gives the overall evaluation of the shared data architecture and the abstract data type architecture. The metrics used in the table is the number of components that need change over the total number of components in the system in each scenario. It is a kind of measurement of the cost needed to make the modification. The weights assigned to the scenarios are the predictions on the probability that such a scenario will happen. Therefore, the overall measurement of the architecture is a kind of expected modification cost. The result shows that abstract data type architecture has a lower expected modification cost than shared data architecture. This result is consistent with our intuition.

Table 10.2 Evaluation of KWIC architectures

Scenario			Modification Cost / Effort	
No.	Description	Weight	Shared data	Abstract data type
2	To operate in an incremental fashion	45%	3/5	2/12
3	To eliminate noise words in shifted lines	35%	1/5	1/12
4	To change the internal representation of lines	10%	4/5	3/12
5	To change the internal representation of intermediate data structure	10%	3/5	6/12
Overall			48	17.9

It should be noticed that such evaluation is subjective in the sense that the selection of metrics for measuring the architecture against each scenario, and the assignment of weights to scenarios. Once such selections have been done, the other tasks of the evaluation are less subjective. In this way, subjectivity can be reduced to the minimum.

The process of performing a SAAM analysis also helps to gain a more complete understanding of the competing architectures. This understanding, rather than just a scenario-based table, is useful for performing comparative analysis.

10.3 CASE STUDY: ANALYSING ARCHITECTURAL DESIGNS OF A KEYWORD FREQUENCY VECTOR EXTRACTION SYSTEM

In this section, we give a complete example of software architectural analysis using the SAAM method. We analyse the architectural designs made in Chapter 7 of the Keyword Frequency Vector extraction system and compare them.

10.3.1 Development of scenarios

The scenarios used in this example are developed based on the quality requirements on modifiability specified in section 7.3. They are listed below.

- *Scenario* 1: Extract keyword frequency vector incrementally as a paragraph is read from the input device;

- *Scenario* 2: Extract keyword frequency vector on the whole text file after it is read;

- *Scenario* 3: Extract keyword frequency vector on demand when the keyword frequency vector is required;

- *Scenario* 4: Change the data representation of text;

- *Scenario* 5: Change the data representation of words;

- *Scenario* 6: Change the data representation of characters;

- *Scenario* 7: Change the data representation of keyword frequency vector;

- *Scenario* 8: Treat synonyms as the same word in the extraction of keyword frequency vectors;

- *Scenario* 9: Delete and insert words from the original text.

The descriptions of the architectures were given in Chapter 7. They are not repeated here. We now analyse the architectural design against each scenario and identify the interactions between the scenarios in each architectural design.

10.3.2 Main program/subroutine with shared data architecture

A. Classification of scenarios

The scenario 2 that extracts keyword frequency vector on the whole text file is a direct scenario. The architectural design of the system is supposed to operate in this way. However, in all the other scenarios, the modifications must be made. Therefore, all other scenarios are indirect scenarios.

B. Assessment on each indirect scenario

For each indirect scenario, modifications on the components must be identified. Sometimes, new components may be introduced. The following discuss the required modifications for each indirect scenario.

(1) Scenario 1: Extract keyword frequency vector incrementally.

In this scenario, the components Input, Statistics and Master Control must be modified as follows.

Input: To modify the component so that it yields control after reading each paragraph.

Statistics: To change the algorithm to be incremental.

Master control: to call the subroutines of Input, Delete Small Words, Reduce and Statistics repetitively until all the paragraphs are processed, then call the Sorting and Output subroutines.

(2) Scenario 3: Extract keyword frequency vector on demand.

Only the Master Control component needs modification.

Master Control: To change the condition under which the subroutines are called.

(3) Scenario 4: Change the data representation of text.

The change of the representation of text affects four components: Input, Delete Small Words, Reduce and Statistics. The modifications on each component are given below.

Input: To change the representation of the output of the component so that new representation of text can be generated.

Delete Small Words: To change the algorithm that tests if a word in the new representation is a small word.

Reduce: To change the algorithm that looks up the dictionary of a word in the new representation to find the original form of the word and to change the algorithm that replaces the word with the original form represented in the new way.

Statistics: To change the algorithm that the frequency of a keyword in the new representation is calculated.

(4) Scenarios 5 and 6: Change the data representation of words and characters.

This is a special case for scenario 4 for this architectural design because the representation of words and characters is a part of the representation of text. Therefore, the required modifications on the components are the same as in scenario 4.

(5) Scenario 7: Change the data representation of keyword frequency vector.

There are three components in the shared data architecture that are affected by the representation of keyword frequency vectors: Statistics, Sorting and Output. The required modifications are given below.

Statistics: To change the output with new representation of keyword frequency vectors.

Sorting: To change the algorithm that sorts keyword-frequency pairs according to the frequency represented in the new format.

Output: To change the algorithm that reads the pairs of keyword/frequency in representation format.

(6) Scenario 8: Treat synonyms as the same word.

In the simple case that only synonymous words are considered as the same, the Reduce component and the dictionary need modification. If phrases are required to be replaced by its synonymous word, Delete Small Words and Reduce must be combined into one component and new algorithm must be used.

(7) Scenario 9: Delete and insert words from the original text.

Since the components Delete Small Words and Reduce operate on the shared data Text, users' interactive deletion and insertion of words into text cannot be easily incorporated into the program. A major redevelopment of the system is inevitable.

The above analysis is summarised in Table 10.3.

C. Reveal scenario interaction

The interactions among scenarios are marked on the architectural design diagrams as shown in Figure 10.8.

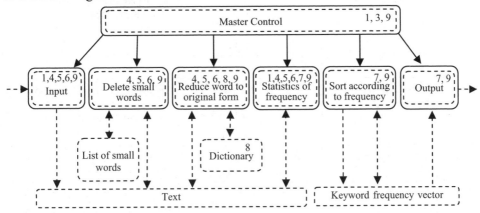

Figure 10.8 Interaction among scenarios on shared data store architecture

Table 10.3 Evaluation of the main program/subroutine shared data architecture

Scenario			Modification	
No.	Description	Type	Component	Change
1	Extract keyword frequency vector incrementally	Indirect	Input	To yield control after reading each paragraph
			Statistics	To change the algorithm to be incremental
			Master control	To call the subroutines repetitively
2	Extract keyword frequency vector on the whole text file	Direct		
3	Extract keyword frequency vector on demand	Indirect	Master control	To change the condition of calling the subroutines
4	Change the data representation of text	Indirect	Input	To change the implementation according to the new data representation of text
			Delete words	
			Reduce	
			Statistics	
5	Change the data representation of words		Input	To change the implementation according to the new data representation of word
			Delete words	
			Reduce	
			Statistics	
6	Change the data representation of characters		Input	To change the implementation according to the new data representation of characters
			Delete words	
			Reduce	
			Statistics	
7	Change the data representation of keyword frequency vector		Statistics	To change the implementation according to the new data representation of KFV
			Sort KFV	
			Output	
8	Treat synonyms as the same word	Indirect	Reduce / Dictionary	Change the dictionary and/or the reduce algorithm
9	Delete and insert words	Indirect	All	A major re-development may be necessary

10.3.3 Abstract data type architecture

For the abstract data type architecture, scenario 2 'extract KFV on the whole text' is the direct scenario; others are indirect. Table 10.4 summarises the required modifications to support each indirect scenario.

Table 10.4 Evaluation of the abstract data type architecture

Scenario			Modification	
No.	Description	Type	Component	Change
1	Extract KFV incrementally	Indirect	Input	To yield control after reading each paragraph
			Master control	To call the subroutines repetitively
2	Extract KFV on the whole text file	Direct		
3	Extract KFV on demand	Indirect	Master control	To change the condition of calling subroutines
4	Change the data representation of text	Indirect	Setup	To change the implementation according to the new data representation of text
			Take word	
			Is text empty?	
5	Change the data representation of words	Indirect	Is small word	To change the implementation according to the new data representation of word
			Reduce	
6	Change the data representation of characters	Indirect	Setup	To change the implementation according to the new data representation of characters
			Take word	
			Is text empty	
7	Change the data representation of keyword frequency vector	Indirect	Initialise	To change the implementation according to the new data representation of KFV
			Add word	
			Take KFV	
			Is KFV empty?	
8	Treat synonyms as the same word in the extraction	Indirect	Reduce	Change the reduce algorithm and the dictionary used by the function
9	Delete and insert words from the original text	Indirect	Master control	Add user interface and corresponding control to allow user to insert or delete text
			Insert word	Additional component as a part of text ADT to allow user to insert word into text
			Delete word	Additional component as a part of text ADT to allow user to delete text
			Delete from KFV	Additional component as a part of KFV ADT to update the KFV after deleting a word from the text

The interactions between scenarios are shown in Figure 10.9.

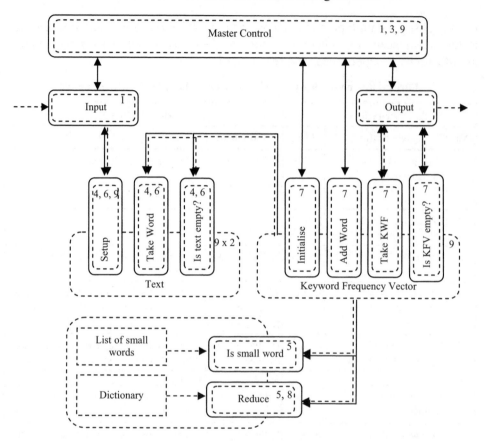

Figure 10.9 Interaction among scenarios on abstract data type architecture

10.3.4 Implicit invocation architecture

For implicit invocation architecture, scenarios 1, 2, and 3 are all direct scenarios. Scenario 9 is also a direct scenario. The required modifications to support other scenarios are summarised in Table 10.5.

Table 10.5 Evaluation of the implicit invocation architecture

Scenario			Modification	
No.	Description	Type	Component	Change
1	Extract keyword frequency vector incrementally	Direct		
2	Extract keyword frequency vector on the whole text file	Direct		
3	Extract keyword frequency vector on demand	Direct		
4	Change the data representation of text	Indirect	Insert	To change the implementation according to the new data representation of text
			Delete	
			Take Word	
			Is text empty?	
5	Change the data representation of words	Indirect	Is small word	To change the implementation according to the new data representation of word
			Reduce	
6	Change the data representation of characters	Indirect	Insert	To change the implementation according to the new data representation of characters
			Delete	
			Take word	
			Is text empty?	
7	Change the data representation of keyword frequency vector	Indirect	Add word	To change the implementation according to the new data representation of KFV
			Delete Word	
			Take KFV	
			Is KFV empty?	
8	Treat synonyms as the same word in the extraction	Indirect	Reduce	Change the reduce algorithm and the dictionary used by the function
9	Delete and insert words from the original text	Direct		

The interactions between the scenarios are shown in Figure 10.10.

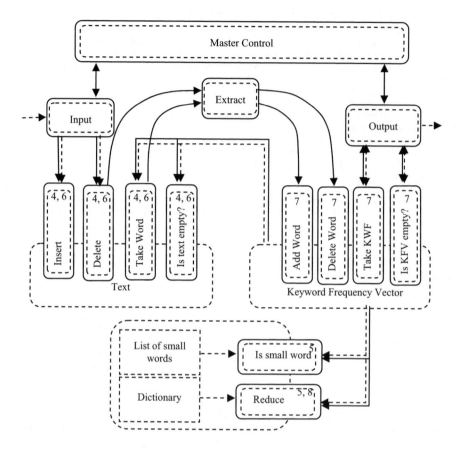

Figure 10.10 Interaction among scenarios on implicit invocation architecture

10.3.5 Pipe-and-filter architecture

For the pipe-and-filter architecture, there are two direct scenarios. They are scenarios 1 and 2. The required modifications on each indirect scenario are summarised in Table 10.6.

Table 10.6 Evaluation of the pipe-and-filter architecture

Scenario			Modification	
No.	Description	Type	Component	Change
1	Extract keyword frequency vector incrementally	Direct		
2	Extract keyword frequency vector on the whole text file	Direct		
3	Extract keyword frequency vector on demand	Indirect	Input / Output filters	To change the condition executing the input filter or output filter
4	Change the data representation of text	Indirect	1 or 2 components	Changing the format of the output streams of a filter will force the downstream filter to be modified
5	Change the data representation of words			
6	Change the data representation of characters			
7	Change the data representation of keyword frequency vector	Indirect	Output	To change the implementation according to the new data representation of KFV
8	Treat synonyms as the same word in the extraction	Indirect	Reduce	Change the reduce algorithm and the dictionary used by the function
9	Delete and insert words from the original text	Indirect	The whole system	No easy way to modify the system to support this scenario. Major re-development is required

The interactions between the scenarios are shown in Figure 10.11.

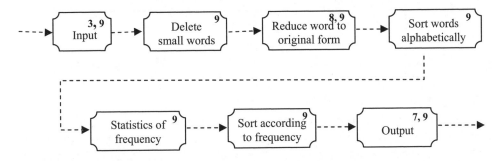

Figure 10.11 Interaction among scenarios on pipe-and-filter architecture

10.3.6 Overall evaluation

Similar to the example of the KWIC problem, we assigned weights to the scenarios according to our expectation on how probable the scenario will happen. The metric for the evaluation of a particular architecture on a given scenario is the number of components needing modification over the total number of components. The result of the evaluation is therefore an estimation of the expected cost of modifications on the architecture.

Table 10.7 Evaluation of KFV architectures

Scenarios		Architectures			
No.	Weight	Shared data	Abstract data type	Implicit invocation	Pipe-and-filter
1	20	5/7	2/12	0	0
2	5	0	0	0	0
3	15	1/7	1/12	0	1/7
4	5	4/7	3/12	4/14	2/7
5	5	4/7	2/12	2/14	2/7
6	5	4/7	3/12	4/14	2/7
7	10	3/7	4/12	4/14	1/7
8	15	1/7	1/12	1/14	1/7
9	20	7/7	4/12	0	7/7
Overall		51.43	19.15	7.49	30.00

The result of comparison shows that shared data architecture is the most expensive design to modify, while abstract data type and implicit invocation are the best with respect to modifiability. Notice that, the overall result of comparison heavily depends on two factors: the set of scenarios and the weights assigned to each scenario.

SUMMARY

SAAM is a scenario-based software architectural analysis method suitable for evaluation and analysis of modifiability. There are two types of input to the analysis: the architectural designs and the quality requirements. The process of SAAM analysis consists of the following activities:

(1) *Development of scenarios.* Scenarios describe the interactions between stakeholders and the system. Quality requirements can be represented in a more detailed context by a set of scenarios.

(2) *Description of candidate architectures.* Software architecture to be evaluated and compared are represented in a form understood by all stakeholders involved in the analysis.

(3) *Classification of scenarios into two types: direct scenarios and indirect scenarios.* Direct scenarios are those that the architecture supports directly without need of any modification to the system. Indirect scenarios are those that the architecture does not support and requires modifications to support the scenario.

(4) *Individual evaluation of indirect scenarios.* Each indirect scenario is further analysed to identify the required modifications of the components and the costs of such modifications.

(5) *Assessment of scenario interaction.* A component may need modifications in a number of scenarios. To support all these scenarios, the component needs to be modified to satisfy all the requirements imposed by these scenarios. Such situations are complicated and difficult to find a solution. The assessment of scenario interaction identifies such scenario interactions.

(6) *Overall evaluation.* Weights are assigned to scenarios according to their importance and costs of the modifications on the components are estimated so that numerical comparison between architectural designs can be made with minimum subjectivity.

In this chapter, we demonstrated how to analyse each individual architectural design as well as the comparison of a collection of designs by using SAAM. Such analysis and comparison does not simply tell us whether an architectural design is good or bad, but also tells us where the problems are and in what scenarios the problem may occur. This provides detailed information for software designers to improve their designs so that the problems are solved, or to take other technical and/or management actions to prevent the problem occurring or to reduce the consequences when the problem does occur.

FURTHER READINGS

SAAM was originally proposed to analyse the modifiability based on information presented in software architectural designs. It has been proven useful for assessing other quality attributes related to the modification of a software system, such as portability, extensibility, integrateability, etc. as well as functional coverage, performance and reliability. However, these aspects were superseded by the ATAM (Architecture Tradeoff Analysis Method), which will be discussed in the next chapter.

SAAM method is presented in [2] and with case studies in Chapter 9 of [5]. The book *Evaluating Software Architectures: Methods and Case Studies* written by Paul Clements, Rick Kazman, and Mark Klien published in 2002 is devoted to the evaluation of software architectures as the title indicated [1]. It discussed and illustrated three methods of evaluation and analysis of software architectural designs in great details. These methods are advocated by researchers at Software Engineering Institute (SEI) at Carnegie Mellon University, including the architecture trade-off analysis method ATAM and software architectural analysis method SAAM and active reviews for intermediate designs ARID method. In addition to the active researchers at SEI, alternative approaches to the uses of scenarios in the analysis and design of software architecture and the elicitation of scenarios have also been investigated by two research groups separately and sometimes jointly. They are the group lead by Prof. Jan Bosch at the University of Karlskrona/Ronneby in Sweden and the group led by Prof. Hans van Vlient at the Vrije University in Amsterdam in the Netherlands. A survey of the current state of art in the research on evaluation of software architecture can be found in [6].

A number of attempts to extend SAAM have been made in the past a few years. SAAMCS extends SAAM by considering the complexity of scenarios and different levels of impact of scenarios on architectural designs rather than just direct or indirect scenarios [7]. There are four levels of the impacts on architecture, which consist of (1) *No impact,* (2) *Affect on 1 component,* (3) *Affect on several components,* and (4) *Affect on the whole architecture.* SAAMER extends SAAM to evaluate architectural designs' evolution and reusability [8]. It also attempted to answer the practical question regarding when to stop generating scenarios. A stakeholder-centric approach was taken [9]. ESAAMI method combines analysis activities and reuse of domain-specific knowledge about the architectural designs by integrating the SAAM in the domain-specific and reuse-based development process [10]. Reusable software architectures are packaged with tailored analysis templates focused on the distinctive characteristics of the architectures.

Jan Bosch's book on *Design & Use of Software Architectures: Adopting and Evolving a Product-Line Approach* also contains a chapter that discusses various methods of assessing software architecture in addition to scenario-based methods [11].

EXERCISES

(10–1) Complete the SAAM analysis of shared data architectural design of KWIC software on scenarios 6, 7 and 8.

(10–2) Apply the SAAM to the architectural design in abstract data type style of KWIC software.

(10–3) Discuss the following questions.

(i) Why a design should be evaluated?

(ii) Is it a good practice to make more than one design and to compare them? Why?

(iii) How should scenarios be selected in the evaluation of a software architectural design? Why?

(iv) Does the granularity of the description of software architecture affect the analysis result? How to avoid unfair comparison caused by description granularity?

(10–4) In the examples given in this chapter, we have seen how quality requirements on modifiability can be expressed in the form of scenarios and analysed by application of SAAM. Discuss whether other quality attributes can be expressed in the form of scenarios. If the answer is yes, give examples in the analysis of the KWIC software.

REFERENCES

1 Clements, P., Kazman, R. and Klien, M., *Evaluating Software Architectures: Methods and Case Studies*, Addison Wesley, 2002.

2 Kazman, R., Abowd, G., Bass, L. and Clements, P., Scenario-based analysis of software architecture, *IEEE Software*, November, 1996.

3 Parnas, D., On the Criteria for decomposing systems into modules, CACM, Vol. 15, Nol. 12, pp1053–1058, 1972.

4 Shaw, M. and Garlan, D., *Software Architecture: Perspectives on an Emerging Discipline*, Prentice Hall, 1996.

5 Bass, L., Clements, P. and Kazman, R., *Software Architecture in Practice*, Addison Wesley, 1998.

6   Dobrica L. and Niemela, E., A survey on software architecture analysis methods, *IEEE Transactions on Software Engineering*, Vol. 28, No. 7, pp638–653, July 2002.

7   Lassing, N., Rijsenbrij, D. and van Vlient, H., On Software Architecture Analysis of Flexibility, Complexity of Changes: Size Isn't Everything, *Proc. Second Nordic Software Architecture Workshop (NOSA'99)*, pp1103–1581, 1999.

8   Lung, C.-H., Bot, S., Kalaichelvan, K. and Kazman, R., An Approach to Software Architecture Analysis for Evolution and Reusability, *Proc. CASCON'97,* Nov. 1997.

9   Bot, S., Lung, C.-H. and Farrell, M., A Stakeholder-Centric Software Architecture Analysis Approach, *Proc. Int'l Software Architecture Workshop (ISAW 2),*1996.

10   Molter, G., Integrating SAAM in Domain-Centric and Reuse-Based Development Processes, *Proc of Second Nordic Workshop Software Architecture (NOSA'99)*, pp. 1103–1581, 1999.

11   Bosch, J., *Design & Use of Software Architectures: Adopting and Evolving a Product-Line Approach,* Addison Wesley, 2000.

11 Quality Trade-off Analysis: The ATAM Method

The techniques of scenario-based evaluation and analysis of software architectural designs that we have learned so far are only good for the evaluation of a single quality attribute. When a set of quality attributes is considered at the same time, an architectural design often has to trade-off between conflict quality requirements. This is because, as we have discussed in Chapter 2, certain quality attributes are inversely interrelated. That is, two quality attributes are in conflict with each other, if an architectural design is good at one quality attribute it implies that it will be inevitably less satisfaction on the other quality attribute. Architectural designs must balance between such conflict quality requirements to achieve overall satisfactory. In the architectural design of software systems, we need to answer questions like the following.

Are there quality attributes that are in conflict with each other within a specific architectural design?

Which design decision or decisions in an architectural design bear the most impact on the quality attributes that are in conflict with each other?

Which component or connector or a set of them are most sensitive to affect or to be affected by the balance between the conflicting quality attributes?

These questions are what quality trade-off analysis methods aim at answering. They are addressed in this chapter. The objectives of this chapter are:

- To understand why quality attributes can be in confliction with each other;

- To learn how to make design decisions to balance between conflict quality attributes in architectural designs through trade-off;

- To learn how to analyse whether an architectural design demonstrates conflict quality attributes, and to identify the location of such conflictions if any.

We will study the ATAM method, which stands for architecture trade-off analysis method. It was developed by a group of computer scientists at SEI in the late 1990s and early 2000s.

The chapter is organised as follows. Section 11.1 gives a brief introduction to the process of ATAM analysis. Section 11.2 describes the activities in ATAM analysis and evaluation in detail step by step.

11.1 ATAM ANALYSIS PROCESS

ATAM is a structured method that aims at achieving repeatability in the analysis of software architectural designs. It is intended to be applied at early stages of software development during requirements and design stages when discovered problems can be solved relatively cheaply. It provides guidelines to various stakeholders to work together asking the right questions regarding the architecture under evaluation and looking for conflicts with the design objectives and resolutions to these conflicts.

ATAM emphasises the anticipation of various stakeholders. They contribute to the analysis and evaluation of architectural design with their specific expertises and various specific quality concerns. Therefore, a wide range of quality requirements can be elicited from them. Table 11.1 shows the specific quality concerns of various types of stakeholders who may participate in the ATAM analysis process.

Table 11.1 Stakeholders for an ATAM architecture evaluation

Stakeholder	Definition	Quality Concerns
Producers of the system		
Software architect	Person responsible for the architecture of the system and responsible for making trade-offs among competing quality pressures	Moderation and mediation of all the quality concerns of the other stakeholders
Developer	Coder or designer	Clarity and completeness of architecture description, high cohesion of parts, limited coupling of parts, clear interconnection mechanisms
Maintainer	Person making changes after initial deployment	Maintainability, ability to locate every place in the system that must change in response to a modification
Integrator	Developer responsible for integrating the components	Same as developer
Tester	Developer responsible for testing the system	Integrated consistent error-handling protocol; limited component coupling; high component cohesion; conceptual integrity
Standards expert	Developer responsible for knowing the details of standards (current and future) to which the software must conform	Separation of concerns, modifiability, interoperability

Performance engineer	Person who analyses system artefacts to see if the system will meet its performance and throughput requirements	Comprehension, conceptual integrity, performance, reliability
Security expert	Person responsible for making sure that the system will meet its security requirements	Security
Project manager	Person who allocates resources to teams, is responsible for meeting schedule and budget, interfaces with customer	Clear structuring of architecture to drive team formation, work breakdown structure, milestones and deadlines, etc.
Product-line manager or 'reuse czar'	Person who has a vision for how this architecture and related assets can be reused for further developing the organisation's long range goals	Reusability, flexibility
Consumers of the system		
Customer	Purchaser of the system	Schedule of completion, overall budget, usefulness of the system, meeting customers' or market's expectations
End user	Users of the implemented system	Functionality, usability
Application builder (in case of a product-line architecture)	Person who will take the architecture and any reusable components that exist with it and instantiate them to build a product	Architectural clarity, completeness, simple interaction mechanisms, simple tailoring mechanism
Mission specialist, mission planner	Representative of the customer who knows how the system is expected to be used to accomplish strategic objectives; has broader perspective than end users alone	Functionality, usability, flexibility
Service of the system		
System administrator	Person running the system (if different from user)	Ease in finding the location of problems that may arise
Network administrator	Person administrating the network	Network performance, predictability
Service representatives	People who provide support for the use and maintenance of the system in the field	Usability, serviceability, tailorability
Persons interfacing or interoperating with the software		
Representatives of the domain or community	Builders or owners of similar systems or systems with which the subject system is intended to work	Interoperability
System architect	Architect of the entire system; person who makes trade-off decisions between hardware and software and who selects the hardware environment	Portability, flexibility, performance, efficiency
Device expert	Person who knows the devices with which the software must interface; can predict future trends in hardware technology	Maintainability, performance

The evaluation takes the form of a workshop. The organisation of the workshop usually consists of the following roles.

- *Team leader*: sets up the evaluation and coordinates with various stakeholders and forms the evaluation team;

- *Evaluation leader*: runs evaluation;

- *Scenario scribe*: captures agreed-upon wording of each scenario;

- *Proceedings scribe*: captures the proceedings in electronic form on a notebook computer or in room workstation computer;

- *Timekeeper*: helps the evaluation leader to stay on schedule;

- *Process observer*: keeps notes on where the evaluation process itself could be improved or deviated from plan;

- *Process enforcer*: helps the evaluation leader remember and carry out the steps of the evaluation method;

- *Questioner*: raises issues of architectural interest that perhaps the stakeholders have not considered.

The structured process of ATAM analysis consists of 9 steps that fall into four groups:

- *Presentation*: ATAM emphasises the involvement of various types of stakeholders in the analysis of software architectural designs. Presentation plays the central role in ATAM to exchange information between different stakeholders.

- *Investigation and analysis*: ATAM is a scenario-based method. It assesses architectural design decisions against quality requirements specified in the form of scenarios. These scenarios are organised and systematically elicited.

- *Testing*: ATAM also contains activities to check the results of investigation and analysis against all stakeholders' needs.

- *Reporting*: It involves presenting the result of ATAM to all stakeholders.

Figure 11.1 illustrates the activities in ATAM analysis and their main outcomes.

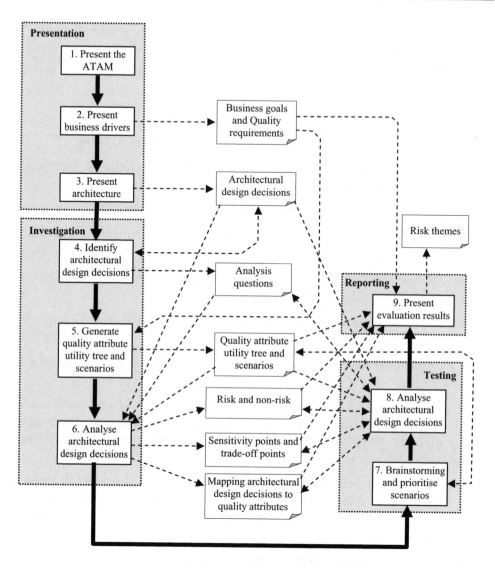

Figure 11.1 The process of ATAM analysis

The following section describes the ATAM process step by step.

11.2 ATAM ANALYSIS ACTIVITIES

We now describe the ATAM analysis activities step by step.

11.2.1 Step 1: Present the ATAM

The ATAM analysis and evaluation process starts with the evaluation leader presenting the ATAM method to all stakeholders participating in the analysis. In this step, the process that everybody will be following is explained, the techniques used in the analysis and evaluation are described, and the output of the evaluation is outlined. In this step, time for stakeholders to ask questions and the evaluation leader to answer the questions is also allowed. This step sets the context and expectations for the remainder of the activities.

11.2.2 Step 2: Present the business drivers

In this step, the project decision maker (ideally the project manager or the system's customer) presents an overview of the system from the business perspective. It aims at a good understanding of the context of developing the system and the primary business goals and motivations of the project by all participants of the evaluation exercise. The presentation should cover the following issues:

- The system's most important functions

- Relevant technical, managerial, economic or political constraints

- The business goals and context of the project

- The major stakeholders involved in the project

- The main quality requirements that shape the architectural design.

11.2.3 Step 3: Present the architectural design

In this step, the lead architect (or architectural design team) makes a presentation describing the architectural design at an appropriate level of detail. The presentation should cover the following issues:

- Technical constraints such as the operating system, hardware or middleware prescribed to use

- Other systems with which the system must interact

- Architectural design decisions made to meet the quality requirements

11.2.4 Step 4: Identify architectural design decisions[1]

The ATAM focuses on analysing an architectural design by understanding how architectural design decisions affect quality attributes. In this step, architectural design decisions are captured by the evaluation team but not analysed.

Here, architectural design decisions include the choice of architectural style or styles used in the architecture, the components and connector and their main functionalities and properties, etc. As discussed in the previous chapters, an architectural style includes a description of component types and their topology and a description of the pattern of data and control interactions among the components. A style can be considered as a set of constraints on an architecture – constraints on component types and connector types in terms of their properties and their interactions. These constraints define the set or family of architecture that satisfy them. From these constraints, we can infer the properties of the systems, especially their quality attributes as discussed in Chapter 7. This approach to the definition of software architectural styles is called *attribute-based architectural styles*. It is particularly useful in the ATAM analysis. It provides an explanation of how architectural design decisions achieve certain quality attributes.

11.2.5 Step 5: Generate the quality attribute utility tree

In this step, the evaluation team works with the project decision makers to identify, prioritise and refine the system's most important quality attribute goals. This is a crucial step that the outcome of the step will guide the remainder of the analysis process. This is accomplished by constructing a utility tree. Figure 11.2 shows a sample utility tree from [1].

A utility tree contains utility as the root node as an expression of the overall 'goodness' of the system. Quality attributes form the second level of the utility tree. Typically the quality attributes of performance, modifiability, availability, and security are the children of utility, although participants of the evaluation are free to name their own quality attributes. Under each of these quality attributes are specific quality attribute refinements. For example, in Figure 11.2, performance is decomposed into 'data latency' and 'transaction throughput'. Each of the refined quality attributes are further refined by a set of scenarios that are concrete enough

---

[1] Notice that, in the literature of ATAM method, architectural design decisions are called *architectural approaches* because not all architects are familiar with the language of architectural styles and so may not be able to enumerate a set of styles used in the architecture.

for prioritisation and analysis. The prioritisation may be on a 0 to 10 scale, or may use relative rankings such as High (H), Medium (M) and Low (L).

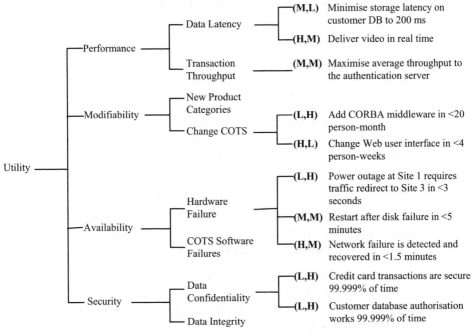

Figure 11.2 Sample utility tree

The ATAM method requires that the prioritisation of scenarios should be done along two dimensions: (a) by the importance of each scenario to the success of the system, and (b) by the degree of difficulty posed by achieving the scenario in the estimation of the architect. For example, in Figure 11.2, the scenario 'Minimise storage latency on customer DB to 200 ms' has priority (M,L). This means that it is of medium importance to the success of the system and the architect expects low difficulty to achieve this.

Constructing a utility tree with prioritised scenarios forces the evaluation team and the customer to define their quality requirements precisely with concrete context. It also serves as a plan for the remainder of the ATAM evaluation. It guides the evaluators to look at the architectural design decisions involved with satisfying the high priority scenarios of the tree.

11.2.6 Step 6: Analyse the architectural design decisions

In this step, the evaluation team use the prioritised scenarios from step 5 and the set of architectural design decisions from step 4 to probe the architectural design on how architectural design decisions realise the important quality requirements. This is done by reviewing the design decisions and identifying their risks, non-risks, sensitivity points and trade-offs. The goal of this analysis activity is to convince the evaluation team that the architectural decision being evaluated is appropriate for meeting the attribute specific requirements for which it is intended. The outputs of this step include:

- *A mapping from architectural design decisions to each relevant high-priority scenario in the utility tree.* All the architectural design decisions identified in step 4 should be covered and associated to the scenarios. If not, the reason for the discrepancy should be explained.

- *A set of analysis questions associated with each design decision in relation to the quality attributes with which its scenarios are associated.* These questions might come from stakeholders' previous experiences, documented design knowledge of the architectural style and the literature on software architecture and architectural designs.

- *The architect's responses to the questions.* These questions and answers form the rationale of the design and justifies why the architectural design decisions can meet the quality requirements.

- *A collection of identified risks, non-risks, sensitive points, and trade-offs.* Each of these is linked to the achievement of one or more quality attribute refinement in the utility tree and the design decisions that the analysis questions concerned.

The utility tree serves as the guideline to tell the evaluation team where to probe the architectural design according to the priority assigned to each scenario. Questions can then be asked according to the quality attribute to probe the architectural design decisions more deeply. The questions help the evaluation team to understand the design in detail and how general design knowledge of the architectural styles was applied in this instance. They also help the evaluation team to look for known weaknesses of the architectural design according to the general knowledge of the architectural style. Moreover, they also help the evaluation team by providing the clues for the sensitivity points and trade-offs between quality requirements made in the design decisions, and suggesting alternative design choices.

The key point in this analysis is to identify the risks and non-risks, sensitive points and trade-off points. These concepts are defined as follows.

A. Sensitive points and trade-off points

Sensitive points and trade-off points are key design decisions. A sensitivity point is a design decision, especially a property of one component or component relationship, that is critical to achieve a particular quality requirement.

For example, the following are sensitive points in architectural designs.

- The level of confidentiality in a virtual private network might be sensitive to the number of bits of encryption.

- The latency for processing a message might be sensitive to the priority of the lowest priority process involved in handling the message.

Sensitive points tell where attention should be paid in the design and analysis of software architecture in order to understand the achievement of a quality goal. Without careful consideration, a sensitive point can become a risk when design decisions are made on the sensitive point. For example, when a 32-bit encryption is decided in the design of a virtual private network, it may present a risk in the architecture with respect to the security requirement. If a very low priority is assigned to a process that is involved in handling the message, the design decision can become a risk to achieve the performance requirements of processing the message.

A trade-off point is a property that affects more than one quality attribute in an inverse way. It is a sensitive point for more than one quality attribute. The improvement of the property will help to improve at least one of these quality attributes, but will inevitably decline the other quality attributes. Therefore, a correct design decision must be made to balance these conflictions between the quality attributes demonstrated in this architectural design.

For example, changing the level of encryption could have a significant effect on both security and performance in an inverse way. Increasing the level of encryption improves the security but requires more computation time to process messages for encryption and decryption. On the other hand, if the level of encryption is decreased, the time required to process each message for encryption and decryption can be reduced and hence improve the performance, but the security is predictably lower. A difficult decision-making situation is when the message processing has hard real-time constraints and requires high security. Trade-off between these two quality requirements must be made. In other words, a balance between these two quality attributes must be achieved.

From this simple example, we can see that trade-off points are critical design decisions, which must be made with great care.

ATAM relies on the evaluation team to identify sensitive points and trade-off points. They are then classified into risks or non-risks.

B. Risks and non-risks

Risks are potentially problematic architectural design decisions. For example, consider the situation that in a design of three-tier client-server architecture of a web-based e-commerce system, the rules for writing the business logic modules are not clearly articulated. Unarticulated rules for writing the business logic can result in unintended and undesired coupling of components. This is a negative effect of the design decision of delaying the articulation of the rules. Consequently, there is a risk of resulting in replication of functionality and thereby compromising modifiability of the third tier.

In contrast to risks, a non-risk is a good design decision that quality attributes that the decision is addressing can be achieved without problem. However, non-risks inevitably rely on certain assumptions, which are often implicit. When the assumptions become no longer true, the non-risk can become problematic. Therefore, it is necessary to understand the assumptions and to explicitly document such assumptions. For example, consider again a web-based e-commence system. Assume that the message arrival rate is one per second. The architectural design of the system assigns the message processing to a server on which the processing time of each message is less than 30 ms and there is only one higher priority process on the server. One can infer that a one-second soft deadline for message processing seems reasonable because the arrival rate is bounded and the pre-emptive effects of higher priority processes is known and can be accommodated. Therefore, the decision has no risk to achieve the performance requirement of one-second soft deadline for message processing (i.e. processing a message within 1 second). This conclusion of non-risk is based on the assumptions that 'the message arrival rate is one per second', 'the server can process each message within 30 ms' and 'the existence of one higher priority process'. For the non-risk to remain a non-risk (i.e. a good design decision) the assumptions must not change. If they change, the designation of non-risk will need to be re-justified and it can become a risk. For example, if the message arrival rate becomes significantly higher than the assumption, or the processing time becomes much longer than 30 ms, or the number of higher priority processes become more than 1, the design decision can be problematic.

By the end of this step, risks, non-risks, sensitivity points and trade-off points are gathered together in separate lists. They are numbered as R1, R2, ..., Rk, for risks, N1, N2, ..., Nj for non-risks, S1, S2, ..., Si for sensitive points, and T1, T2, ..., Tn for trade-off points. The association of these with scenarios is captured and recorded in a file, of which a template was provided by the method's developers [1]. The template is shown in Figure 11.3 and an example record of the analysis of architectural designs in ATAM, also from [1], is given in Figure 11.4.

Analysis of Architectural Design				
Scenario #: *Number*	Scenario: *Text of scenario from utility tree*			
Attribute(s)	*Quality attribute(s) with which this scenario is concerned*			
Environment	*Relevant assumptions about the environment in which the system resides, and the relevant conditions when the scenario is carried out*			
Stimulus	*A precise statement of the quality attribute stimulus (e.g. function invoked, failure, threat, modification ...) embodied by the scenario*			
Response	*A precise statement of the quality attribute response (e.g. response time, measure of difficulty of modification)*			
Architectural Decisions	Sensitivity	Trade-off	Risk	Non-risk
Architectural design decisions relevant to this scenario that affect quality attribute	*Sensitive point #*	*Trade-off point #*	*Risk #*	*Non-risk #*
...	...	...	...	...
...	...	...	...	...
Reasoning	*Qualitative and quantitative rationale for why the list of architectural decision contributes to meeting each quality requirement expressed by the scenario*			
Architectural Diagram	*Diagram or diagrams of architectural views annotated with architectural information to support the above reasoning, accompanied by explanatory text if desired*			

Figure 11.3 Template for analysis of architectural designs

Analysis of Architectural Design				
Scenario #: A12	Scenario: Detect and recover from hardware failure of the primary CPU			
Attribute(s)	Availability			
Environment	Normal operation			
Stimulus	One of the CPUs fails			
Response	0.999999 availability of the switch			
Architectural Decisions	Sensitivity	Trade-off	Risk	Non-risk
Backup CPUs	S2		R8	
No backup data channel	S3	T3	R9	
Watchdog	S4			N12
Heartbeat	S5			N13
Failover routing	S6			N14
Reasoning	• Ensure no common mode failure by using different hardware and operating system (see Risk R8) • Worst-case rollover is accomplished in 4 seconds as computing state takes that long at worst • Guaranteed to detect failure within 2 seconds based on rates of heartbeat and watchdog • Availability requirement might be at risk due to lack of backup data channel (see Risk R9)			
Architectural Diagram	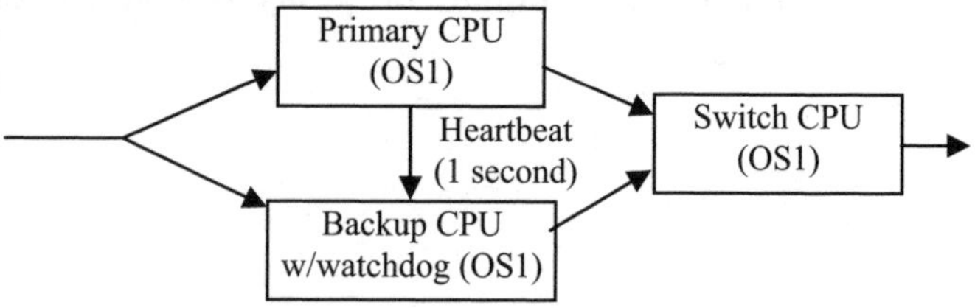 Primary CPU (OS1) — Heartbeat (1 second) — Backup CPU w/watchdog (OS1) — Switch CPU (OS1)			

Figure 11.4 Example of analysis of an architectural design on a scenario

At the end of this step, the evaluation team should have a clear picture of the most important aspect of the entire architecture, the rationale for key design decisions that have been made, and the risks, non-risks, sensitivity points and trade-off points of the architectural design.

11.2.7 Step 7: Brainstorm and prioritise scenarios

This step and the next form the testing phase of the ATAM process. In this step, a set of scenarios are generated as test cases by the stakeholders to represent their interests and understanding of quality requirements. The main purpose of scenario brainstorming is to take the pulse of the larger stakeholder community. It was claimed to work well in large groups for creating an atmosphere in which the ideas and thoughts of one person stimulate others. The process fosters communication and creativity and serves to express the collective mind of the participants. The list of scenarios generated from brainstorming are then prioritised and compared with those generated via the utility tree exercise. If the sets of scenarios do not agree with each other, for example, additional driving scenarios are discovered, this is also an important outcome.

In the brainstorming process of scenarios, three kinds of scenarios are asked for the stakeholders to consider. They are as follows.

- *Use case scenarios*. They represent the ways in which the stakeholders expect the system to be used. In each use case scenario, the stakeholder is an end user, using the system to execute some function.

- *Growth scenarios*. They represent the ways in which the architecture is expected to accommodate growth and change in the moderate near future, including expected modifications of functionality, changes in performance or availability requirements, porting to other platforms, integration with other software, and so forth.

- *Exploratory scenarios*. They represent the extreme forms of growth, i.e. the ways in which the architecture might be stressed by changes, such as dramatic new performance or availability requirements, e.g. improvement by an order of magnitude, major changes in the infrastructure or mission of the system, and so forth.

Once scenarios are collected, they are prioritised by the stakeholders through voting. A subset of the scenarios is selected for carrying forth to the subsequent steps according to the votes.

The result of scenario prioritisation is then compared with the result of utility tree exercise carried out in step 5. Each high priority scenario is placed into the utility tree and associated to an appropriate leaf node. Three things may happen when a scenario is placed into the utility tree.

(a) The scenario matches well to an existing leaf node. This means that the scenario is essentially a duplicate of a scenario that has already been considered in utility tree exercise.

(b) The scenario does not match with any existing leaf node in the utility tree, but it can be associated with an existing branch of the utility tree. This means that the scenario addresses a quality attribute that has been covered by other scenarios in the utility tree. Notice that, a scenario may be associated to more than one quality attribute. In that case, it will be placed into the leaves of several branches. Usually, this requires the scenario to be carefully reworded to ensure its relevance to the quality attributes is clear.

(c) The scenario cannot be associated to any branch of the utility tree. This means that the scenario expresses a quality requirement that has not been addressed previously in the utility tree exercise. It suggests that the architect may have failed to consider an important quality requirement. Therefore, further analysis of the architectural design on this scenario must be carried out as in step 6.

It is worth noting that although both step 5 and step 7 generate scenarios, prioritise them and associate them to various quality attributes, they serve two significantly different purposes. Step 7 is a testing step. Table 11.2 highlights the differences between these two steps.

Table 11.2 Utility tree versus scenario brainstorming

	Utility Tree	Scenario Brainstorming
Participants	Architects, project leaders	All stakeholders
Typical group size	Evaluators; 2–3 project personnel	Evaluators; 5–10 project-related personnel
Primary goals	Elicit, make concrete and prioritise the driving quality requirements Provide a focus for the remainder of the evaluation	Foster stakeholder communication to validate quality attribute goals elicited via the utility tree
Approach	General to specific: begin with quality attributes, refine until scenario emerges	Specific to general: begin with scenarios, then identify quality attributes they express

11.2.8 Step 8: Analyse the architectural design decisions

In this step, the evaluation team performs the same activities as in step 6 to analyse the architectural design against scenarios. The difference is that the set of scenarios used in this step comes from step 7 rather than step 5. When step 7 did not produce any high priority scenarios that are not covered by the set of scenarios generated in step 5, the analysis activity is simply a testing activity. Otherwise, the architectural design decisions are examined in the new scenarios and new information about the design is uncovered.

11.2.9 Step 9: Present the results

The last step of ATAM process is to summarise and report the analysis results to all stakeholders who participated in the evaluation process. It is typically in the form of a presentation by the evaluation team leader and accompanied by a more complete written report. The report should cover all aspects of the output from the ATAM analysis activities, including:

- The architectural design decisions documented;
- The set of scenarios and their prioritisation;
- The set of attribute-based questions;
- The utility tree;
- The risks discovered;
- The non-risks documented;
- The sensitivity points and trade-off points found.

In addition to these, step 9 also generates the very important final output of the ATAM: the *risk themes*.

A risk theme is a general concern of a group of interrelated risks in a design. A set of risks contained in an architectural design can often be grouped together based on some common underlying concern or system deficiency. For example, the risk of inadequate documentation and the risk of out-of-date documentation might be grouped into a risk theme stating that documentation is given insufficient consideration. The risks that the system's inability to recover from various kinds of hardware and/or software failures might be grouped into a general risk theme that insufficient attention has been paid to backup capability.

For each recognised risk theme, the evaluation team will then identify the business drivers listed in step 2 that are affected. Identification of risk themes and relating them to the business drivers enable ATAM analysis to give overall assessment of architectural design with regards to its business goals. It elevates from technical details to business and management strategic goals. Without this step, the results of the previous analysis activities would not be so useful and meaningful.

Therefore, it might be better to call this step 'overall assessment against business goals'. Alternatively, this step can be split into two steps, one focuses on the identification of risk themes and relating them to the business drivers, and the other for just reporting the results of the whole evaluation process.

SUMMARY

ATAM is a method to evaluate and analyse software architectural designs against a set of quality requirements of different quality attributes. It has the following features.

- ATAM analysis process involves various stakeholders and organises the analysis activities in the form of workshops.

- ATAM is a structured method aim to achieve repeatability of the analysis. It consists of 9 steps of well-defined analysis activities, which fall into 4 types, including *presentation*, *investigation*, *testing* and *reporting*.

- In ATAM analysis process, quality requirements are elicited from the stakeholders and represented in the form of a *utility tree*, of which the root represents the whole utility of the system, the branches represent the top level quality attributes, which can be further refined into more specific quality attributes. On the leaves of the utility tree are *scenarios* that represent the context and expected results of the quality requirements.

- During ATAM analysis, an architectural design is recognised as a set of *design decisions*, such as the selection of architectural style or styles, the functions assigned to each component and connector as well as the properties associated to each component and connector, etc.

- The ATAM analysis of architectural design is performed by mapping scenarios to design decisions that affect or are affected by the scenario. *Risks*, i.e. problematic design decisions, are identified, and *non-risks*, i.e. good design designs, are also recognised and understood by explicitly expressing their underlying assumptions. *Sensitivity points*, which are key design decisions that are critical to each quality requirement, and *trade-off points*, which affect more than one quality requirement in an inverse way, are identified and recorded. These can significantly improve the understanding of the architectural design and the way it meets the quality requirements.

- An important final step of ATAM analysis is to summarise the risks contained in a design by grouping sets of risks with a common concern and abstracting each group of risks into a *risk theme*.

- ATAM method also contains the testing of evaluation and analysis results as an integral part of its activities to check the consistency between the understandings of the design quality requirements by the architects and the other stakeholders.

FURTHER READING

The ATAM method was proposed and developed through a number of technical reports of SEI at CMU, which include [2, 3, 4, 5, 6]. Detailed description of the method and case studies can be found in [1]. The method builds on the bases of understanding software quality and software architectural styles' impacts on them. A model that related architectural styles and quality attribute is called attribute-based architectural style (ABAS) and is presented in [4]. A study of scenarios in this framework can be found in [7] and in Chapter 5 of [1].

EXERCISES

(11–1) Discuss the following questions:

(i) What does it mean by repeatability of a software development method?

(ii) What are the factors that may affect the repeatability of a software development method?

(iii) How can repeatability be achieved in software development in general, in software design, and in the analysis and evaluation of software architectural designs in particular?

(11–2) Refer to the literature on the ATAM method such as [1], to find how each activities of ATAM are normalised to achieve better repeatability.

(11–3) Discuss the following questions.

(i) What is the role of presentation activities in ATAM analysis?

(ii) What are the alternative approaches that may achieve the same purposes of presentations?

(iii) In comparison with alternative approaches, what are the advantages and disadvantages of presentations?

(11–4) (i) Give a brief definition of the concept risk and give some examples.

(ii) Discuss why an architectural design may contain risks.

(iii) Explain why risks in an architectural design should be identified.

(11–5) (i) Give a brief definition of the concept non-risk and some examples.

(ii) Discuss if non-risk may become risk and under which circumstances.

(iii) Explain why assumptions underlying a non-risk design decisions should be identified and explicitly stated.

(11–6) Explain the concept of sensitivity points and trade-off points, and give some examples.

(11–7) (i) Explain the concepts of use case scenarios, growth scenarios and exploratory scenarios and give some examples.

(ii) For each type of scenario, discuss their roles in the analysis and evaluation of architectural designs.

(iii) Classify the examples of scenarios given in Chapter 9 into use case scenarios, growth scenarios and exploratory scenarios.[2]

(11–8) Utility tree is essentially a hierarchical software quality model as discussed in Chapter 2. In the context of analysing and evaluating software architectural designs, discuss the following questions.

(i) What are the advantages and disadvantages of using a hierarchical quality model?

(ii) Whether other kinds of quality models, such as a relational model, can be used to replace utility trees?

(11–9) ATAM include testing activities as an integral part of the method.

(i) Discuss the importance of such testing activities in the analysis and evaluation of software architectural design.

(ii) Discuss why a different set of scenarios must be generated using a different way to test the correctness of the outcomes of the investigation activities in ATAM.

(11–10) In the final step of ATAM analysis, the outcomes of the previous steps are not only reported to all participants, but also summarised, especially, risk themes are formed.

(i) Explain the concept of risk themes and give some examples.

(ii) Discuss the importance to classify risks into groups and abstract from a set of individual risks into risk themes in ATAM analysis.

---

[2] Notice that, many scenarios given in Chapter 9 are stated without expected outcomes. In such a case, you may need to add a suitable expected outcome of the scenario from the specified interactions between the stakeholder and the system.

REFERENCES

1 Clements, P., Kazman, R. and Klein, M., *Evaluating Software Architectures–Methods and Case Studies*, Addison Wesley, 2002.

2 Barbacci, M., Klein, M., Longstaff, T., Weinstock, C., *Quality Attributes*, Technical Report, CMU/SEI-95-TR-021, Software Engineering Institute, Carnegie Mellon University, Dec. 1995.

3 Barbacci, M. R., Klein, M. H., Weinstock, C. B., *Principles for Evaluating the Quality Attributes of a Software Architecture*, Technical Report, CMU/SEI-96-TR-036, Software Engineering Institute, Carnegie Mellon University, March 1997.

4 Barbacci, M., Carriere, S., Feiler, P., Kazman, R., Klein, M., Lipson, H., Longstaff, T. and Weinstock, C., *Steps in an Architecture Tradeoff Analysis Method: Quality Attribute Models and Analysis*, Technical Report, CMU/SEI-97-TR-029, Software Engineering Institute, Carnegie Mellon University, May 1998.

5 Klein, M. and Kazman, R., *Attribute-Based Architectural Styles*, Technical Report, CMU/SEI-99-TR-022, Software Engineering Institute, Carnegie Mellon University, Oct. 1999.

6 Kazman, R., Klein, M. and Clements, P., *ATAM: Method for Architecture Evaluation*, Technical Report, CMU/SEI-2000-TR-004, Software Engineering Institute, Carnegie Mellon University, August 2000.

7 Kazman, R., Carriere, S. J. and Woods, S., Toward a discipline of scenario-based architectural engineering, *Annals of Software Eng.*, vol. 9, 2000.

12 Model-Based Analysis: The HASARD Method

In the previous chapters, we have studied the methods of scenario-based analysis and evaluation of software architectural designs. They enable us to find out how well a software architectural design meets quality requirements specified in the form of scenarios. A common weakness of these methods is that they have limited power to discover unknown problems that are not elicited and explicitly specified by quality requirements. To discover unknown problems of a software design is of particular importance especially when the software is for a new application domain or the design explores a new architecture. In this chapter, we will study a model-based approach to address the problem of how to analyse an architectural design in order to discover its quality features without pre-specified requirements.

We will study a method called HASARD, which stands for *Hazard Analysis of Software ARchitectural Designs*. As its name suggests, the method is based on a kind of system analysis technique called hazard analysis that is widely used in analysing safety related systems in various industry sectors. The HASARD method was based on the work initially proposed by the author and his colleague and students in [1] for analysing software architectural designs, but significant changes have been made to improve its repeatability. Further research on the development of software tools to support the uses of the method is now in progress.

The objective of this chapter is:

- To study the model-based approach to the analysis of software architectural designs, which include

  - how to represent the quality models of software systems;

  - how to construct quality models from software architectural designs;

- how to systematically analyse a quality model to derive quality features of software designs.

The chapter is organised as follows. In section 12.1, we will first generalise the notion of quality models introduced in Chapter 2 and devise a diagrammatic notation to represent quality models to enhance their expressiveness so that the specific features of the architecture and its application domain can be expressed and analysed. Section 12.2 presents a systematic method to derive software quality models from architectural designs. Section 12.3 discusses various types of quality features that can be derived from a given quality model. Section 12.4 is a case study of client-server architecture of websites that gives an example to illustrate the application of the method.

12.1 REPRESENTATION OF QUALITY MODELS

As discussed in Chapter 2, software quality models are models of software systems specifically developed for understanding, measuring and predicting the qualities of software systems. Existing quality models are generic in the sense that they are models of all software systems. However, being generic, they do not provide detailed information about a specific system.

As discussed in the previous chapters, software designers would like to know the quality of a designed system before it is implemented. For example, it is desirable to know whether a design meets a specific performance requirement under certain operation profile, and which component is crucial to meet such requirements. For an internet and world wide web based application, we also want to know whether the design of a system has a security problem, and if yes, which component or connector needs to be modified or where to add new components and/or connectors to solve the problem, etc. The ATAM method studied in Chapter 11 can be applied to obtain such information. In Chapter 10, we have also seen that SAAM can provide information about the modifiability of a software system from its architectural design. Such information is very useful for software designers to solve design problems associated with modification and maintenance problems at architectural design stage. However, both SAAM and ATAM are scenario-based methods, which are effective to analyse and evaluate architectural designs against elicited and specified quality requirements specified in the form of a set of scenarios. They use a generic quality model, in fact a hierarchical model, to guide the analysis activities in order to answer quality questions rather than to build a system specific quality model.

Existing software quality models have been represented using simple and intuitive notations. For example, hierarchical models are represented in the form of a tree with nodes as quality attributes and arcs as positive relations between the attributes. Relational models use matrices that each row and column represents a quality attribute and the values of the matrix represent the stereotype relations between the corresponding attributes. Such representations do not refer to any elements of the software product whose quality is under investigation. Hence, they are independent of the software product. These representations are suitable for generic quality models that are intended to be applicable to all software systems.

Although such generic models play significant roles in software development, quality models that make no explicit references to the product specific features have limited usefulness. A way to overcome this weakness is to follow the Dromey's principle [2, 3], which is stated below.

- *Dromey's principle.* In a quality model, abstract quality attributes must be linked to the tangible software properties through the quality-carrying properties of the components.

Notice that, in the statement of Dromey's principle, the 'components of a software product' refer to the elements of the product. In the context of software architectural designs, it can be any components and connectors of the architecture, etc. The 'quality-carrying property' means any property of the element that may affect the quality of the element and/or the whole system somehow. The way that a quality-carrying property of a component affects a quality attribute of the system is important because it often provides some insight information that can significantly improve the usability of quality models.

For example, safety is a property of software systems that ensures the physical system controlled by the software will not harm human life and damage environment and property. It is an important quality attribute of safety critical systems. It is of extreme importance for engineers to understand how faults and failures of the components are related to the safety of the system. Only when such information is available, can design solutions be put forward to eliminate the specific types of faults of the component and to prevent the occurrences of the specific types of failure modes that may contribute to safety. Moreover, testing of the system can then directly target the safety-related components and events to ensure system safety.

A quality attribute, such as usability, modifiability and maintainability, are usually abstract. Consequently, the links between two abstract properties cannot be easily established or validated. However, abstract properties usually demonstrate themselves through various concrete events and observable phenomena, which are tangible and observable. For example, the poor usability of a web page is clearly demonstrated if the user cannot find the required information via following hyperlinks. While relationships between abstract properties are difficult to establish and validate, the relationships between observable phenomena are often self-evident in the context of the system. For example, when the incorrectness of an HTML file of a web page is demonstrated by the fact of containing broken links, the usability of the system will suffer because the user would not be able to find the information through the hyperlinks. This example shows that if the observation of one phenomenon implies the occurrence of another phenomenon, the corresponding abstract properties must have a causal relationship. Many authors have used such rationale in the construction of generic quality models. Unfortunately, such rationale has never been included in existing quality models. Such information is useful not only for design but also for many other software development activities. For example, in the design and analysis of safety critical systems, we not only need to know if the system is safe, we also need to know how the system will behave if a certain event happens. This provides the crucial information for software testers to develop test cases to check if the system correctly implements the safety as designed.

In [1], a diagrammatic notation to represent quality models was proposed that enables all the information discussed above to be included into a quality model. As shown in Figure 12.1 below, in the graphic notation of quality models, a quality model is a directed graph, which consists of two kinds of elements: the *nodes* and *links*.

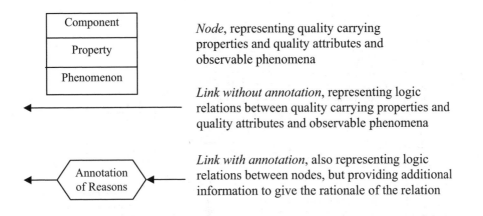

Figure 12.1 The notation for HASARD representation of quality models

Each node contains three parts specified in three compartments:

(1) an element of the system, which can be a component, a connector, a subsystem, or the system itself, etc;

(2) a quality-carrying property of the element; and

(3) an observable phenomenon of the property.

The links are directed arcs between the nodes. A link from node A to node B means that the observation of the phenomenon on node A implies the occurrence of the phenomenon on node B. Each link may contain an optional annotation for the reasons why the two nodes are related.

Figure 12.2 gives a fragment of quality model of web-based information systems. This fragment of quality model shows that the usability of a web-based system is related to the correctness, responsiveness, HTML files' property of well structured, compatibility, and the usability of the online help sub-system. For example, it shows that the compatibility of the code on the client side will affect the usability, while there is no compatibility issue associated to the server side code. It also indicates in detail how these properties are related to whether the user can find the required information. For example, if a file's size is large, it will increase the response time. If the response time is longer than the time-out setting, the browser will regard the requested file as unavailable. The designer can use this quality model to ensure that each page is in a reasonable size so that a quick response time can be achieved.

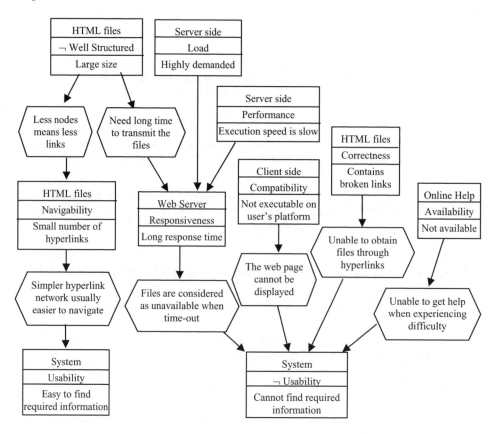

Figure 12.2 A fragment of a quality model of web-based information systems

It should be noticed that, the links between the nodes must be understood as the implications of one phenomenon to another, rather than simply the relationship between two quality attributes. For example, large sized HTML files may contain fewer hyperlinks between them than smaller sized files. This makes the navigation between the files easier. Consequently, the user may find it is easier to use. Therefore, it is positively related to the usability of the system. On one hand, the size of HTML files determines the response time and, in extreme cases, over sized

HTML files may cause poor usability. On the other hand, the sizes of HTML files determines the complexity of the hyperlink network, hence the navigability of the system. Large sized HTML files may help to reduce the complexity and improve usability. Such complicated relationships between two quality attributes cannot be represented in an existing quality model that only relates two abstract quality attributes. As we will see later in the chapter, the size of HTML files is a trade-off point that can be identified by analysing the quality model.

12.2 CONSTRUCTION OF QUALITY MODELS

In the HASARD method, the construction of quality models takes software architectural models as the input and consists of four steps as shown in Figure 12.3. The first step is to apply hazard identification methods to identify all quality sensitive observable phenomena of the components, connectors or the system. The second step is to establish the causal relationships between the phenomena. In the third step, these pieces of information are then assembled together and represented in the diagrammatic notation given above. Finally, the quality carrying property/ quality attribute that a phenomenon demonstrates is then identified according to the nature of the phenomenon.

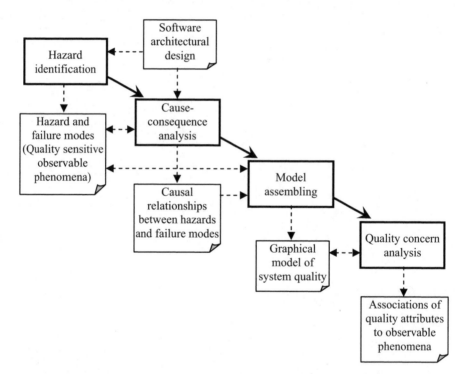

Figure 12.3 The process of HASARD quality model construction

The following describes these steps in detail.

12.2.1 Hazard identification

Hazard analysis techniques have been widely used in the development and deployment of safety critical systems that involve computer software or not. It intends systematically identifying, assessing and controlling hazards before a new work process, piece of equipment, or other activity is initiated. In such a context, a hazard is a situation in which there is actual or potential danger to people or to the environment. Associated with each hazard is a risk, which is related to the likelihood of the event occurring and its consequences. Once the hazards are identified and analysed, safety as well as other quality requirements can be specified for each component. Risks can be avoided or reduced ultimately through technical design, management and organisational means. Consequently, the quality and reliability of the system are improved [4, 5, 6, 7].

In order to analyse a wide range of software quality attributes not just safety, the concept of hazard must be extended and hazard analysis methods must be adopted. Therefore, in the context of software design, the word *hazard* has its widest meaning, which means any situation that may cause undesirable effect or system failure. The more likely a hazard occurs and more serious the consequences of the hazard, the more important is corresponding quality attribute, and *vice versa*. Under this understanding and definition of hazard, safety is one of the quality concerns that hazard analysis is capable of dealing with.

The process of hazard analysis starts with the identification of hazards of a system. One of the most effective methods of hazard identification is the so called hazard and operability studies, or shortly HAZOP.

The HAZOP technique was developed by ICI in the 1960s as a method of analysing hazards within chemical and process control plants. It is adopted by the MOD Defence Standard 00-58 for programmable electronics [8]. The method relies on determining answers to questions of a what-if nature. For example, in the analysis of a chemical reactor, a typical what-if question is 'what would be the effect of an increase of temperature?' The method provides a set of guide words to systematically develop a collection of what-if questions when applied to the attributes of various components of the system being studied. If a deviation from the normal working of the component is credible, then the causes, consequences and recommendations of the investigation are documented, and the behaviour of the component is considered as a possible hazard.

Table 12.1 lists the guide words for hazard identification in the analysis of software architectural designs. Each guide word can be applied to one or more attributes and have different meanings depending on the type of attribute and the context in the system. For example, the guide word 'NO' can be applied to any data produced by a component of a software system. In such a context, it means no data is produced by the component. The hazard identification will ask the what-if question that 'what would happen if the data is not produced by the component?'. The same guide word can also be applied to an architectural component. In such a context, it means that the component is not contained in the system, for example, a dynamic link library is not available when the system is initialised at run-time. A what-if question can be asked to identify the consequences of missing such a component.

Table 12.1 Guide words for hazard identification of software design

Guide word	Applicable attribute	Interpretations
No	Date or control signals	No data or control signal exchanged through a connector; No data or control signals produced by a component; No data or control signal received from input.
	Component property or function	The component or connector does not have the designed property or function.
	Component or connector	The system does not contain the component or connector.
More	Quantitative parameters of a component, connector or the whole system	The value of the parameter is too large.
Less	Quantitative parameters of a component, connector or the whole system	The value of the parameter is too small.
As well as	Event or activity	The intended event or activity occurs, but in addition to this, …; For example, redundant data are sent to the designated receiver in addition to intended value. Data is sent to the designated receiver as well as an unintended receiver.
Part of	Structured data	Only a part of the data produced, stored or received.
	Structure events	Only a part of the events happened.
Reverse	Direction of information flow	The information flow in the opposite direction.
	Event	The opposite event happened.
Other than	Data and control signals, any quantitative and qualitative parameters	Incorrect data or control signals produced; The parameter has a value different from the designed ones.
	Component or system's functionality and property	The component has a functionality or property different from the designed ones.
Early	Periodical events	The event happened earlier than expected.
Late	Periodical events	The event happened later than expected.
Before	Temporal orders between events	The event happened before an event in temporal order as designed.
After	Temporal orders between events	The event happened after an event in temporal order as designed.

Notice that, not all applications of a guide word to an attribute are meaningful. Moreover, even if the application of a guide word to an attribute is meaningful in the sense it produces an error or hazard, the probability that the hazard occurs may be so low, or practically impossible, that its consequences need not be further investigated.

For example, consider the Internet connection between the client side and the server side in a web-based application. By applying the guide works given in Table 12.1, we can identify a number of hazards shown in Table 12.2.

Table 12.2 Hazards of the Internet connection in client-server architecture

Ref	Guide word	Failure mode	Causes	Consequences
I1	No	The internet connection passes no messages between the client and server.	Physically disconnected; Traffic jam; Software failure; Network server is down.	Client cannot communicate with the server.
I2	More	More messages are delivered than the clients and the server send out, e.g. duplicated messages.	Hacker's attack; Heavy traffic on the Internet caused resending packages.	System clash; Overload on the server or the client.
I3	Less	Fewer messages are delivered than the server and the clients send out, i.e. lost messages.	Discontinued Internet connection; Heavy traffic on the Internet; Software failure.	Incomplete transactions; System clash; Damage the integrity of the data and program on the server and/or client.
I4	As well as	Messages are delivered to other destinations in addition to the correct designated receiver.		Leak of sensitive information.
I5	Part of	Only a part of the packets of a message is delivered to the destination client or server, i.e. an incomplete message is delivered.	Discontinued Internet connection; Heavy traffic on the Internet; Software failure.	Software failure; Production of incorrect computation results if incompleteness is not detected.
I6	Reverse	Not applicable		
I7	Other than	A message not from the client or the server is passed to the server or client.	Hacker's attack; Other software system's failure	System failure; Damage the integrity of the data and the program.
I8	Other than	The message is in a different format.	The client or the server is modified; Fault in the software.	System failure.

I9	Early	Not applicable.		
I10	Late	Not applicable.		
I11	Before	A sequence of messages is delivered in a wrong order.		Actions taken by the server and/or the client are in a wrong order.
I12	After	A sequence of messages is delivered in a wrong order.		Actions taken by the server and/or the client are in a wrong order.

From the hazards identified in the above table, we can recognise some common hazards of all web-based applications. For example, hazard I4 has a potential security problem since a message could be delivered to other receivers if the hazard occurs. Hazard I2 also has a potential security threat, if a large amount of messages from an unidentified source are delivered to the server. It could be a denial of service attack. Hazard I11 and I12 state that there is a hazard in which messages could be delivered in the reverse order of their departure. This requires the implementation of the server and the client not to rely on the temporal order of receiving messages.

The consequences of a failure, i.e. an occurrence of a hazard, depend on the particular application of the system, not just the structure and behaviour of the architecture. For example, if hazard I4 occurs, a message is delivered to other destinations. It does not always cause security problems unless the message contains sensitive contents and the message is not encrypted. Certain hazards represent potentially intended scenarios in the future operation and maintenance of the system. For example, hazard I8 represents a scenario of modifying the representation of messages passed between the clients and the server. Such a scenario is not necessarily a failure of the system.

HAZOP study not only requires the engineer to identify the failure modes of a system, but also to analysis the effects and causes of the hazards. Table 12.2 also shows the possible causes and the consequences of each hazard of the Internet connection between the server and clients. Such analysis is preliminary, but indicates which hazard is important and deserves further investigation, which is the focus of the next step.

12.2.2 Cause-consequence analysis

The second step of quality model construction is the cause-consequence analysis of each hazard identified in the first step.

For example, consider the hazard I2 given in Table 12.2. There are several possible causes of the hazard, which include that the traffic on the Internet results in duplicated packages being generated, a malicious source generates false request messages on purposes, etc. A direct consequence of a large number of false request messages is a high load on the server. This in turn, could lead to poor performance of the server, even the clash of the server system. Consequently, the clients cannot get the requested services responsively.

In the above analysis, we can see a sequence of hazardous phenomena or events is identified so that one is the consequence of another:

(a) the large number of false request messages,

(b) the high load on the server computer,

(c) the poor performances of the server, and

(d) the slow responses (or no responses at all if the server clashes) to client requests.

Some of the hazards may have already been identified in the initial hazard identification step. However, some are new to the list of hazards generated in step 1. These new hazards should be added into the hazard list and assigned with a unique identification number. The cause-consequence relationships between hazards can be recorded in a form for the use in the assembling of a graph quality model at the next steps. A template of the form is given below in Figure 12.4. It can also be directly represented in the graph model via drawing a diagram in the graph quality model's notation.

Cause-Consequence Analysis Record

System : system name				**Analyst:** Name	**Date:** Date of completion		**Version:** Version No.
Ref	**Cause**			**Consequence**			**Explanation**
	Hazard Ref.	Description		Hazard Ref.	Description		
		Component	Phenomenon		Component	Phenomenon	

Figure 12.4 Template of cause-consequence analysis record form

The cause-consequence analysis progressively selects the hazards identified in the hazard identification step and investigates their causes and consequences until the analyst is satisfied with the coverage of the most threatening hazards. Such an analysis process can also be focused on a specific type of hazard, such as security, usability, modifiability, etc. In such cases, a subset of hazards that are identified with a consequence in the specific quality aspect is used as the starting point of the analysis.

In the process of cause consequence analysis, the effects of a hazard or failure mode are determined for the unit itself and for the other components as well as the complete system. Each cause of a failure of a component indicates what quality attribute that the system is sensitive to from developer's point of view. The corresponding consequences of the failure indicate what quality attributes the system is sensitive to from the users' point of view. Both causes and their consequences are observable phenomena and events of the system. Therefore, the relationships between the quality attributes or quality-carrying properties can be established.

The cause-consequence analysis can be performed in backward and forward directions and a combination of both.

- *Forward*: from a hazard to search for potential effects.

- *Backward*: from an observable hazard to search for the causes of the hazard.

For example, consider a simple website that consists of a number of web pages. Suppose that we start with a failure mode that the user cannot find the required information on the website. By performing a backward search, a cause of the failure mode is that the website is unable to obtain a file through a hyperlink. Further causes of the failure are: (1) the hyperlink is broken; (2) the web server is down. [1]

In the application of cause consequence analysis, each of the causes and consequences of a failure mode may become a new entry to the hazard chart. These causes and consequences are further investigated until the cause is primitive and the consequences are terminal.

A failure mode is primitive if its causes cannot be further identified without additional knowledge about the system. A failure mode can also be considered as

---

[1]   Notice that, there are more causes of the failure than have been given in the example.

primitive if we are not interested in its causes. For example, in Figure 12.5 the failure 'broken link' can be considered as primitive. However, in a different context, we may well be interested in its causes and to find out why the hyperlinks are broken.

Cause-Consequence Analysis Record

System : A Web page			Analyst: HZ			Date: 6/5/04	Version: 1.00
	Cause			**Consequence**			
Ref	Hazard Ref.	Description		Hazard Ref.	Description		**Explanation**
		Comp.	Phenomenon		Comp.	Phenomenon	
R1	W2	Web page	Unable to obtain a file through a hyperlink	U8	The user	Cannot find required information	When the user searches for information by browsing through hyperlinks
R2	H1	HTML files	A hyperlink is broken	W2	Web page	Unable to obtain a file through the hyperlink	The file cannot be found due to the broken link
R3	S6	Web server	Server is down	W2	Web page	Unable to obtain a file through the hyperlink	The file cannot be retrieved and transmitted
R4	S7	WWW server	Under maintenance service;	S6	Web server	Server is down	Maintenance shutdown
R5	S8	WWW server	Hacker's attack;	S6	Web server	Server is down	Due to hacker's attack
R6	S9	WWW server	Software failure;	S6	Web server	Server is down	
R7	S10	WWW server	hardware failure;	S6	Web server	Server is down	
R8	P1	Power supply	Power cut;	S6	Web server	Server is down	

Figure 12.5 An example of a cause-consequence analysis record

A failure mode is terminal if it does not affect any other component of the system or does not cause any other failures. In many cases, we consider a failure mode as terminal simply because we are not interested in its further consequences. For example, in the example shown in Figure 12.5, the consequence of 'user cannot find required information' is considered as terminal, because we are not interested in what would happen afterwards. However, in certain context, what happens afterwards may become a serious problem. For example, if the system is for storing and retrieving patients' medical records, the situation that a doctor cannot find a patient's record may lead to serious consequences in the treatment of the patient.

The failure mode that 'the server is down' is neither terminal nor primitive. Its causes can be: (a) the server is under maintenance services; (b) the server is clashed due to hacker's attack; (c) the server is clashed due to software faults; (d) hardware failure; (e) power cut; etc.

12.2.3 Assembling graphic model

The construction of a quality model takes the information charted in the cause consequence analysis records and translates the information into graphical representation. Each hazard or failure mode in the record becomes a node with the component and phenomenon as specified in the record. Each row in the record becomes a link from the node that represents the cause to the node that represents the consequence. The explanation column of the row forms the reason of the link. For example, for the first row in Figure 12.5, the following nodes and link are generated.

Figure 12.6 The fragment of diagram derived from row 1 of Figure 12.5

Similarly, from the second and third rows in Figure 12.5, we can derive the following nodes and links.

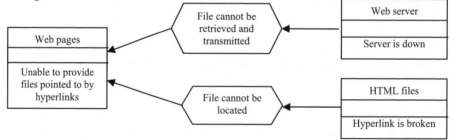

Figure 12.7 A fragment of diagram derived from Figure 12.5

Assembling these nodes and links together, we can obtain the following diagram.

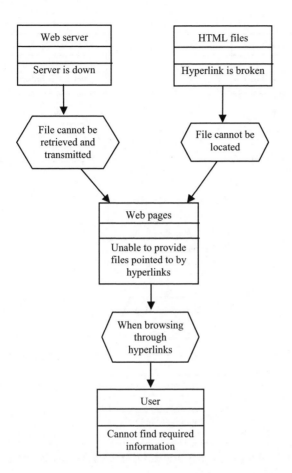

Figure 12.8 The diagram derived from Figure 12.5

12.2.4 Identification of quality concerns

The diagram generated from a causeconsequence analysis record as above is incomplete. The property slots need to be filled in. Therefore, for each node in the diagram, the observable phenomenon is compared with the definitions of a set of quality attributes and quality-carrying properties of the components. The quality attribute or quality carrying property that the phenomenon demonstrates is, then, identified, or a new attribute or property is recognised. This property is filled into the slot of each node. For example, 'a hyperlink is broken' demonstrates the quality attribute correctness. 'Server is down' is related to the reliability of the system. 'User cannot find required information' is associated to the usability of the system. Therefore, we can derive the following quality model from Figure 12.5.

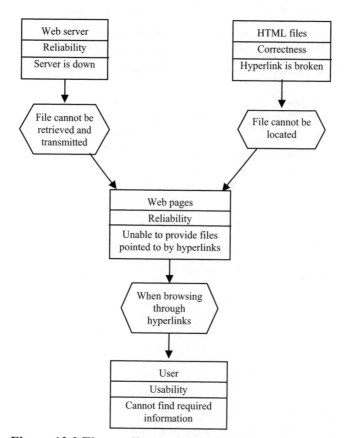

Figure 12.9 The quality model derived from Figure 12.5

In the examination of each node in the diagram, the significance of the risk of the hazard represented by the node must also be considered. Two factors must be taken into consideration in the examination of risk levels of each hazard. The first is the likelihood of the occurrences of the hazard and the second is the consequences of the hazard. The information about the consequences has been identified in step 2 and presented in the diagram as the result of step 3. The likelihood of the hazard must be justified according to prior knowledge of the development team etc. If the risk level is high, i.e there is a high probability of the hazard to occur and the consequence of the hazard is significant, the hazard should be included in the final quality model. Otherwise, the hazard can be ignored and omitted from the quality model.

12.3 DERIVATION OF QUALITY FEATURES

Given a graphic quality model described above, we can derive a number of different types of quality features of an architectural design. The following discusses a few such quality features.

12.3.1 Contribution factors of a quality concern

In the analysis of a software architectural design, we often want to know how a quality issue is addressed in the design. We want to know which components or connectors in the system are related to the quality issue and how they collectively provide the solution to meet the quality requirements. A set of components and/or connectors and their specifically designed properties that are related to the quality issue are the contribution factors of the quality attribute demonstrated in the design. Such information can be derived from a quality model by using the following algorithm.

Algorithm 1 {* Derivation of contribution factors to a quality attribute *}

Input: M – a quality model;

Q – a quality attribute that we want to know its contribution factors.

Variables: S – a subset of nodes in the quality model M;

L – a subset of links in the quality model M.

Output: G – the sub-graph of M that represents the contribution factors to the quality attribute Q.

Begin

Step 1: Search for all nodes in M that has Q as the quality attribute. Let S be the set of such nodes. Let L to be set of links between the nodes in S, if any.

Step 2: If there is a link X to a node N in the set S from a node Y in M such that X is not in L, add the node Y into S and the link X to L.

Step 3: Repeat step 2 until there is no more node and link that can be added into the sets S and L.

Step 4: Output sub-graph G that consists of S as the nodes and L as the links.

End

For example, the fragment of quality model depicted in Figure 12.2 represents the contribution factors to the usability of a web-based system. From this sub-graph, we can see that the usability depends on (a) the well-structuredness of HTML files, (b) the navigability of HTML files, (c) the responsiveness of the WWW server, (d) the compatibility of the client side code, (e) the correctness of HTML files, and (f) the availability of Online Help. The responsiveness of the server further depends on (a) the load on the server, (b) the performance of the system, and (c) the size of the files to be processed and transmitted. The sub-graph not only tells us what are the contribution factors to a quality attribute, but also the specific ways that each factor affects the quality of the system on that attribute. From the quality model depicted in Figure 12.2, we can derive the following sub-graph for the contribution factors of a server's responsiveness property.

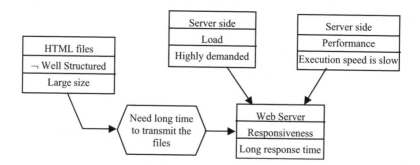

Figure 12.10 Contribution factors of server's responsiveness

12.3.2 Sensitive quality attributes of a component

Another frequently asked question in the analysis of a software architectural design is what are the consequences of a design decision on the properties and functionality of a component or connector? In such cases, we need to find out what are the quality attributes that are affected by the design decision no matter whether the effect is positive or negative. Such information can also be derived from a well constructed quality model very similar to the algorithm 1 above. The following describes the algorithm for this purpose.

Algorithm 2 {* Derivation of sensitive quality attributes of a design decision *}

Input: M – a quality model;

                 N – a node in M that we want to know the quality attributes that N affects.

Variables: S – a subset of nodes in the quality model M;

                 L – a subset of links in the quality model M.

Output: G – the sub-graph represents the quality attributes that design decision N affects.

Begin

 Step 1: Search for all nodes in M that the component is N. Let S be the set of such nodes. Let L to be set of links between the nodes in S, if any.

 Step 2: If there is a link X from a node N in the set S to a node Y in M such that X is not in L, add the node Y into S and the link X to L.

 Step 3: Repeat step 2 until there is no more node and link that can be added into the sets S and L.

 Step 4: Output sub-graph G that consists of S as the nodes and L as the links.

End

For example, consider the quality model depicted in Figure 12.2. The size of HTML files affects the navigability and responsiveness of the system, which further affects the usability of the system. Apply the algorithm above to Figure 12.2, we can obtain the following sub-graph in Figure 12.11 that represents the sensitive quality attributes of the quality carrying property of HTML files' size.

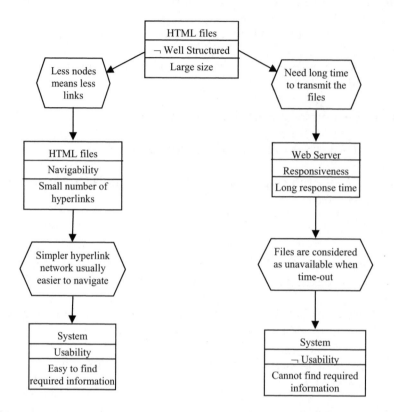

Figure 12.11 Quality attributes that are sensitive to the size of HTML files

12.3.3 Quality risks

A design decision may have positive affects on a quality attribute, but can also have negative effects. The negative effects may impose quality risks to the system. Therefore, it is often desirable to know where the quality risks are within an architectural design. This can be derived from a well constructed quality model.

The negative effect of a design decision can be recognised by searching for links in the quality model that have a negative effect. For example, in the quality model depicted in Figure 12.2, there is a link between the node of HTML with the property of large file size and the node of web server with a property of responsiveness. The link is negative since the larger the size of the file, the poorer the responsiveness of the web server. Therefore, a design decision of large file size is a risk to the quality attribute of responsiveness.

The further consequences of a quality risk can be identified and analysed using the algorithm for deriving sensitive quality attributes of the node, i.e. *Algorithm 2* above. Therefore, we can derive that a further consequence of having large sized HTML files is poor usability of the whole system from the quality model depicted in Figure 12.2.

In certain cases, a negative effect, i.e. a quality risk, is not a simple design decision. Instead, it can be the consequence of a number of other design decisions. In that case, its causes must also be identified so that a better design can be made. In this case, the algorithm to deriving the contribution factors, i.e. *Algorithm 1*, can be applied to identify the causes.

12.3.4 Trade-off points

In many situations, a quality risk cannot be resolved without compromising the quality of the system on other quality issues because these quality issues are conflicting with each other. In such cases, trade-offs between the quality attributes must be made and a balance between them must be achieved through appropriate design decisions.

For example, consider the quality model depicted in Figure 12.2. The size of HTML files positively affects the navigability of the hypertext network, but negatively affects responsiveness of the web server. Therefore, navigability is in conflict with responsiveness. Therefore, a trade-off between them must be made so that responsiveness is within a tolerable range while navigability is also acceptable. Such a trade-off occurs in the form of deciding on a suitable size of HTML file.

From this example, we can see that a trade-off point is a node in the quality model that has a negative effect to one or more quality attribute and at the same time it has effects on one or more positive quality attributes.

To make a right decision on a trade-off point, we need to understand all the consequences of the design decisions. Therefore, we need to apply the algorithm that derives all quality attributes that the trade-off point affects, i.e. using algorithm 2 above. For example, from the quality model depicted in Figure 12.2, we can derive that the size of HTML files affects the usability of the system both positively and negatively as shown in Figure 12.11.

In certain complicated situations, a trade-off point is a consequence of a number of other design decisions. In such cases, we need to apply algorithm 1 to find all contribution factors to a trade-off point.

12.4 CASE STUDY: CLIENT-SERVER WEB SYSTEMS

This section illustrates the application of the HASARD method by analysing a simple software architecture.

12.4.1 Description of the architecture

The following diagram in Figure 12.12 depicts the architecture of basic two-tier web-page systems.

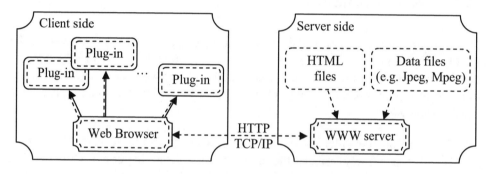

Figure 12.12 The two-tier client-server architecture

In this architecture, the software running on the client side computer consists of a *web browser* and a set of *plug-in software applications*. The browser provides a graphical user interface to the user by displaying the data contained in the HTML files as well as data in other formats, which are interpreted by calling the corresponding plug-in software. It also receives user's commands from the graphical user interface, such as clicks on hyperlinks, and requests files from the server through the HTTP and TCP/IP communication protocols. Running on the server computer is the *WWW server* software, which has access to a set of *HTML files* as well as some *files in other data formats*, such as JPEG and MPEG files. The WWW server receives requests of files from the clients and transmits the corresponding files to the clients through the Internet connection using the HTTP and TCP/IP protocols.

12.4.2 Construction of quality model

To construct the quality model, we first apply the HAZOP method to identify the hazards of the system. Table 12.3 below gives all the hazards identified by HAZOP study of the architecture.

Table 12.3 Application of guide words to the client-server architecture

Ref	Guide word	Failure mode
Component / Attribute: Client side: Service Request		
C1	No	The client side sends no service requests.
C2	More	The client side sends more requests than the designed capability of the server can handle.
C3	Less	The client side sends less requests than it should.
C4	As well as	The client side sends service requests to other destinations as well as the server.
C5	Part of	The client side sends incomplete service request information.
C6	Reverse	Not applicable.[2]
C7	Other than	The client side sends messages that are not service requests to the server.
C8	Other than	The client side is a different component, i.e. a modified version.
C9	Early	Not applicable, assume there are no periodic events on the client side.
C10	Late	Not applicable, assume there are no periodic events on the client side.
C11	Before	The client side sends service request messages in a wrong order, such as payment information before product selection.
C12	After	The client side sends service request messages in a wrong order, such as login after a request of information.
Component / Attribute: Client side: output to the user		
G1	No	The client side displays no information on the screen.
G2	More	The client displays more information than the user requested.
G3	Less	The client displays less information than it should.
G4	As well as	The client side stores and/or processes the information as well as displays information to the users.

---

[2] The hazard is that the client side performs an event that is the opposite of what it should do. It is not applicable in a basic website that only contains a set of interlinked HTML files. However, in more complicated applications, such as e-commerce, this can be a significant hazard. For example, the user wants to transfer money from account A to B, but the system transfers money from B to A.

G5	As well as	The client side displays the information to other users as well as displaying the information to the correct user.
G6	Part of	The client side displays only a part of information.
G7	Reverse	Not applicable.
G8	Other than	Client displays information that is not user required.
G9	Early	Not applicable.
G10	Late	Not applicable.
G11	Before	The client side displays information in a wrong temporal order.
G12	After	The client side displays information in a wrong temporal order.

Component / Attribute: Client side: plug-ins

P1	No	There are no plug-ins.
P2	More	There is more than one plug-in for some data formats.
P3	Less	There are some plug-ins missing.
P4	As well as	Not applicable.
P5	Part of	Not applicable.
P6	Reverse	Not applicable.
P7	Other than	Not applicable.
P8	Early	Not applicable.
P9	Late	Not applicable.
P10	Before	Not applicable.
P11	After	Not applicable.

Component / Attribute: Internet connection: Messages

I1	No	The Internet connection passes no messages between the client and server.
I2	More	More messages are delivered than the clients and the server send out, e.g. duplicated messages.
I3	Less	Fewer messages are delivered than the server or the client send out, i.e. lost messages.
I4	As well as	Messages are delivered to other destinations in addition to the correct designated receiver.
I5	Part of	Only a part of the packets of a message is delivered to the destination client or server, i.e. an incomplete message is delivered.
I6	Reverse	Not applicable.
I7	Other than	A message not from the client or the server is passed to the server or client.
I8	Other than	The message is in a different format, i.e. the representation of messages is modified.
I9	Early	Not applicable.
I10	Late	Excessive delay in the delivery of messages.
I11	Before	A sequence of messages is delivered in a wrong order.

I12	After	A sequence of messages is delivered in a wrong order.
Component / Attribute: HTML files and Data files		
H1	No	There are no HTML files and Data files.
H2	More	There are more HTML files and Data files than should be.
H3	Less	Some HTML files or Data files missing.
H4	As well as	Not applicable.
H5	Part of	Some HTML files or Data files are incomplete.
H6	Reverse	Not applicable.
H7	Other than	Some HTML files or Data files are incorrect.
H8	Early	Not applicable.
H9	Late	Not applicable.
H10	Before	Not applicable.
H11	After	Not applicable.
Component / Attribute: Server: Service Reply		
S1	No	The server produces no reply to the service requests.
S2	More	The server produced results more than necessary.
S3	Less	The server produced results less than necessary.
S4	As well as	Reply messages are sent to other destinations in addition to the correct designated receiver.
S5	As well as	The server performed additional function in addition to the requested service.
S6	Part of	Only a part of the requested service is performed and/or a part of the result is produced.
S7	Reverse	The server does the opposite function of the requested service.
S8	Other than	The server performed a function other than requested.
S9	Other than	The server is a different component, i.e. the server is modified.
S9	Early	The server performed periodic event (such as backup, virus check, etc.) earlier than scheduled.
S10	Late	The server performed periodic event (such as backup, virus check, etc.) later than scheduled.
S11	Late	Excessive delay in giving reply to a service request.
S12	Before	A sequence of events, such as sending a set of messages, is performed in a wrong order.
S13	After	A sequence of events, such as sending a set of messages, is performed in a wrong order.

To construct the quality model, we start with the hazards in the client-side group that affect the end-user's operation of the system, that is, the hazards G1-G12. For each of these hazards, we first analyse their consequences, and then their causes. The results of the analysis are directly represented in the graph notation of quality models given in section 12.1. For the sake of space, we have omitted the reasons for the links between the nodes, which in our context are very obvious. For each node in the diagram, further analysis of their causes and consequences were identified and added into the diagram. The hazards identified in the application of guide words were checked against their coverage in the quality model. If a hazard is not covered in the quality model, it is investigated for whether the hazard will cause any failure mode included in the quality model, or its possibility as a consequence of the failure modes in the quality model. As shown in Figure 12.13, the quality model has a good coverage of the hazards in Table 12.3.

Finally, for each node in the diagram, the quality attributes that the phenomenon of the node represents is recognised and annotated on the node. As shown in Figure 12.13, there are phenomena that cannot be easily associated to a known quality attribute. For example, the situation that the data file of the web-based system has a format that is not commonly used may cause the failure that the client side cannot display the data on the user's screen due to the client side computer not having installed the plug-in application for the data format. The problem of data file format can hardly be associated to any of the quality attributes discussed in Chapter 2. Therefore, such node in the quality model has no information filled in the quality attribute compartment. There is another situation when the quality attribute compartment of a node is not filled. It is when the phenomenon of the node is about an external entity of the system, such as the user. In such cases, the quality attribute compartment is meaningless.

The resulting quality model is shown in Figure 12.13.

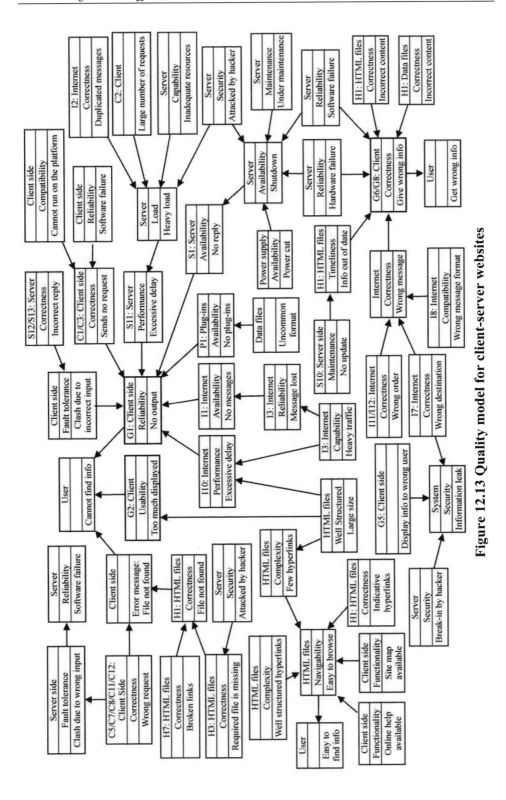

Figure 12.13 Quality model for client-server websites

12.4.3 Analysis of quality features

From the quality model in Figure 12.13, we can derive a number of quality features of the client-server architecture of websites.

For example, we can derive the contribution factors to a number of quality attributes. For instance, the navigability of the HTML files depends on the following factors:

- the complexity of the HTML files;

- the property of well structured HTML files with reasonable sizes;

- the HTML file's correctness in terms of the hyperlinks are indicative;

- the availability of site map;

- the availability of the online help system.

Similarly, we can derive that the user gets correct information depending on the following factors:

- the HTML files are correct in terms of the contents are correct;

- the data files are correct in terms of their contents are correct;

- the server hardware and software do not fail;

- the HTML files are up to date, which is updated timely by the server;

- the Internet delivers the messages correctly.

The performance of the server depends on the load on the server, which in turn depends on the following factors:

- the number of requests made by the clients;

- the server's computational capability and resources;

- the security of the server in sense of the possibility of being attacked by hackers;

- the correct behaviour of the Internet in terms of duplicated messages delivered.

From the quality model, we can also derive the main risks of the architectural design, which include:

- the use of a new format of data file could cause the information not to be displayed in the client computer;

- the compatibility problem of the client code may mean that the system could not be executed on the client's computer, and consequently, the system unusable;

- the heavy traffic on the Internet may hinder the usability of the system;

- hackers' attacks may cause the system's poor performance, and in extreme cases, the systems clash, information leak, data integrity be damaged when HTML/Data files are removed or replaced with incorrect ones, etc.

- poor indicative hyperlinks may cause bad navigability, which in turn hinder the user to find required information; etc.

The main trade-off point in the design of a website is the decomposition of information into HTML files. Too many HTML files may cause a complexity in the hyperlink network. However, too few HTML files may cause large files to be transmitted over the Internet and result in poor responsiveness.

SUMMARY

In this chapter, hazard analysis methods originally developed for the analysis of safety critical systems are adopted for the analysis of software architectural designs. The method can be used to construct quality models of software systems from their architectural designs. The quality model is represented in a diagrammatic notation. It enables the explicit references to the components of the system whose quality-carrying properties affect the system quality attribute. It also enables the explicit annotation of the reasons why two properties or attributes are related. Containing such information in quality models can significantly improve the usability of quality models in software development. It provides a logic that bridges the gap between abstract system quality attributes and the tangible quality-carrying properties of components and connectors and the observable behaviour of the systems and their components. The model can be used to derive quality features of the design, such as the contribution factors to a quality attribute, the quality attributes that a design decision affects, the risks of a design decision imposed on quality attributes, and the trade-off points that affect conflict quality concerns.

FURTHER READING

This chapter was based on the author and his colleague and students' research work reported in [1]. Hazard analysis techniques in the context of safety-related systems are covered in the textbooks of on safety critical systems, such as [5] and [7]. The adoption of the hazard analysis method HAZOP to the analysis of software safety can be found in [8], which applies to software design and requirements specifications represented in data flow diagrams, state transition diagrams, entity relationship diagrams, and object access models. Prof. Nancy Leveson and her colleagues also adopted the fault tree analysis method, which is a hazard analysis method for investigation of the failure modes that can cause a specific failure, to the analysis of software safety at program source code level [5].

EXERCISES

(12–1) Use the graph notation to represent the following relationships between quality aspects.

(i) A server's availability is affected by the maintenance of the software if the server must be off-line when the software is updated;

(ii) A hacker's attack to a server may cause the server to shutdown because of hacker's damage to the integrity of the program and/or the data;

(iii) The reliability of a system can be improved if multiple versions of a key component are used for fault tolerance, while the complexity of the system may increase as well;

(iv) A fault tolerance causes lower performance because computation resources are used to detect failures and when failure occurs, the program is rolled back to the recovery point and calls a second version of the component;

(v) In a system ABC, the change of component A's output format will result in a huge effort to modify the software because the format is used by 2/3 of the other components.

(12–2) Translate the information contained in Figure 12.5 into a quality model represented in the graph notation defined in section 12.1.

(12–3) Apply the HAZOP method to identify the hazards (potential failure modes) of the following software components and connectors.

(i) The frequency and value of data passing through a pipe;

(ii) The frequency of data arrival at the input to a filter;

(iii) The functionality of a procedure;

(iv) The size and format of a passive data component;

(v) The a mount of input to an event handler in an independent component architecture;

(vi) The number of clients in a system of shared data architecture;

(vii) The number of layers in a system of layered architecture;

(viii) The frequency of data passed through a data flow in a data flow architecture;

(ix) The number of filters in a pipe-and-filter architecture;

(x) The value that a client produces in a system of shared data architecture.

(12–4) Use the quality model given in Figure 12.13 to derive the quality attributes that are affected by each of the following:

(i) the maintenance of the server;

(ii) the hacker's attack on the server;

(iii) the incorrectness of the contents of an HTML file or a data file;

(iv) an HTML/data file of very large size;

(v) the server receives a large number of requests;

(vi) an HTML file contains a broken link;

(vii) the information stored on the server is not updated timely.

(12–5) Consider an architectural design for the keyword frequency vector extraction problem. Use HASARD method to analyse the modifiability of the architectural design. (*Hint*: first apply guide words to the functionality of the system to identify possible changes of the functions, apply guide words to the data representations of each passive data component to identify possible changes of data representations. Then, use cause-consequence analysis to identify the necessary modifications to the components and connectors. Finally, construct the quality model and analyse its quality features.)

(12–6) Business to business (B2B) e-commerce systems are different from the business to customer (B2C) or customer to customer (C2C) e-commerce systems, as they have a number of special characteristics including high volume of goods traded, high value of goods traded, multiple electronic payment methods, and involvement of business bidding, contracts and agreements [9]. These features make the B2B systems more complex to manage than B2C or C2C systems.

At the highest level of abstraction, a B2B e-commerce system consists of three parties, the buy-side, the virtual market and the sell-side. Information is exchanged among these parties in certain orders. A cycle of activities must be completed before a deal can be made. The information exchange process within the systems can be decomposed into four phases: information searching, purchasing requisition, signing contract, and receiving goods and make payment. The typical architectural structure of the virtual market part of an e-commerce system consists of four components: product information manager, purchasing requisition processor, contract manager and payment manager. The architecture of such a system is given in Figure 12.14.

Apply the HASARD method to construct a quality model of the system and analyse its quality features.

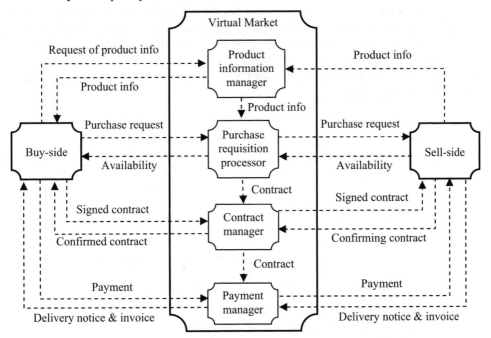

Figure 12.14 Architecture of B2B e-commerce systems

REFERENCES

1   Zhu, H., Zhang, Y., Huo, Q. and Greenwood, S., Application of Hazard Analysis to Quality Modelling, *Proc. of IEEE COMPSAC'2002*, Oxford, UK, 26–29 August, 2002, pp139–144.

2   Dromey, R. G., A Model for Software Product Quality, *IEEE Transactions on Software Engineering*, Vol. 21, No. 2, Feb. 1995, pp146–162.

3   Dromey, R. G., Cornering the Chimera, *IEEE Software*, Vol. 13, No. 1, Jan. 1996, pp33–43.

4 Kletz, T., *Computer control and Human Error*, Rugby: Institute of Chemical Engineers, 1995.

5 Leveson, N. G., *Safeware: System Safety and Computers*, Reading, MA: Addison Wesley, 1995.

6 Neumann, P. G., *Computer-Related Risks*, ACM Press, New York, 1995.

7 Storey, N., *Safety-Critical Computer Systems*, Reading, MA: Addison, 1996.

8 Ministry of Defence, HAZOP Studies on Systems Containing Programmable Electronics, Part 1 Requirements; Part 2: General Application Guidance, Defence Standard 00-58, Issue 2, 19 May 2000.

9 Chan, H., Lee, R., Dillion, T. and Chang, E., *E-Commerce*, Chichester: John Wiley & Sons, 2001.

Index